PIKE'S PORTAGE
Stories of a Distinguished Place

Edited by Morten Asfeldt & Bob Henderson

Foreword by James Raffan

NATURAL HERITAGE BOOKS
A MEMBER OF THE DUNDURN GROUP
TORONTO

Published by Natural Heritage Books
A Member of The Dundurn Group
www.dundurn.com

Library and Archives Canada Cataloguing in Publication

Asfeldt, Morten, 1963-
    Pike's Portage : stories of a distinguished place / by Morten Asfeldt and
Bob Henderson.

Includes bibliographical references and index.
ISBN 978-1-55488-460-5

    1. Pikes Portage Route (N.W.T.)--History. 2. Pikes Portage Route (N.W.T.)--
Description and travel. I. Henderson, Bob, 1956- II. Title.

FC4161.A84 2009   971.9'3   C2009-902991-X

1   2   3   4   5   14   13   12   11   10

Conseil des Arts   Canada Council
du Canada   for the Arts

ONTARIO ARTS COUNCIL
CONSEIL DES ARTS DE L'ONTARIO

We acknowledge the support of **The Canada Council for the Arts** and the **Ontario Arts Council** for our publishing program. We also acknowledge the financial support of the **Government of Canada** through the **Book Publishing Industry Development Program** and **The Association for the Export of Canadian Books**, and the **Government of Ontario** through the **Ontario Book Publishers Tax Credit** program, and the **Ontario Media Development Corporation**.

Back cover image: Portaging between Artillery and Toura lakes on Pike's Portage. *Photo by Morten Asfeldt.*
Front cover image: Descending Pike's Portage in April 2004; the journey that inspired this project. *Photo by Morten Asfeldt.*
All maps by Chrismar Mapping Services Inc.

Cover design by Jennifer Scott
Text design by Courtney Horner
Edited by Jane Gibson
Copy edited by Allison Hirst
Printed and bound in Canada by Transcontinental

Dundurn Press
3 Church Street, Suite 500
Toronto, Ontario, Canada
M5E 1M2

Gazelle Book Services Limited
White Cross Mills
High Town, Lancaster, England
LA1 4XS

Dundurn Press
2250 Military Road
Tonawanda, NY
U.S.A. 14150

PIKE'S PORTAGE

To our children:
Jasper and Kaisa Asfeldt
Ceilidh, Meghan, and Quinn Henderson
"May they see the beauty and know the stories of this place."

Table of Contents

Acknowledgements

When I think about the origins of this book, I have a recurring image of sitting at my sister's computer in Fort McMurray, Alberta, on November 1, 2003. I opened my email and found a message from Kristen and Dave Olesen with the subject heading "Hoarfrost River, McLeod Bay, Great Slave Lake." Kristen and Dave's email was an invitation to consider some form of collaborative outdoor education experience based at their Hoarfrost River homestead. I joined Dave for an exploratory trip in April 2004, and, as is said, the rest is history. I thank Dave and Kristen for that 2003 invitation and their unending welcome, hospitality, and growing friendship. Without their invitation, I may never have discovered this distinguished place and its endless stories.

Bob and I also thank the contributors to this book. At one time we thought we would write all the stories included here ourselves, but quickly realized that we would be seeking advice and information from the many friends and colleagues who in the end wrote the chapters themselves. They each have specific expertise and experience far beyond ours — and far beyond anything we could hope to gain in just a few years — which made having them do the writing an obvious choice.

Chrismar Mapping Services Inc. made the seven fine maps in this book. Their thoughtful and professional advice made each visit and phone call a delight. As well, Ken Duncan of Kela Graphics graciously made time — on short notice — to scan many of the slides on the pages that follow.

In the North, there are many people to thank who have assisted us along the way: my lifelong friends Cathie and Kevin Bolstad, who have opened their home to us and to our students before and after our trips to the Hoarfrost, and provided room, board, and the best of company on our research forays to Yellowknife; Susan Irving, Robin Weber, and Ian Moir at the Prince of Wales Northern Heritage Centre in Yellowknife — Robin and Ian of the NWT Archives for their expertise in tracking down images and helping us understand the differences between an *item*, an *accession*, and a *fond*, and Susan for her wealth of knowledge, eagerness to pull many items from the museum collection for us to see, for the stories that she shared with us and our students, for her expert feedback on an early version of our manuscript, and for her willingness to answer many questions over the phone. We are greatly indebted to her. Thanks also to Air Tindi pilot Ted Studer for a thrilling flight to the Hoarfrost with the window of the airplane open to accommodate my aerial photography desires (much to the discomfort of my wife Krystal, who sat in the back seat absorbing the full blast of the cold April air and having her stomach do somersaults as we buzzed up, down, around, and sometimes back again to get *the shot*); and to Roger Catling for sharing his story, demonstrating his craft, answering many questions, and annotating our maps from his precise and enthusiastic memory of a lifetime in the country.

At Augustana Campus, I have been supported by a research grant that assisted in a 2006 canoe trip over Pike's Portage and a sabbatical leave in 2008–09 that allowed for a dedicated focus on this project. I also thank my friend and colleague Dr. Ingrid Urberg, who helped to design and co-teach the course that finds us and our students at the Hoarfrost; Dr. John Johansen for reading and providing feedback on some of my writing; librarian Paul Neff for helping to track down obscure sources and in some cases scanning and emailing them to me in Norway; Lois Larson for her secretarial expertise; and Dylan Anderson for his technological wizardry.

Acknowledgements

Much of my writing happened in a little office at Telemark University College in Norway. Thank you to my friends and colleagues there who were a constant source of curiosity and who welcomed me and my family into their Norwegian way of life for nine months that we will never forget.

Much of the co-ordination, correspondence, and editing happened with the assistance of Greer Gordon — a source of stability, patience, and encouragement.

Thanks, also, to Margot Peck and Jacqueline Akerman for being such good sports as the four of us made our way over Pike's Portage in 2006 and we asked them to stop, or go ahead, or come back and do that one more time — usually with a pack on their backs and a canoe on their heads — as we needed just *one more picture.*

To Jane Gibson, Barry Penhale, Allison Hirst, Jennifer Scott, and the rest of the crew at The Dundurn Group and Natural Heritage Books go our thanks for taking on this project and for their suggestions along the way.

Much appreciation goes to James Raffan for the book's inspired foreword. Jim knows this country and many of its characters well.

Bob and I, of course, thank our families for their support and encouragement and for tolerating the many suppertime phone calls that became routine. We especially thank Krystal for reading and providing gentle yet insightful feedback on the many drafts of our work and Margot for her encouragement and excitement for this project.

And finally, I would like to thank my fine friend Bob Henderson for his instant support and enthusiasm for this book when I first shared the idea with him. Bob has mentored me through the book editing and writing process and his vast network of contacts and his unwavering belief in me and for this project have been an endless source of motivation and confidence.

Morten Asfeldt
Camrose, Alberta.

Foreword

In the flurry of first responses to this celebration of Pike's Portage in manuscript form, I found myself thinking about a game travellers of the wild play when we have nothing better to do (and even sometimes when we *do*). It's called "Who would be part of the ultimate group on your ultimate wilderness journey?" There's the dead-or-alive version — Barbara McClintock and Copernicus always figure largely on that list — and then there's the do-you-think-they-would-come-if-we-asked list. In thinking broadly and creatively about the kind of voices they wanted to hear around this campfire, veteran wilderness travellers Morten Asfeldt and Bob Henderson have put together a truly remarkable group of collaborators on this literary journey to a singular Canadian place.

There are names, like David Pelly and Gwyneth Hoyle, who have contributed regularly to wilderness literature. There is historian Randy Freeman whose research is reported regularly on radio and in *UpHere* magazine but not often enough in a bookish context — he provides a very exciting first-ever glimpse at this level of detail into the Beaulieu clan, who led so many outsiders into the Barrens. There are many lively voices that come directly from the North. Among them are the enduring poetic wisdom of Father René Fumoleau, a cameo appearance by Guy Blanchet in his own hand, and a glimpse inside the life of the last Barrenlands wolf hunter, Roger Catling. And then a contribution from Professor John Wadland, who knows as much about Canada as anyone around but who commits rarely to print, and, in an engagingly self-conscious critique, takes us back into the world of Ernest Thompson Seton, one of the many characters in this book united only by shared experiences through time, on the storied path between Great Slave and Artillery lakes.

Absent, of course, are the voices of the people for whom this land was, and *is*, home, but through the engaging narratives of archaeologist Peter Carruthers, lawyer Larry Innes, and especially ethnologist Brenda Parlee, the struggle to find and embrace a post-colonial perspective is abundantly evident and serves as proxy for the first person, First Nation, and Métis voices still to be heard. Remarkable in this eclectic volume is the fact that names like Beaulieu, Drybones, Catholique, Saltatha, and Barromie carry equal load in the telling of the story of Pike's Portage as do the more familiar names like Hornby, Blanchet, Anderson, and Ingstad, etched so clearly in the historical record. And perhaps the most delightful surprise of all in Morten and Bob's group is Dave Olesen, dog musher, pioneer, pilot, and philosopher, whose clear and unfettered account of life at the mouth of the Hoarfrost River grounds or anchors the whole volume in authentic and un-romanticized experience on this land.

In any worthy book, a reader must find at least three types of people. They must find the writer(s) who, in this instance, constitute a unique and maybe even unlikely cast of characters, but who, in every instance, provide fresh perspectives even on older stories such as the Hornby tale, that have been told ad infinitum. Secondly, a reader must find the protagonists and relate to them in a way that allows them to rise from the page with a genuine ring of authenticity. With such a range of characters who have walked, snowshoed, skied, crawled, flown, snowmobiled, tobogganed, sledded, skipped, or been carried over Pike's Portage, there is something here to engage just about every reader's taste or sensibility — no doubt about that. Finally, in any good book a reader must find him/herself, and that's where I would like to admit being beguiled by this collection.

Foreword

I have been over Pike's Portage several times, in winter and in summer, and, in fact, was invited to contribute a story to this collection. What took me there in the first instance, nearly twenty years ago, was research into a place that allowed me the privilege of meeting, living among, and travelling with a number of the characters in this book. As luck or circumstance would dictate, the nature of what happened in a series of cross-cultural experiences was, in some instances, so profoundly moving or inspiring or, in other instances, so conflicted and confusing, that to this day I am still trying to make sense of what happened on those lands in and around Pike's Portage. Oh, yes, there was beauty to behold in friendships and in a land whose character shifted with the seasonal winds. And there were rubs of packs, boots, and preconceived notions. There was the taste of siphoned ice-cold gasoline. There was the smell of firewood and raw fear, the sustaining warmth of black tea, raw meat, and there was a love of land and a respect for the sanctity for life and living expressed in the most unusual ways. There was the map that blew away on the Barrenland winds. Try as I have over the years, words have never come to articulate anything much at all about the raw and transformative power of these experiences. Maybe one day they will: Maybe not. Certainly not now. So, I had to respectfully decline Morten and Bob's kind invitation to contribute.

But now that their work is done, I have to say that joining this remarkable group of fellow travellers for a journey back through the imagination to Kache — the place at the end of the lake — has provided new context and a rich new frame for appreciating my own experiences in and around Pike's Portage. But the work has also clearly demonstrated that a book with one locale at its core can work as a foil to uncoil the tangled complexities of place. With maps and photos thrown in for good measure, and with Jane Gibson's steady hand on the editing pencil, I suspect that for other readers it will do just the same.

James Raffan
Kingston, Ontario

List of Maps

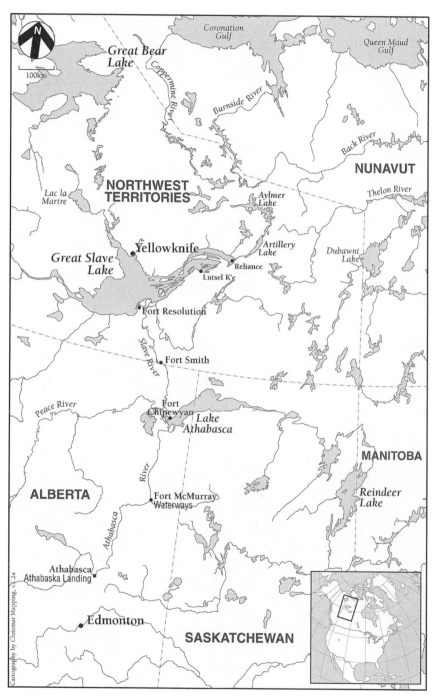

Map 1. Overview of Region.

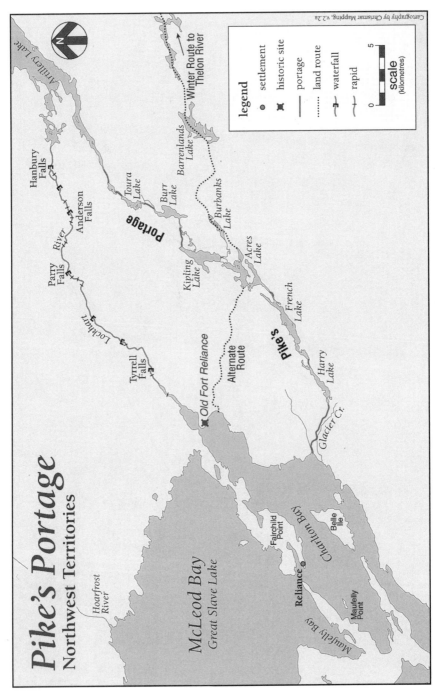

Map 2. Pike's Portage.

Photo by Morten Asfeldt/Chrismar Mapping Services Inc.

Pike's Portage is seen here from a mile and a half above Artillery Lake. The view looks west toward Great Slave Lake.

19

We had to make use of a chain of lakes, eight in number, lying to the south of the stream. This is by far the prettiest part of the country that I saw in the North, and it was looking its best under the bright sunshine that continued till we reached the fort. Scattering timber, spruce and birch, clothed the sloping banks down to the sandy shores of the lakes; berries of many kinds grew in profusion; the portages were short and down hill; and caribou were walking the ridges and swimming the lakes in every direction. A perfect northern fairyland it was, and it seemed hard to believe that winter and want could ever penetrate here; but on the shore of a lovely blue lake Pierre the Fool pointed out a spot where the last horrors of death and cannibalism had been enacted within his memory.[1]

— Warburton Pike, *The Barren Ground of Northern Canada*

Introduction

Pike's Portage is more than a trail leading from Great Slave Lake to Artillery Lake at the edge of the Barrens in the Northwest Territories. It is an age-old trail that has been used by Native people for centuries as an access route to the Barrens and to the herds of caribou that sustained their lives. It is a route that *makes sense* geographically in this land, avoiding the canyons and waterfalls of the nearly impassable Lockhart River.[1] It is a route that reflects the intimate and necessary knowledge of the Dene and Métis people that allowed them to survive in this remote and often harsh place. More recently it has served as a transition to and from the remote windswept Barrens and the more hospitable and inhabited shores of Great Slave Lake for early explorers, sportsman, and adventurers who travelled east and west across northern Canada. In the early twentieth century it was a trapper's rite of passage, marking a commitment to a long, cold winter in the pursuit of white fox and wolf furs and the unending quest for caribou to fend off starvation for themselves and their dogs. Today, few dog-team or snowshoe tracks are seen on Pike's Portage; rather, in late winter and spring, the trail is packed hard by snow machines carrying hunters from the nearby community

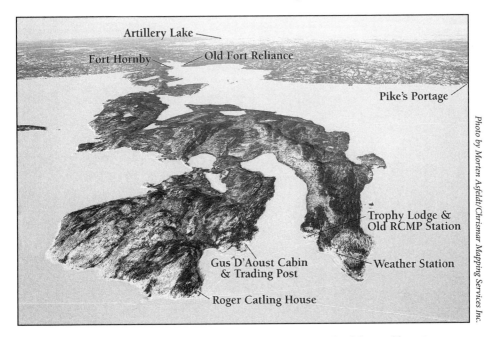

Fairchild Point separates McLeod and Charlton bays. The mouth of the Lockhart River and the Barrens can be seen in the distance.

of Lutsel K'e[2] in search of caribou and muskox. In summer, only a few footprints mark the path: those of the most committed and adventurous canoe parties, who carry heavy loads uphill through a series of lakes and portages before reaching Artillery Lake, where they launch their canoes and set out for Baker Lake, Chantrey Inlet, or perhaps Kugluktuk — journeys that will take them most of the ice-free summer months.

Navigating the ocean of Great Slave Lake and struggling over Pike's Portage is an experience shared by most people whose stories linger in the East Arm, and for us, as for many others, knowing these stories has given voice to the rocks, hills, trails, sandy beaches, and old, weathered cabins of this historically rich and geographically unique and beautiful place — this distinguished place. As we have travelled by snowshoe, dog team, canoe, and even airplane, our experience and imaginations have been filled with images and stories that breathe life into the land and enable us to travel with a heightened curiosity that would otherwise be missing. While we are both mesmerized by this region and its stories, and some of our experiences of the place are shared, we come to it along two separate and unique paths. Let us explain.

Morten's Path

My first glimpse of the East Arm of Great Slave Lake came early one July morning in 1995 as I sat in the cockpit of a Twin Otter headed for Lynx Lake at the headwaters of the Thelon River. We were flying above a broken layer of clouds as I chatted away with the pilot, who I had come to know after numerous northern canoe trips. I had read many of the stories included in this book and knew well of Pike's Portage and the route to the Thelon down the Hanbury River, yet, as I peered out the cockpit window that early July morning, I was unable to piece together the geographical puzzle as we flew above a layer of cloud that resembled Swiss cheese.

In planning this canoe trip, our group had considered portaging over Pike's Portage and following the traditional route to the Thelon, but, in hindsight, I think we were intimidated by the experiences of the early explorers, surveyors, sportsman, and trappers, who described the ruggedness of the country and great effort required to make that journey. I wish now that we had gone that way.

In April 2004, I finally made my first trip over Pike's Portage. I had joined Dave Olesen on a dog-team trip that took us up the Hoarfrost River to Walmsley Lake, overland to Artillery Lake, down Pike's Portage, and across McLeod Bay to Dave and Kristen's homestead at the mouth of the Hoarfrost River. Dave, who I had met fifteen years earlier on a first-aid course and then crossed paths with a number of times on the float-plane docks in Yellowknife, had contacted me to see if we could work together to provide a winter outdoor education experience for students from Augustana Campus, where I teach. After a busy semester of teaching, rescheduling final exams, and drying my sleeping bag from a recent ski-touring trip, I made my way to Lutsel K'e, where Dave met me in his two-seater Husky airplane on skis. We flew in bright sunshine over Christie Bay, the Kahochella Peninsula, and McLeod Bay, before landing on the ice in front of a dog yard of barking huskies at their homestead. This time the geographical puzzle began to fit together. I knew only that I was headed out on an eight-day dog-team journey that would take us beyond the treeline — I had no idea that our route would include Pike's

Portage, or that it would be the beginning of my passion for this place. I have now made six journeys to the East Arm and three trips over Pike's Portage — two by dog team and one by canoe — and countless more imaginary ones.

So, I ask myself: What is it about this place that has such a grip on me? I am not sure I fully understand, but I have a few ideas. As a child, I came by boat from Denmark to New York, and then drove with my parents and older brother in a Volkswagen Bug to Kansas City, where my father completed his medical training. In 1967, we moved, of all places, to St. Anthony, Newfoundland — a small community of 2,500 people on the northern tip of the Great Northern Peninsula, a few miles from L'Anse aux Meadows. We spent five years in this rugged landscape, and it made a great impression on me that I now see as the origin of my love of wilderness travel, wild places, and their associated stories. It was here that I read a narrative about Sir Wilfred Grenfell, who travelled up and down the coast of Newfoundland and Labrador providing medical services to remote and isolated communities. That experience of reading about his life and adventures remains vivid today. My father also travelled up and down the coast of Newfoundland and Labrador providing medical services to many of those still remote and isolated communities, although by modern ship, plane, or helicopter rather than the more primitive means that Grenfell used. I was fortunate to be allowed to skip school and travel with my father on many occasions — these trips were a highlight of my childhood.

As I made my way over Pike's Portage in April 2004, it was as if I was transported back to my Newfoundland childhood; the landscape was remarkably similar, with stunted black spruce and birch trees, granite outcrops, and rolling hills covered with snow and bathed in the warm spring sun. Memories of spring snowmobile outings and hospital parties with ice fishing and bonfires in the White Hills of Newfoundland flowed easily from deep within my memory.

The morning I was to fly back to Yellowknife from Dave and Kristen's homestead, we sat drinking tea and making plans for me to bring a group of students to Hoarfrost River homestead for two weeks in February 2005.[3] In the weeks and months that followed, I tried to envision a course that would be more than just a fun dog-team trip in the Northwest Territories

Two unidentified men carry loads over Pike's Portage in the early 1900s.

in the deep and cold of winter. As I had been travelling south on Artillery Lake a few days earlier, being pulled along by a team of seven dogs, I could sense the rich history of the place and felt as if I was travelling with the ghosts of John Hornby, the Norwegian, Helge Ingstad, and elder Noel Drybones; and as I rode the brake as hard as I could down the last steep section of Pike's Portage, passing stumps in the forest, I began to wonder what the story of those stumps were. Could George Back and his crews have cut them? Maybe it was Gus D'Aoust or Guy Blanchet. Who knows? That day we also stopped to visit Roger Catling. He wasn't home as we pressed our snow hooks into the spring snow and flipped our sleds over to hold the dogs; nevertheless, at least now I know where this man I had heard so much about lived, and whose cabin on the Thelon River I had visited in 1995.

In preparing for the course, Dave sent me a bibliography of books and narratives from the region. It was a long list, most of which I have now read. At the same time, I began to ponder which of my colleagues at Augustana might be interested in partnering with me to develop and teach this new course and provide an additional lens to help students understand their northern experience. I wanted this course to be something more than just another fun trip to satisfy the adventure-junkies in the program. It took only ten minutes of conversation with my friend and colleague, Dr. Ingrid Urberg, associate professor of Scandinavian Studies, who has spend much of her research life studying personal narratives from Norway's remote Svalbard, to know that she could add a whole new dimension to the course. Together we gathered narratives from the region, as well as from the wider circumpolar world of Canada and Scandinavian; the pile of books became staggeringly tall. Slowly, after teaching the course a few times, more reading, more travelling in the region, and coming to know Roger Catling and his story, I realized that, while the region has a rich and diverse history that is partially captured in the published narratives, nowhere were they gathered together providing a focused and comprehensive sense of its storied past. In fact, some stories weren't published at all. With a goal to remedy these facts in mind, we began this project.

However, perhaps this project really began more than forty years ago and thousands of miles to the east in the storied ruggedness of northern Newfoundland, where my father tells me I met Helge and Anne Stine Ingstad in 1967. I was five years old at the time, and we were on one of our frequent outings to L'Anse aux Meadows, a few short miles from St. Anthony. While I have no specific memory of meeting the Ingstads, I do have clear memories of people on their hands and knees digging with small shovels and sweeping carefully with tiny brooms as they excavated the Viking site. I also remember my father's enthusiasm at meeting these other Scandinavians, whom he had read about in a recent issue of *National Geographic*.[4] It wasn't until the summer of 2007, when on a pilgrimage of sorts with my father and younger brother back to St. Anthony — our first visit since leaving thirty-five years earlier — and we stood listening to the stories of our park interpreter at L'Anse aux Meadows, that I began to wonder: Had I meet Helge Ingstad here as a child? By then I knew the story of his trapping life on the Barrens, and when my father confirmed that I had met him and Anne Stine here, I began to wonder if perhaps those first glimpses of Great Slave Lake in 1995, that first trip with Dave Olesen in 2004, and my subsequent fascination with the East Arm of Great Slave Lake had not been long in the works — if not inevitable.

Bob's Path

> Had a stop with coffee in thermos for a long "look where I am"
> moment. Good view of great distance over to Reliance from hills
> over the Hoarfrost.

> — journal entry, February 2008

As a map-reader, or rather a traveller who dreams into
maps, I have long been an admirer of McLeod Bay and the East Arm
of Great Slave Lake with its hills rising to the plateau eight hundred
feet above the lake. Seemingly endless waterways (all challenging) exist
on this plateau above Great Slave Lake, taking one out of the treeline
and onto the Barrens: Warburton Pike's winter route north, involving
the Mountain and McKinlay rivers, which still confounds trail seekers;
George Back's "crazy" route up the Hoarfrost; the Anderson and Stewart
1855 climb "out of the lake" with plans to search for Franklin and crew at
the mouth of the Back (Great Fish) River. These are all *byways* — a phrase
used to describe the lesser-known and lesser-used routes to the Barrens
from the East Arm of Great Slave Lake. Pike's Portage, the ancient canoe
and dog-team highway, is now a *travel way*.

The portage rises from a beautiful beach that once showcased an
impressive lobstick spruce tree[5] in Tyrrell's 1900 photograph (see page
77). Here Hornby wandered with his companions; Blanchet worked
steadily as a surveyor; many regional trappers carved out a living with
plenty of stories; E.T. Seton, Buffalo Jones, and Warburton Pike all
looked for muskox with an imposing local Dene and Métis guiding
presence — in this capacity, the Métis Beaulieu clan stand tall. Here, too,
Pike had the support of the Yellowknife guide Saltatha, Buffalo Jones had
the watchdog Sousie Barromie, Guy Blanchet travelled with companion
Sousi Beaulieu, and the list goes on. These Native companions and guides
involve a particularly challenging stretch of my imagination. They were
not the writers. I must *dream into them* like the tripper dreams into
maps. I'm always adding fuel to my internal fire. It transports my mind
to places where I will eventually travel if the fire grows large enough. This

This is a long-awaited view of Great Slave Lake from Pike's Portage after leaving Harry Lake.

Photo by Morten Asfeldt.

distinguished place has become my bonfire. This is a landscape that fills the imagination like few others in the Canadian North for its wealth of stories and characters.

Then there is its transitional geography, from Taiga spruce forests to the land of the little sticks at the edge of the treeline, up to the Barrenlands in an 820-foot rise twenty to thirty miles of travel north or east from McLeod Bay. Like Pike's Dene and Métis guides, the edge of the treeline is what I like best. It is a northern landscape, remarkable for its history and geography.

While sitting on my skis high over McLeod Bay with a crystal-clear twilight overhead and a blanket of new snow shimmering like a million lights from the lake below, I realized that sitting and staring made more sense than continued skiing. Wow! What a place! Despite the twenty-below conditions, I had dressed for a ski with a long sit and was reminded of the reworked saying, "Don't just do something, sit there." Staring widely and wondering was a great privilege here, and I thought, *how exciting is history when sitting amidst its geography*. Here the two fitted together like hot coffee and a twenty-below day. The hills were beautiful and the lake massive, its scale frightening. There is geography here like in no other place and a history also like no other.

Earlier, in August of 2006, while with Morten, Margot Peck, and Jacqueline Akerman, I'd felt this geography/topography directly with a humiliatingly easy load for the downhill portage from Artillery Lake to Great Slave Lake. No stove on my back heading up to the Thelon River as Hornby had done in 1926.[6] No carrying of supplies uphill for a full summer out on the Barrens. No, just a friendship group out for ten days to participate in this blending of history and geography and to brainstorm a possible Pike's Portage book. This time I wanted to do something. *Sit there* was not an option — it was my first time in the region and there was just so much to see. Would the weather allow us time to get over to Old Fort Reliance[7] and Back's chimneys? Yes! Would we have the time and energy to hike into Parry Falls and share a telling of the legend of the old lady who sits in the falls? No. Would Roger Catling be home so we might enjoy a time hearing about his life as a wolf hunter and his travels on the Barrens? Yes!

To date, I have taken two trips in this country and I'm certain it will be a place of repeat visits for me. As I write, I'm planning a 2010 summer trip along the Lockhart River to Timber Bay on Artillery Lake, with a visit to Hornby and Critchell-Bullock's 1924–25 esker cave, or maybe a paddle from Old Fort Reliance with that visit to Parry Falls, many hikes onto the McLeod Bay hills, and perhaps a paddle all the way to Taltheilei Narrows — the "place of open water."[8] Or maybe, with John McInnes's help, I might canoe and hike and search for Pike's winter route onto the plateau. *Hmmm*, that's ambitious. Whatever trip it is to be, it will evoke the same feeling — a swell of calm excitement and satisfaction for simply being there, sitting, and then moving over that storied land. Knowing when to pause and stare and wonder, and when to go steady: this is a traveller's skill learned over time.

With each visit, I'll get to know all these people better: Charles Jesse Buffalo Jones, Ernest Thompson Seton, Helge Ingstad, Gus D'Aoust, and locals Roger Catling and Dave and Kirsten Olesen, even Souci "King" Beaulieu. Each visit will involve another read of the journals and reports or one or more of the stories provided here. This book will help me and others advance our thinking of how to blend history and geography with our own combination of active sitting and moving. This is a book founded in the notion of activeness and activity.[9] We hope it propels a *felt* experience of activeness first — activeness being *present* in a place, and investing that place in meaning. Such activeness creates a sharpened attention and "aliveness." This is a region worthy of such special attention and, as noted by Larry Innes in his chapter, special attention is likely forthcoming.

In the main, though, there is activity. Activity alone, simply the doing of something — paddling a canoe, gathering winter wood — maybe

Photo by Morten Asfeldt.

Bob Henderson looks northeast over Artillery Lake as we begin to make our way over Pike's Portage toward Great Slave Lake. This is also the first view of Artillery Lake when coming uphill from Great Slave Lake.

shallow or undirected, yet such activity can be advanced with imagination and thoughtfulness, leading to a bigger picture. With activeness, activity — such as travel — can come alive within us as understanding and even wisdom. Part of the wisdom is putting oneself in the right place within this landscape. When compared with the trips made by Warburton Pike and his guide Saltatha, mine hardly measure up — yet that's part of the point. It is easy, and wise, to be regularly astonished in this landscape. Just think of George Back and crew climbing with gear up the Hoarfrost!

There is a saying: "If you learn a skill without learning the way, you've learned nothing."[10] We hope this collection of stories will enhance "the way" of activeness within this distinguished place. Perhaps we need to look no farther for the advancement of "the way" than the often quoted — for good reason — passage that closes Warburton Pike's 1892 book, *The Barren Ground of Northern Canada.* I turn to my treasured 1892 copy and write out this passage, knowing I have shared it often with students along more southern Canadian Shield waterways:

To the man who is not a lover of Nature in all her moods the Barren Ground must always be a howling, desolate wilderness; but for my part, I can understand the feeling that prompted Saltatha's answer to the worthy priest, who was explaining to him the beauties of Heaven. My father, you have spoken well; you have told me that Heaven is very beautiful; tell me now one thing more. Is it more beautiful than the country of the musk-ox in summer, when sometimes the mist blows over the lakes, and sometimes the water is blue, and the loons cry very often? That is beautiful; and if Heaven is still more beautiful, my heart will be glad, and I shall be content to rest there till I am very old.[11]

What's Coming in This Book

The stories of the people who have struggled over Pike's Portage are many and varied. They include sport hunters Warburton Pike, Ernest Thompson Seton, and Buffalo Jones; surveyors Guy Blanchet and the Tyrrell brothers; the eccentric John Hornby and his one-time partner James Critchell-Bullock; a long line of trappers including Helge Ingstad, Gus D'Aoust, and Roger Catling; Noel Drybones and the Métis guides of the Beaulieu clan; homesteaders Dave and Kristen Olesen; explorer George Back, who chose the nearly impossible Lockhart River route to Great Slave Lake over the traditional Pike's Portage route; Hudson's Bay Chief Factor James Anderson and James Stewart, who made their way over one of the *other* byways to the Barrens; and John McInnes, who has been retracing many of these lesser-known and hard to follow byways in a Sherlock Holmes manner as only he can. These are the stories that are included in this book. There could have been more — many more — like those of sportsman and wanderer David Hanbury; those of the RCMP who were stationed at Reliance; of Billy Hoare and Jack Knox, who established Warden's Grove on the Thelon River; of a number of other trappers from the early twentieth century; of countless recreational canoe trips; of Chris Norment and crew, who spent the winter of 1977–78 at Warden's Grove and had the Russian Cosmos satellite fall into their isolation; of the Norwegian Lars Monson, who spent three years travelling from Alaska to Goose Bay, Labrador, and passed through Reliance in 2001; or of polar explorer Will Steger and crew, who pushed their way over Pike's Portage in 2004 as a part of the Arctic Transect Expedition.

We also humbly acknowledge that the endless and largely unrecorded travels of Native people rightly dominate this place and are under-represented in our collection, yet not completely absent. Sadly, many of the Native stories remain only in the memories of an aging generation, and as each year passes, more are lost. Even so, to acknowledge and honour that Pike's Portage, known to the local Denesoline as *Ka a Ku*, meaning "Place where you go up to the lake,"[12] we include René Fumoleau's poem, "Wolf," as the prologue to this book.

Father René Fumoleau spent most of his adult life living with Aboriginal people along the Mackenzie River, beginning in 1953, before retiring to Lutsel K'e. Father Fumoleau is a Catholic priest who has a deep understanding of traditional Native life and has worked tirelessly on their behalf while sharing his experiences and insights through poetry, story, and photography. We selected this poem on René Fumoleau's recommendation as reflective of traditional life in this region.

So why *these* stories? There are many reasons. First, there is only so much room in a book before you need a freighter canoe just to cart it around. Second, we feel our collection of stories provide a diverse representation over time, beginning with archaeological discoveries and followed by early explorers, sports hunters, surveyors, trappers, as well as those few who live there today. Third, the stories include some that are reasonably well-known and central to the region's history, such as George Back and John Hornby, some that are less well-known like Buffalo Jones, Gus D'Aoust, and Dave and Kristen Olesen, as well as a few that have yet to be published, including those about the Beaulieu clan, Noel Drybones, Lawrence Catholique, and Roger Catling. However, we acknowledge that the collection is incomplete and that two other editors may rightfully have chosen a different collection of stories that could be equally representative, interesting, and telling of the region. Nevertheless, these are our selections.

And what about these people we have selected? Aside from their travels and lives that, for the most part, include journeys over Pike's Portage, they all share an element of mystery and complexity. As Harry, a fictional Yellowknife radio station manager in Elizabeth Hay's prize-winning novel *Late Nights on Air* suggests, there is more than one way of looking at people. Harry was reading *The Legend of John Hornby*[13] as he prepared for a canoe trip on the Thelon River, and had this to say about Hornby:

> If you took his life as a series of disasters in rapid succession, if you saw him as a distillation of his shortcomings, then you'd call him a loser, feckless, under-prepared, dangerous. If you saw him, instead, in all his complexity, in the fullness of his extraordinary life, then he was no less irresponsible, but he was also astonishingly vivid, driven, solitary, intense, endearing. Harry was all for seeing people in their complexity and having them return the favour.[14]

The stories in this book are about complex people who have lived extraordinary lives. We have attempted to capture this complexity and encourage readers to see past the surface of their stories so that you might see the many layers that compose these people and their distinctive lives — and trust that same favour will be returned to you.

Prologue

Wolf

Antione is fifty years old.
He and his eight brothers and sisters
were born in a tent somewhere
in what is called the Barren Land.

How many times the Denes have told me
with love, passion, or nostalgia:

"The Barren Land, it's so beautiful!
There is nothing!"

And, after all, it is not barren:
Grass, moss, lichens, and shrubs grow there,
and there is enough food for caribou herds
numbering 50,000, 100,000, or more.
Who could count the grizzlies, wolves, black bears,

foxes, wolverines, hares, ravens,
and many other small inhabitants?

I was twelve or thirteen years old,
Antione told me.
My dad had set a long trapline to catch white foxes.
Me, I was learning with a few traps
not so far from our tent.

One December morning,
when the sun never rises even at noon,
I started with my four dogs.
I had already visited a few traps
when wind, snow, and blizzard enfolded us.
Stretching out my arm, I couldn't see my hand.

I turned my toboggan upside down,
and crawled underneath.
The dogs, too, knew their trade:
they curled themselves along the toboggan
on the protected side.
The "evening," the whole "night"!

Finally the storm tired itself out
and a pale daylight appeared.
The dogs shook themselves free of snow,
and crawled out from under my toboggan.
The clouds reached the ground.
The frozen waves of the snowdrifts
looked totally unfamiliar.
Not one usual landmark!

'Where is North? South?
Where is our camp?'

My dogs had often shown better flair than me.

Prologue

I harnessed them.
I faced the team in one direction, in another one,
but they didn't move.
Nowhere to go.

Then I heard some noise and I turned my head.
Twenty metres behind us
a white wolf walked quietly,
a barren land wolf, two metres long.

The wolf walked by us
and veered a bit to the left.
I don't know why, but the dogs heeled.
I jumped onto the toboggan
and we followed the wolf,
one hour, two hours?
I don't know, I don't know.

At one point, the wolf turned his head
and looked at me and the dogs.
Then he galloped away toward the left.

I looked ahead. I looked around
to the right, to the left:

'Oh, I know where we are.
Our tent is behind that hill,
ten minutes away, straight ahead.'[1]

René Fumoleau
Yellowknife, Northwest Territories

Part I

A Storied Trail

I've heard it said that the country makes men and the city uses them and I know it is so … and in my mind there is a huge difference between men who did big spectacular things and men who were great in themselves. Probably some of the greatest men who ever lived have never been heard of, never had one line written about them, they were of the earth and returned to the earth …[1]

— Elliott Merrick, *True North*, 1942

Chapter 1

Pike's Portage: A Story in Deep Time

Only a massive body of water like Great Slave Lake could give rise to the mighty Mackenzie River. Like most lakes with historical and geographical significance, Great Slave is a rich source of sustenance and provides many reasons and avenues for arrival and departure. Like a pinwheel, it centripetally and centrifugally draws people in and sends them out again, and has for millennia. The route followed by Warburton Pike in 1889–90 along the Lockhart and the portage which strangely took his name was an ancient route with many paths, most of them worn by the uncountable caribou that enjoyed this neck of the woods and by the people who depended on the herds during the past five to eight thousand years. Pike's book, *The Barren Ground of Northern Canada*,[1] of course, brought the old trail to wider attention.

Early accounts of the eighteenth-century inhabitants of the Mackenzie Basin have come down to us from Mackenzie and Hearne,[2] and late-nineteenth-century accounts by such men as Diamond Jenness and Bryan Gordon,[3] summarized in 1932 and 1996 respectively, describe the impact on the local cultures of the Euro-intervention. Nonetheless, the Slavey Dene, Dogrib (Tłįcho), Yellowknife (Tatsanottine), and

This is a view of the beach that marks the beginning of Pike's Portage from a high rocky outcrop to the south.

Courtesy of Russell/NWT Archives/N-1979-073-0831.

Chipewyan (Denesoline) people have survived and still occupy the territory of their ancestors. Their Na-Dene language family, which has links across the Bering Strait and includes language variants that extend all the way from northwestern Canada to the American southwest, continues to be spoken.

The area was archaeologically unknown until the middle of the last century, when Richard McNeish,[4] from the National Museum of Canada, and his guide, Sam Otto,[5] went on a quick canoe and bush-plane survey in 1949 and realized that there were several cultural periods represented north and east of Great Slave Lake that covered quite a span of time. I was fortunate to be part of the follow-up to this pioneering work in 1966. My work had been primarily Great Lakes oriented up till then, but I had quite a bit of bush experience and was happy to accompany Bill Noble,[6] a distinguished northern archaeologist and professor of anthropology at McMaster University in Hamilton, Ontario, on the first of his many trips to the Barrenlands.

As a student, Bill had worked with Jim Wright from the National Museum in 1964–65, surveying in parts of Manitoba, Saskatchewan, and Alberta. Bill and I spent two months, from late July to the end of August, working around Great Slave Lake, initially travelling by truck — since our canoe hadn't yet arrived by barge in Hay River — and then by air and water. After July 25, much of our time was spent at the east end of the lake. When archaeologists use the term *survey* they mean "looking around for and documenting artifacts and sites." Of course, the process is informed by background research and levels of strategy, but one of the techniques used in the early stages of the process is talking to people who have been out there. For McNeish, Sam Otto of Yellowknife was one of those informants. He also happened to have several documented collections of artifacts.

Aside from using informants, archaeology is aided by the reality that a place that was a good campsite hundreds of years ago is likely a good campsite today. Any of us who have travelled in the bush know the difference between a good campsite and a mediocre one. Consequently, geologists and other field people, such as hunters and anglers — whether Native or non-Native — notice the remains of past human use of the land at attractive campsites, and know that talking to people familiar with such places can save a lot of time. Also, it is hoped that no one who has passed that way has removed important artifacts because they are few and far between, and one arrowhead of a particular type in its original location can tell researchers a lot.

Archaeologists discover, contribute to, and use data from many other fields, including history, geology, and biology. By using a broad range of information, archaeology is one way of proving that time exists, and demonstrating that geography and the environment change over time, and that human societies, which are based on environmental opportunities, also evolve. In the same way that geologists understand time by describing different layers and sequences of rock, or biologists describe groupings of species and subspecies in their environmental context, archaeologists organize their findings using terms such as *cultures, cultural complexes, periods, stages,* and *traditions.* Remains of human activity can take the form of different tools, and of tool or artifact clusters within various types of settlements. Settlement types can be recognized as forming similar groups or patterns, and are useful in distinguishing one group from another. Where similar settlement types and styles of living occupy a generally similar zone, they can be referred to as a cultural *complex.* When a group of roughly similar complexes are broadly distributed through space and time, they are referred to as *traditions.*

Settlement types in the North can be radically different from those that existed around the same time in the south, due to distinct opportunities and the effect of contrasting influences. For example, people who were hunter-gatherers would be part of different traditions than horticultural people. The artifacts and settlements of cultures hunting bison in the south ten thousand years ago can be very similar to those hunting similar species in the North several thousand years later, because flora and fauna, including people, were following a retreating ice front. These people could be part of a similar tradition.

Once our canoe arrived in Hay River, Bill and I went to the Bay store and bought 110 dollars' worth of food — enough to last two men for a month — and fourteen dollars worth of lures and other gear, which included thirty-five gallons of gas, and four gallons of naphtha. From a modern perspective, it seems like a ridiculously small cost.

On July 25, Willy Laserich, a renegade northern pilot,[7] flew us down the lake and into Charlton Bay, following the massive MacDonald Fault that is the source of the impressive cliffs of the East Arm. Anyone who knew Willy would understand when I say that he followed the ruggedly breathtaking valleys and fault lines at somewhere just slightly higher than treetop level, buzzing Native camps, cemeteries, the occasional post, a young moose, and the town of Snowdrift (now Lutsel K'e). As the elevation rose toward the east, we were treated to a sense of geological turmoil that was absolutely out of this world.

Landing at the government float-plane dock in Reliance, we were met by Gus D'Aoust,[8] the well-known free trader, and Gene Rasminsky from the weather station. Gus and Delphine, his Chipewyan wife, lived in a beautifully situated log house that was furnished exactly as a log house should be, with rustic furniture, a big wood stove, white wolf heads, and guns and bearskins on the walls. We talked for a while, had some pie and tea, then gingerly loaded our eighteen-foot Chestnut square-stern canoe. Gus said that if we managed to make it to the portage with all our gear, we would find that arrowheads were pretty common around there.

We carefully headed east down the bay to Belle Island, between Reliance and Pike's Portage, where we set up camp and cached half our food. The water was cold, green, and clear like Lake Superior, and the mountainous terrain was spectacular. Our campsite was littered with caribou skull fragments, mandibles, lower limbs, vertebrae, and antlers,

Photo by Peter Carruthers.

Peter Carruthers's canoe and tent rest on the sandy beach on Great Slave Lake that marks the beginning of Pike's Portage. This photo was taken in 1966.

as well as the remains of several structures. Among the hearths that remained, we found several children's boats hanging from strings.

The next day, after making sure our gear and supplies were in order, we tied on our new Red-Devil lures and trolled around. A strike slowed the canoe, and after considerable time we saw we had caught a huge lake trout that would have to be pulled up on the beach because it was too big to lift into our canoe. The trout provided enough meat to feed six people, and so began our habit of fishing, eating, and smoking meat to eat later — a nice way to spend the evening, and a practice that became a common purposeful pastime. The next day, wind and rain gave us an opportunity to explore the island, identify and record some sites, and, from the rocky summit above the slate-grey water, see the sands at the western terminus of Pike's Portage.

We travelled from Belle Island to the mouth of a creek with extensive sand formations and erosional features just north of the beginning of the portage. On the side of the valley were sixty-five to eighty-foot pinkish bedrock, quartzite bluffs. And gazing up the valley,

Photo by Morten Asfeldt.

Bob Henderson admires a copper pot found by Roger Catling on an island near Reliance.

on the south side you could see terracing, which had been formed by the rising of the land due to glacial rebound or changing water levels in Great Slave Lake. Seeking an overview of the terrain, we climbed up through the woods to the high rocky ridge north of the little river, where the sheer cliffs rose two to three hundred feet above the lake. From there was a beautiful view toward Charlton Bay, Fairchild Peninsula, Belle Island, and, in the distance, Reliance. More importantly, we had a cross-sectional view of the portage route, upslope toward Harry Lake, with bedrock cliffs bounding it on the south side and a steep drop into a river valley on the north.

As we climbed north we found, well above the shore and nestled in an open exposure of sand surrounded by large boulders, a camp littered with slate flakes, scrapers, quartz and quartzite tools, as well as larger fleshing and chopping tools made from local bedrock, and beautiful flakes of a soft green translucent chert (a rock that flakes when broken and is commonly used for making arrowheads) — all just lying there as they were left hundreds of years ago. There was also a light covering of reindeer moss around old lichen-covered

46

hearthstones. Sites like these are like moments frozen in time, as if the people had heard us coming, and silently vanished. After setting up camp on a perfect parabolic beach of coarse sand nicely sheltered by a bedrock bluff to the south, we returned to what we initially called Pike's Portage number one — the name we gave to this first of many archaeological campsites along the trail.

The beginning of the portage lies on the side of an outwash valley confined by bedrock cliffs and defined by a small river along the north side. We called it Lobo Creek because of the huge wolf tracks that we kept seeing every morning near our tracks from the day before. From here the beach strands rise like steps back from shore, scantly wooded with birch and spruce. The lower levels are sparsely grass-covered and the upper reaches support reindeer moss.

The first three beach terraces were scattered with gear from the recent multi-seasonal Native occupation, including sledges, backpack frames, one toboggan, hearths, caribou remains, traps, tin cans, washtubs for fish nets, tent stakes, both round and square tent outlines, and many fish clubs whose use we now understood clearly. Hanging from the central trunk of a spruce, under dense branches, were about fifty muskrat traps. Although there were clear caribou trails heading east up the hill, we had no knowledge of the lay of the land or how this portage worked.

After dinner that day, we walked east, upslope, past an historic cemetery, and discovered one of the most compact records of post-glacial rebound and lake-level change that I had ever seen. Like benches, these raised beaches curved, nesting concentrically up along braided caribou trails through the moss. And on many of the terraces, beginning just above the recent Dene campsite, archaeological remains littered the sand exposures. In a classic way, the raw materials and tool types seemed to vary with elevation, and we had the sensation of walking through time, since there was a very real likelihood that each occupation occurred on a beach beside a lake, the shore of which had long since dropped to the present level — two hundred feet below. I had previously documented lake-level changes in Michigan and Ontario, and we had noticed several raised beaches during our work to that point. But the nature of a portage is such that travellers

Photo by Peter Carruthers

Peter Carruthers excavated this old campsite in 1966. The trail of Pike's Portage can be seen behind the campsite.

tended to land, get organized, and move, as opposed to staying for long periods. Campsites would be adjacent to the water at either end, temporary but habitual. Depending on the length of the carry, there might be resting places along the way, but generally activities would be concentrated at either end. The nature of this end of the portage meant that the record was confined to relatively narrow strips of beach strands rising from the lake.

Time is a tricky thing to determine in the absence of organic cultural materials, which in the subarctic tend to disappear in the acid soils and as a result of the gnawing of rodents. Very little of the organic material on the lower beaches, for example, would survive more than a century, leaving only stone, metal, and buried bone. This portage was like a multi-layered, linear, stratified site.

As a result of the beach-strand campsites, the focus of our work had suddenly changed from simply documenting sites to one of doing a contour survey of the beaches so that we would have some basis for associating these former campsites with time and each other. It quickly became clear that we would not make it to Artillery Lake this time. Using driftwood, measuring tapes, and string, we made a line level and set out to plot the terraces and record the cultures from Great Slave to Harry Lake. There were twenty-five beaches in all. About twelve of the terraces had complex sites on them. Several of these camps had material dating over several hundred years, indicating variability in rebound or periods of stability in lake levels.

In 1969, Bill Noble had the chance to travel the route from Artillery Lake to Charlton Bay and found only four sparse little sites along the trail east of Harry Lake. However, other evidence suggests that Artillery Lake has been at the treeline since 3000 B.C. and there are several important archaeological sites on its shores.

The earliest sites, up to 130 feet above the lake, at the highest part of our beach sequence, suggested penetrations as far as Artillery Lake by people from the grasslands to the south of Great Slave Lake looking for caribou or bison during the 2500 to 1500 B.C. period. From one hundred feet on down are sites exhibiting strong evolving Athapascan traditions focused on the caribou herds and fishing.

Those who are interested in the evidence on which these interpretations are based are directed to Bryan Gordon's book *People of Sunlight, People of Starlight*. He makes sense of the vast amount of research that has gone on since 1950 and the bewildering array of raw materials and tools such as lanceolate points (long narrow spearheads used for hunting big game animals) and *chithos* (crescent-shaped chopping tools made of stone, used to butcher animals), microblades, burins and snub-nosed scrapers, and copper and bone tools found within the treeline and out on the Barrens. Gordon also includes excellent historical photographs of the people and useful anthropological interpretation.

Pike's Portage was not a centre of occupation but rather a means to an end and only one of many routes to and from the Barrens (see chapter 5). But the evidence from the trail indicated wide-ranging relationships throughout Dene territory during at least four thousand years and no doubt longer. And during the six to eight thousand years that the territory was ice-free, there were huge changes in drainage, flora, and fauna as the glaciers shrank away. Glacial Lake McConnell became present-day Great Slave Lake by 8,500 years before present. Forests expanded and contracted. Wood bison (*Bison,*

bison athabascae) evolved from thousands of years of inter-mingling between *Bison, bison occidentalis* and *Bison antiquus,* and began to inhabit the region.[9] Caribou herds, prey to the arctic wolves and the barren land grizzly, developed territorial migration patterns. These predators, along with the vast migrating herds of caribou, were all formidable challenges to hunters.

The Dene people lived in a tough and uncertain environment, which, although immensely rich in resources, was a difficult place to exist. Their close relationships spanned an area from the Mackenzie River to the lower Thelon, and from north of Great Bear Lake down to the Churchill River. Hunting bison and caribou and fishing for whitefish and lake trout with boats and equipment made from bone, hide, stone, bark, and wood was no small feat. A twenty-five-mile portage was all in a day's work.

Peter Carruthers
Toronto, Ontario

Chapter 2

The Denesoline: Where Are All Their Stories?

We come to truly know the places we dwell through what we have read and the stories told to us, but ultimately through our own experiences. Our experiences, woven together with the knowledge and experiences of others produce a sense of place that informs our identity as well as the way in which we engage with the places we call home.[1]

— Hugh Brody

Hugh Brody, scholar and anthropologist, recently gave a lecture at the University of Alberta, during which he recounted some of his experiences in Sanikiluaq, Nunavut.[2] He lived in this tiny Inuit village for several years during the 1970s, and became intimately connected to the landscape and the people of the community. Although he has had numerous research experiences since that time, he confessed that they all seemed shallow and short-lived when compared to the feeling of being part of the life of Sanikiluaq. The confession resonated with me, not only because it seemed an honest and self-critiquing reflection on a long and illustrious career, but because I share similar feelings about my own research experiences. Although I am currently involved in many challenging projects, I continue to feel as if nothing I have done since living in Lutsel K'e or nothing I am likely to do in the future will be as meaningful or powerful.

Lutsel K'e is a community of 340 people located on the East Arm of Great Slave Lake, about one hundred miles southwest of Pike's Portage. The community was located there in the 1960s; however, the traditional territory of the Denesoline (the Dene name for themselves, the Chipewyan people) extends many hundreds of miles beyond the community. Pike's Portage was historically, and continues to be, an important travel route from the community into the Barrenlands and to *Eda Cho* (Artillery Lake), which is a traditional site for barren ground caribou hunting.

Part of the power of my experience comes from the romance and exhilaration of youth and the adventure of being in a place little known to other Canadians. The belief in *community* and the impossibility of anonymity was also a draw — Lutsel K'e is so small that everyone, for better or for worse, becomes a part of your life. Despite its *tough* reputation, it was and is a romantic place.

The so-called history of the North, idealized in the glory and demise of northern explorers like Mackenzie and Hearne, is fraught with stereotypes of ice and snow and barren lands. The voices of northern Dene, Inuit, and Métis communities are seldom heard in the south — the details of their history and experience continue to be a footnote in our discourse about the North. The stories told by those of us who — for one reason or another — have become a part of a northern community offer another kind of perspective. If we are lucky, the relationships forged through random encounters and interactions deepen and continue over many years and open up boundless possibilities for learning. Not all of the learnings are, however, transferable segments of data or information. As noted by environmental educator Janet Pivnick, we come to learn in many different ways:

> We must listen to the land, observing it for a sufficient length of time to learn about wind patterns, to understand its response to cold, to watch the movement of water along its surface. This listening requires an immersion and an opening to what the land has to teach. Second,

we must read the signs that the place is offering and we must come to the place with a knowledge that allows for a thorough and sensitive reading. Third, we must come to the place with questions, and with the tools to find answers…. Finally, and underneath all of these tasks, is the requirement to care about and for this place. Love is required in order to "respond to the place as it really is" and "imagine possibilities that are really in it."[3]

The emotional and spiritual knowing of a place may be the most powerful, but it is also the most difficult to explain. How do we communicate ideas and experiences that transcend the structured and ordered ways of knowing? In writing this piece, I have struggled with determining what part of the story belongs to me, will belong to the reader through the reading, and what claim can be made by others to that same story? What part of the story is necessarily a discrete and self-sustaining phenomenon knowable only to those fortunate to have had the same or a similar experience?

Some of the initial sense of place or place identity I found in Lutsel K'e came from the feeling that I had been there before. Growing up in a small town in northeastern Ontario, I was immediately taken by the similarity of the landscape of Great Slave Lake and the boreal stands of spruce and pine to Temagami, Algonquin, and Superior. This Canadian Shield country, revered in song, prose, and paint by folk singers and the Group of Seven, is what I consider to be the essence of home. I grew up canoeing those Shield lakes I now know to be Anishinabe land — singing songs that were evocative of northern spaces and northern peoples.

Although I sought to return to northern Ontario to carry out graduate work, I was sidelined by an offer by the Canadian Arctic Resources Committee and Lutsel K'e Dene First Nation to document community perspectives about the potential socio-economic and environmental effects of diamond mining in the region. It was a small project that was to become a passion for more than five years. As a Master's student, eager to learn about the North, I initially found myself wandering through the University libraries in an effort to learn more about this place called Lutsel K'e. Developing an understanding of Lutsel K'e through text wasn't a straightforward or easy task. So it was that I jumped on a plane knowing little of historical figures like Samuel Hearne, John Hornby, Matonabee, and Thanadelther,[4] or about contemporary scholars working in the community, such as geographer and writer James Raffan[5] or professor and anthropologist Ellen Bielawski.[6]

I also knew little about the stories of white trappers who arrived in the 1920s and 1930s; their stories, which transpired over a period of less than a decade, seemed peripheral to the real Dene history of the region. Few elders I came to know offered comment about the persons or personalities that arrived in search of their fortunes during this time — perhaps because it was a dark period. It was the beginning of a change in the Dene way of life — of loss. In addition to the disease and forced sedenterization of the Dene and residential school policies, the relationship that people had to the land and resources they had depended on for thousands of years was also to change. As noted by environmental historians such as John Sandlos,[7] the relationship between government, non-Aboriginal trappers and hunters, and the Dene and Inuit people of the Northwest Territories at that time was fraught with conflict, and precipitated what Peter Usher, a geographer and northern scholar, has described as the "criminalization of subsistence."[8]

Although of limited interest and value to the people of Lutsel K'e, the tales that were written about the town and the surrounding area by Norwegian trapper Helge Ingstad appear to have much greater significance in his homeland.[9] I came to discover Helge's cult-like status there through meeting and entertaining a northern European woman seeking *Helge Ingstad's Dene* — the Dene of loincloth, caribou-skin teepees, and peace pipes. Having left her family and spent considerable dollars to travel to Canada, the misguided traveller was aghast to discover that the Dene wore parkas from the Sears catalogue, had running water, and ate Cheerios, not unlike her own family. I listened to her bold critique on the demise of Dene culture at a Band Council meeting and the patient but dismissive responses of the chief. I came away from the encounter awestruck by the lack of education of a seemingly very well-educated woman. But then again, how much do I really know about Norway? It does seem, however, that even within Canada we are a bit naive. The contemporary North is imaged by icebreakers and Coca-Cola commercials; any references to Native peoples are constrained by stereotypes of what is *traditional*. Where were all the stories of the elders who were born, lived, raised families, and died on the land we now know as Pike's Portage? Where are all the stories of the Denesoline youth who imagine their futures there?

Part of my purpose in Lutsel K'e was to work with elders and youth to document Lutsel K'e Dene history of the lands and resources of places like Pike's Portage. I came to know the Chipewyan (Denesoline) names and oral histories associated with the major lakes, landscape features, and spiritual sites in the area. Over several years, community members documented and mapped their history to preserve it for future generations. Youth, trained through the Wildlife, Lands and Environment Office, were able to interview their grandfathers and grandmothers, moms and dads, aunts and uncles, and transfer their stories into digital maps for land-use planning, environmental assessment, Treaty Entitlement negotiations, and protected area and park planning.

The most powerful teachings came from being on the land with elders, many of whom have now passed away. We came to know each other over five or more years — the relationship was built on the recognition that as an educated non-Aboriginal person with academic knowledge and skills, I could potentially translate the elders' experiences and perspectives into a language and context with influence over social and environmental policy. They in turn would teach me how to be "a good Dene woman." The idea was always said with a chuckle, obviously comic to those who considered my presence as a necessary but fleeting imposition. Plucking feathers and singeing black duck over the open fire in spring was my initiation. Having passed the test, I was soon invited to participate in spiritual ceremonies, shown how to gut and fillet lake trout, cut up moose meat for elders, and soak and stretch caribou hides to tan in the summer months. I learned to make dry-meat from caribou thighs — not too thick so that it would not dry and not too thin that it would tear and fall to pieces when hung over the wood stove to dry.

I also came to know this place through the eyes and heart of Lawrence Catholique. As a Dene man, a trapper, and a caribou hunter, his identity and sense of purpose emerged from his relationship and experiences living on the land with his grandfather. I first met Lawrence in Ottawa during a meeting about the potential environmental and socio-economic effects of Canada's first diamond mine. At the time, in 1995, there was grave concern not only about the effects on barren ground caribou populations but on communities and the well-being of current and future generations. Lawrence offered quiet but emotional perspectives based on his own experiences as a trapper and a hunter. Although not feeling quite himself in the Lord Elgin Hotel, he was determined to have an impact on decisions that would so clearly affect his life and livelihood. The land was known to him as Kache — "the place at the end of the lake."

We would often travel across to the north shore of Christie Bay; the summer trips to Kache were common for many families. The fastest route to Kache is through a small portage on the East Arm — for those with smaller boats, such as a seventeen-foot Lund, the portage could be easily passed with some muscle and determination. Lawrence was often among the first each spring to use the portage and would help clear and reconstruct the pulls so as to make it easier to pass. We would be followed by several others, including elders, and so it was a community effort to get everyone across. After being boxed in all winter, the warm breezes and physical challenge was welcome — although the spring blackflies were not.

In winter the route was fast; by skidoo we could make it in less than three or four hours. It was always amazing to me, those first few trips, how easily he could find his way *across* (meaning to the other side of the lake), around the open water of the Snowdrift River, through the narrows of the lakes and the tree-lined trails that led to Kache, and finally to the white light in the distance. Sometimes we would stop for tea and bannock and a rest from the noise of the skidoo. In the really cold weather he would find a dried spruce, fallen some years before, that would light in seconds into a magnificent bonfire. After I rubbed my feet until they were warm, we would venture out again to find Reliance. I would travel behind on the sled from time to time, particularly when it was empty and he feared it would tip or swing sideways — uncertain of its path. The total journey was less than fifty miles.

The white light belonged to Noel Drybones — the old man at Reliance. Although there was once a thriving community there, Noel was the only remaining Dene man living there year round. To say he lived at Reliance is somewhat of an understatement. Noel spent much of his life travelling by dog team, by skidoo, boat, and on foot from Fort Resolution, about 185 miles west of Reliance. Pike's Portage was the access route to *Eda Cho* (Artillery Lake), *Tla Kai Tué* (Aylmer Lake), *Tha K'ai Tué* (McKay Lake), and *Gah Cho Kue* (Kennedy Lake). A challenging personality, Noel felt most at home at Reliance in his later years. Although difficult, even those less than enamoured would defer to his knowledge and experience on the land. It was through watching Noel, other elders, and younger hunters sitting and talking together — making decisions about where and when to spend resources on a community hunt — that I developed a greater understanding of traditional knowledge. It was not only the information that was being shared that I found so instructive, but also the process by which the elders came to their decisions. Anyone with the opportunity to witness such a meeting of minds would be hard-pressed to suggest that traditional knowledge is not a "peer-reviewed" body of knowledge. Although not overt or typed up memo style, it became obvious over the three-day meeting that the perspectives shared by those with limited experience in the places of interest for the hunt were subtly dismissed. Although Noel was very quiet and reserved when participating in such meetings, his voice was among the most powerful.

Reliance was also the home to many community members as well as visitors who would journey to the spiritual site of *Ts'ankui Theda* — "the old lady of the falls." The gathering at Old Fort Reliance is a transformative experience for many who go there seeking healing, direction, and solace. For myself, the deep canyons and fast-running waters of the Lockhart River were a marvel, but they seemed no less spectacular to those who had been there a hundred or more times before. Historically, the site was important for trade and political ceremony; contemporary gatherings at Old Fort Reliance are now no less important to the community, who gather to celebrate birthdays and weddings and to grieve the loss of loved ones. Although the area has been staked, surveyed, and studied decade after decade for metals, diamonds, and hydroelectric power, the familial ties that bind the Denesoline to this place are far stronger and richer than any lease or title.

Lutsel K'e is located within the fall and wintering grounds of both the Beverly, *Qaminurjuaq*, and *Ahiak* barren ground herds (caribou from the east), and the Bathurst herd (caribou from the west). Caribou were historically, and continue to be, fundamental to the health and well-being of the community. In addition to being a main source of food, caribou and caribou hunting are the basis of individual and cultural identities and community. The organization of hunting parties, including their travel north through Pike's Portage to *Eda Cho* (Artillery Lake), was key to ensuring that hunters would be able to find caribou on the fall and winter ranges. Hunters travelling into the Barrens would periodically reconnect at familiar camps close to areas where caribou were known to have passed in previous years. Landscape features, such as Pike's Portage, played an important role in the distribution of the hunters within the range. Like the caribou, hunters would travel along lake shorelines, eskers, and other heights of land. Use of these landscape features not only made travel in the Barrens easier for hunters, but also increased the likelihood of their encountering caribou. The narrows of the big lakes, or *eda*, were key areas where the Denesoline knew they could find caribou.

Having had no real experience with hunting and hunters prior to travelling north, I knew little of what to expect when invited to participate in a community hunt. Like many other women in their twenties, I expected to be unimpressed; I had little to go on save the images of camo-gear and Budweiser commercials broadcast on weekend cable television. Hunting with Lawrence and his family was by contrast an unexpected and intensely spiritual experience.

Travelling over Pike's Portage as far as Eda Cho in winter is a rite of passage for many young people in the community and for "outsiders" like myself. During the fall hunt, people would arrive by float plane; first the young men who were able to prepare the site, and later the elders and young families. As I stepped off the plane, it was hard not be overwhelmed by the beauty of the landscape — the tundra's floor was intense with white and grey caribou lichens and the bright reds of the bearberry, cranberries, and blueberry bushes. No one spoke of it though; as if to state the obvious was too disrespectful. But the caribou trails etched deeply into the hillsides told their own story of the ecological significance of the area. The Denesoline legends I had heard about in meetings in the community hall suddenly came to life as I stood facing the rocky island formations described as part of the journey of the giant *Hachoghe*,[10] the big man in the legend of the beaver lodge and old lady of the falls.[11] The edict to "respect the land," so often heard at kitchen tables and community meetings, took on new meaning as I walked silently with the elders to various cultural and sacred sites and marked the graves of loved ones who had been born and died at Eda Cho. I was completely overcome by the power of the place and the history of the Denesoline in that place.

I spent a great deal of time exploring the area on my own; however, I did not move too far from the site of the camp in the event of meeting up with wolves or grizzlies. But there was also work to be done. Once camp was made, we were able to set off in stride in small groups in search of caribou. These excursions typically did not involve many women (although there are many historic and contemporary Dene women known to be extremely skillful hunters). I was happy to tag along behind Noel, often peppering Lawrence with questions about the cultural significance of particular sites or to interpret Noel's decisions to head in one direction or another. Somewhat embarrassing was the fact that Noel, almost four times my age, could out-walk me across the hummocky tundra. As we moved from one *ts'u dzaii* (pockets of spruce trees) to another, I wondered how many times Noel had hunted here before, and how these spaces were likely to be interpreted by his grandchildren and great-grandchildren and other visitors.

After Lawrence passed on in 2009, one of the elders said, "I guess you won't be coming around here anymore," to which I replied, "I will be around." Yet, I offered the assurance cautiously. I find I am still in the process of reinventing myself into something other than the unlikely "Dene woman in training." Regardless of my current place, I am continuously guided by the words and stories of the elders, my experiences on the land, and the relationships I developed there and struggle to nurture from afar. For better or for worse, I also continue to measure my contributions and the depth and meaning of my northern experiences — scholarly and otherwise — to my years in Lutsel K'e.

Now at the University of Alberta, living vicariously through students travelling to Lutsel K'e and other northern communities, I also tend to measure their success by the relationships they build in communities more so than by the data they collect. Although not a conventional academic deliverable, I believe these relationships are of upmost importance to communities as partners in research and learning. As noted by Pivnick, knowing a place is not simply a cognitive process but is equally an emotional and spiritual journey. As Pike's Portage becomes part of the imagination and experiences of other Canadians and northern travellers, I hope that it does not become transformed into something "other" and those who happen upon it are able to experience it and love it as it really is, in its meaning to the Denesoline.

Brenda Parlee
Edmonton, Alberta

Part II

On the Trail

There is something exciting in the first start even upon an ordinary journey. The bustle of preparation — the act of departing, which seems like a decided step taken — the prospect of change, and consequent stretching out of the imagination — have at all times the effect of stirring the blood, and giving a quicker motion to the spirits. It may be conceived then with what sensations I set forth on my journey into the Arctic wilderness. I had escaped from the wretchedness of a dreary and disastrous winter — from scenes and tales of suffering and death — from wearisome inaction and monotony — from disappointment and heart-sickening care. Before me were novelty and enterprise; hope, curiosity, and the love of adventure were my companions; and even the prospect of difficulties and dangers to be encountered, with the responsibility inseparable from command, instead of damping rather heightened the enjoyment of the moment. In turning my back on the Fort, I felt my breast lightened, and my spirit, as it were, set free again; and with a quick step, Mr. King and I (for my companion seemed to share in the feeling) went on our way rejoicing.

— journal entry, George Back[1]

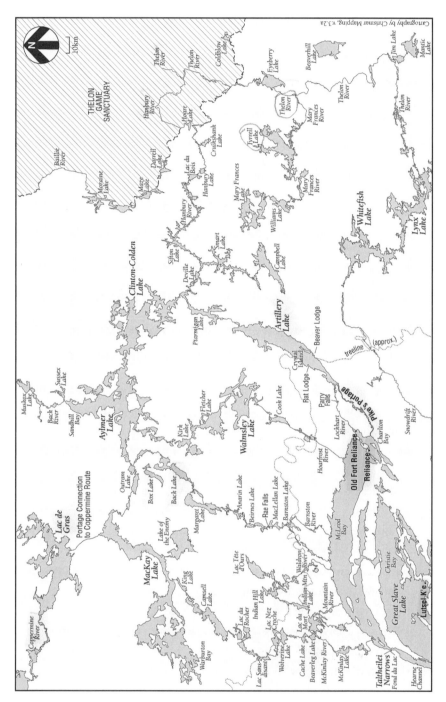

Map 3. Early Travels.

Chapter 3

Warburton Pike: No Ordinary Shooting Expedition

In the spring of 2006, we (Bob Henderson and Morten Asfeldt) read and re-read Warburton Pike's book *The Barren Ground of Northern Canada*. By the time we were paddling down Artillery Lake on the edge of the treeline, headed for Pike's Portage, we had grown to like Mr. Pike intensely. His writing brought a new understanding to the idea of North and northern travel as it was in 1890, and provided a sound basis for experiencing our travels over the portage that now bears his name. Pike's book has become a classic work describing travel north and east of Great Slave Lake. If you only read one book about this region and its exploration, Pike's would serve you well. Considering the cultural context in which Pike travelled and wrote, he expresses himself gracefully and thoughtfully as he is being immersed in the age-old practices of traditional life on the Barrens. Nevertheless, he is openly critical about his encounters with Native people, especially his guides and travel companions.

One biographer has called Pike a noble character, able writer, keen sportsman, and exceedingly modest man.[1] Another commented that "few were as explicit about their borrowing and dependence [on local Native people] as the English adventurer."[2] It is not surprising then, that

Courtesy of the Royal British Columbia Museum, BC Archives/A-01897.

This is a classic portrait of Warburton Pike, the sporting gentleman.

a rare moment of imaginary bliss should strike me (Bob) that summer of 2006, as we entered Pike's 1889–90 world — and it is not surprising that it was not Pike himself that was the subject of my flash of insight.

It was a mirage of sorts, but I am not really sure what to call it. The day was warm and sunny; the mood was excited yet calm. It was the first day of our journey. I looked up from my canoe into the hills that form the southern lip of Artillery Lake and saw walkers — perhaps a Chipewyan family. It wasn't Hearne, who had passed this way with the Chipewyan chief Matonabee and his family in 1772. Nor was it a caribou or summer canoeist. It was the families, relatives, and friends of Pike's Dene and Métis guides. It was a fleeting moment — a mirage wavering in the hills in a weird vision. It was pleasing and fitting for me to not see Pike as the central player on the land; something he never strove to be. The mirage faded as my eyes searched for the portage trail leading up the steep hill that rises from the southern extent of Artillery Lake. My experience was a bit eerie, and I thank Pike for that moment that made the land come alive.

Pike had a knack for directness, capturing relationships and moments with clarity. He is not, as Farley Mowat once suggested of early northern writers, "seized by an inarticulate paralysis when they tried to put their deepest impressions into their writing."[3] Rather, Pike shares a charmed wandering on the land that offers extraordinary insights. His discoveries are

Courtesy of Russell/NWT Archives/N-1979-073-0797.

These unidentified men use an early prototype of a canoe cart on Pike's Portage. At Harry Lake today, there are remnants of all sorts of wheeled contraptions people have used to try to ease the uphill grind from Great Slave Lake.

replete with his understanding that he was an interloper in the homeland of others who were wiser to the ways of the animals, geography, and spirits of the land than he was. Learning from a true learner and student traveller such as Pike is always a good read — he is a fine teacher.

Warburton Pike (1861–1915) was born in England and came to Victoria, Canada, in 1884 at the age of twenty-one after having participated in hunting trips in Africa and Wyoming. The youngest of seven children, Pike had lost both his parents before his seventh birthday. He did, however, receive a significant inheritance from the family estate that financed his life of travel and entrepreneurial ventures. Pike left Oxford University in 1880 at age nineteen without completing a degree, and it is believed that, after Oxford, he spent time in Germany studying mining engineering. Regardless of his education, Pike went on to be recognized as an author, hunter, explorer, and mining engineer.

Pike had a youthful wanderlust that never left him. As a man of means, he explored the interior of British Columbia and purchased land in the Gulf Islands between Victoria and Vancouver before deciding on his 1889–90 trip to northern Canada. The goals of this fourteen-month adventure, largely inspired by the writings of Samuel Hearne, were, in Pike's own words, "to try and penetrate this unknown land, to see the musk-ox, and find out as much as I could about their habits, and habits of the Indians who go in pursuit of them every year."[4] This sounds standard enough but, in 1889, Pike stood as a landmark for recreational travellers beginning to enter the *interiors* of the North. The Yellowknife chief Zinto acknowledged that Pike was the first white man he had seen away from the forts that were dotted along the common travel routes.[5] Pike himself was aware of his rare status as a white sport hunter and traveller, yet also aware of his unique position as a forerunner of sport hunters and leisure travellers — although his travels were anything but leisurely. He writes in the preface to his book that "no great political reformation depended upon my report," and "my only excuse for publishing this account of my travels is that the subject is a reasonably new one, and deals with a branch of sport that has never been described."[6]

Long recognized as a man "rather out of place in civilization," Pike once arrived at the prestigious Victoria Union Club on a wet, rainy day and proceeded to take off his moccasins and old socks and hang them to dry in front of the fireplace — to the immense displeasure and disgust of the "more proper" club members. Perhaps it is understandable that nicknames abounded for Pike. Throughout the scant literature concerning his life, he has been called "Crazy Pike," "Dirty Pike," "One-Shirt Pike," and our favourite, "Moccasin Pike."[7]

Soon after his Barrens hunting trips of 1889–90, he headed into the northern British Columbia interior (1892) for a four-thousand-mile canoe journey down the Yukon River to the Bering Sea and then farther along the Alaska coast.[8] Soon after this trip, mining endeavours — mostly failed initiatives — dominated his travels and entrepreneurial ventures. He travelled as a prospector and miner in northern British Columbia to such places as Telegraph Creek, Dease Lake, Stikine River, and Cassiar, with regular return trips to Victoria. At the same time, he continued his travels as a hunter extraordinaire. In 1909, Pike read his own obituary following a river run and hunting trip down the Colorado River — he was late reporting back from the trip and presumed dead.

In 1910, Pike was hired as commissioner for a Provincial Natural History Museum exhibit to promote British Columbia at the International Shooting and Field Sports Exhibition in Vienna, Austria.[9] Around this same time, he began to turn more toward writing and photography. In October 1915, he died at the age of fifty-four, leaving a massive debt owing from his failed mining endeavours. Returning home from a hunting trip in northern British Columbia and hearing the news of the First World War, he had hoped to enlist in the military and serve his country. He was first turned down in Canada and then again in England, finally accepting a job as a mine sweeper in the English Channel. Friends and family knew that he was suffering from an undisclosed ailment that was affecting his eyesight and brain function, and on October 19, 1915, he was admitted to a nursing home in Bournemouth, England, near his childhood home. He escaped from here the next day and was found dead on the town beach the next morning with rocks in his pockets and numerous stab wounds to the heart — from a pocket knife he had been repeatedly opening and closing the afternoon of his escape.

Perhaps the strong desire to enlist in the military at age fifty-three was an attempt to die honourably in combat before his ailment worsened and became public.[10] He had earlier acknowledged to friends and family that he was "no more good."[11] In his eulogy, he was described as "a rare old sport, game all the way through, a gentleman within a veneer of old clothes."[12] Of all his ordinary shooting expeditions and other adventures, his 1889–90 expedition to hunt muskox on the treeless tundra has always stood alone because of the success of the hunt, his first as a recreational traveller and sport hunter, and the quality of his written account, which has survived the passage of time to remain a classic book on northern adventure.

This expedition was comprised of five distinct adventures. The first was a canoe trip more or less up the McKinlay River through a series of lakes and portages onto the Barrens and north beyond the Coppermine River, where he killed the first muskox on September 27. The second was by dog team and snowshoe following this same route. The third was an interlude in Fort Resolution where he embarked on a short winter bison-hunting foray before heading back to the Barrens in June by canoe using Anderson and Stewart's 1855 route,[13] which eventually brought him over the age-old portage from Artillery Lake to Great Slave Lake that now bears his name. The fifth and final component of this fourteen-month adventure was almost fatal. He travelled from Fort Resolution to Hudson Hope, British Columbia, where he arrived in late October. From there he was headed to McLeod's Lake — typically an eight- or nine-day journey — yet Pike and his crew of four lost their way and starved for nearly two months. Murdo Mackay, one of the crew, described their bleak situation well: "Lost and starving in the mountains with no guns to procure food, no snow-shoes with which to travel over the increasing depth of snow, and no clothes to withstand the cold of mid-winter which was already upon us."[14] This portion of his return trip was indeed a survival epic wrought with poor decisions and dire consequences.

En route to his muskox-hunting venture in 1889–90, Pike arrived in Fort Resolution on Great Slave Lake the usual way of the fur trade, via Edmonton and Athabasca Landing, by river steamer north through Forts McMurray, Chipewyan, and Smith. In Fort Smith, Pike met King Beaulieu, a member of the famous Métis Beaulieu clan,[15] who agreed to serve as his

Photo by Morten Asfeldt.

Taltheilei Narrows as it looked in April 2009, the site of Plummer's Great Slave Lake Fishing Lodge. In Warburton Pike's time, the Beauleau camp, called Fond du Lac, was somewhere nearby.

expedition guide. Pike understood there were "arts of travel with canoes and dog-sleighs"[16] and that the Beaulieu clan could mentor him in these arts. He learned soon enough that King Beaulieu and his sons would test his diplomacy — and his patience. In fact, Pike found the Beaulieus so difficult to work with that he advised E.T. Seton to have nothing to do with them on his 1907 journey into the region. After experiencing similar frustrations with the Beaulieus' pace of work and constant attempts for more food and pay, Seton comments, "Oh! why did I not heed Pike's warning and shun all Beaulieus; they rarely fail to breed trouble."[17]

The party left Fort Resolution in three large birchbark canoes, with over twenty Beaulieu family members, bent for Fond du Lac near Taltheilei Narrows.[18] From here, on September 7, with a smaller party in two canoes, they followed a chain of lakes and streams north. Pike describes the country:

> Ahead of us, to the north, lay a broken rocky country
> sparsely timbered and dotted with lakes, the nearest

69

of which, a couple of miles away, was the end of our portage; a bleak and desolate country, already white with snow and with a film of ice over the smaller ponds. Three hundred miles in the heart of this wilderness, far beyond the line where timber ceases, lies the land of the musk-ox, to which we were about to force our way, depending entirely on our guns for food and for clothing to withstand the intense cold that would soon be upon us.[19]

They depended on the gun admirably but were right to expect a period of *les miseres* — a time without meat — until they reached the Barrenlands.

Heading north onto the plateau, hunger was an issue. Along the way they named Lac du Lard for the last piece of bacon eaten from their stores. From here they went without food until they reached Camsell Lake, where a base camp was established and caribou were plentiful. With food in their bellies and a base camp established, Pike turned his attention from the demands of travel to recording wildlife descriptions, hunting, and related superstitions.

On September 17, now with King Beaulieu and some of his sons, in only one canoe — others in the party had returned to Great Slave Lake to prepare for a winter trip — he continued, well-fed, into muskox country further north and deeper into the Barrens. They travelled without food and shelter, relying on caribou for meat and seeking shelter for sleeping behind large boulders. They travelled by foot, carrying a small canoe they had picked up along the way (caching canoes for future use was a common practice) and crossed the Coppermine River just west of its headwaters at Lac de Gras around September 23. Food remained plentiful, but winter was embracing the land, and cold was now their constant companion. On September 27, Pike killed a muskox and commented, "His fate was not long in doubt, as my first shot settled him, and the main object of my trip was accomplished; whatever might happen after this, I could always congratulate myself on having killed a musk-ox, and this made up for a great deal of misery that we afterward had to undergo."[20]

Soon after, the frost intensified, and the daunting task of not being able to cross MacKay Lake by canoe was looming. North on the Coppermine River, King Beaulieu explained, "It is not far from here that the white man died from cold and starvation at this time of year."[21] It is interesting to note that oral history was keeping the 1819–21 Franklin Expedition alive in their memories. One can be certain that Warburton Pike took particular comfort in his travel companions that night for their "arts of travel" that kept him alive. After making several dangerous lake crossings in the fragile birchbark canoes through forming ice and freezing spray, the canoes were abandoned near the first grove of trees, where the men enjoyed the warmth of a big fire — the first in some time.

From here the group returned on foot, eating meat cached on the northward journey. At trip's end, Pike commented, "I cannot help think that we were lucky in getting through it without more trouble: it was just the wrong time of year to be travelling, too late for open water and too early for dogs."[22] Within weeks of returning to Fond du Lac on Great Slave Lake, they harnessed up their dogs and headed north once more on November 11. The first foray into the Barrens with King Beaulieu and sons had been an austere introduction.

The November trip included Michel and Paul Beaulieu, along with five Yellowknife men — Chief Zinto and Saltatha prominent among them. With twenty-four dogs they began the long climb over the rolling, lake-studded hills of McLeod Bay. With his experience from the previous trip, Pike now took time to consider the finer aspects of travel and the aesthetics of the landscape. He commented early of the sunrise "throwing a beauty over the wilderness that is useless for me to attempt to describe."[23] We suppose these are the sort of remarks Farley Mowat was referring to. But Pike regularly attempts to capture his feelings for the land. After the first muskox hunt of this expedition, on November 21, Pike celebrates with a climb to the top of a high hill for a grand view:

> [A]nd was rewarded for my trouble by a good view of probably the most complete desolation that exists upon the face of the earth. There is nothing striking or grand in the scenery, no big mountains or waterfalls, but a monotonous snow-covered waste, without tree or scrub, rarely trodden by the foot of the wandering Indian. A deathly stillness hangs over all, and the oppressive loneliness weighs upon the spectator till he is glad to

shout aloud to break the awful spell of solitude. Such is the land of the musk-ox in snow-time.[24]

One can't help get the feeling that this sublime description aptly captures Pike's mood and a certain quality he was seeking. This was what he wanted — a profound northern reality few white men had yet to experience.

The hunting was successful, at times too successful. At one point Pike describes the hunt as "a sickening slaughter, without the least pretence of sport to recommend it."[25] Aside from the hunting, bickering among the Beaulieus seemed never-ending, but the virtues of the reliable Saltatha tempered the Beaulieu malaise. On the return trip south, the joys of the "pine-brush instead of the hard snow" were celebrated, but the Beaulieus had proved more than he could bear. Pike originally planned to winter at the treeline on the edge of the Barrens,[26] but instead turned his sights to the distant comforts of the Hudson's Bay fort at Resolution.

On December 7 they arrived back at Zinto's camp, west of Fond du Lac, and Pike rejoined the Beaulieu camp on December 10, before departing the next day for Fort Resolution. Here he enjoyed a meal, sitting "like a white man, and eat[ing] white man's food with a knife and fork, after the long course of squatting in the filth of a smoky lodge, rending a piece of half-raw meat snatched from a dirty kettle."[27] He spent the rest of the winter enjoying the comforts of the Fort, hunting buffalo with Hudson's Bay Company factor James Mackinlay, and planning his summer trip to the Great Fish River, apparently not yet called the Back River.

On May 7, a small party left Fort Resolution in a company boat for Fond du Lac. Here they found "[t]he whole tribe of Yellowknife's awaiting us with King Beaulieu and his family … there were five and twenty lodges." Begrudgingly, Pike comments, regarding his meagre supply of tobacco, that "there was no peace till pipes were going in every lodge."[28]

From Fond du Lac, familiar by now as an important staging area, a new group of Dene and Métis guides were identified for the summer journey — a task that was always a struggle. The Yellowknife Capot Blanc now became the main guide and source of advice, but Saltatha's presence and support continued to be a mainstay for Pike and his new Hudson's Bay partners Mackinlay and Murdo. They left Fond du Lac on May 21 with dog teams and snowshoes and headed north, detouring from their familiar canoe route to a more easterly course used by Anderson and Stewart on their 1855 trip to the Great Fish River. Here Pike provides important insight for future travellers:

> From this time, all through the summer till we again reached the Great Slave Lake late in August, we had no difficulty about provisions; although there was many a time when we could not say where we might find our next meal, something always turned up, and we were never a single day without eating during the whole journey. I really believe it is a mistake to try to carry enough food for a summer's work in the Barren Ground, as the difficulty of transport is so great, and after the caribou are once found there is no danger of starvation.[29]

On June 7 they experienced the last winter-like storm, and four days later they were forced to camp due to considerable water on top of the ice that made travel slow and miserable. Snow blindness was also a serious issue and "[t]he Indians smeared their faces with blood and wood ashes"[30] to keep off the dangerous bright glare. By June 16, the water had run off the ice and the group "solemnly burn[ed] some thirty pairs of used-up snowshoes"[31] — as old friends, they were hard to part with. Soon on the trail again, Pike commented that he believed the more easterly and familiar route (the McKinlay River) was better. They reached Lake MacKay on June 25, where they joined the fall route and travelling became easier. Once again, Pike found himself travelling during the difficult time that occurs each fall and spring during freeze-up and break-up. Pike describes some of the challenges of his spring journey:

> From this point [the camp on Lake MacKay] we sent Moise with three Indians and our own dogs to bring up the big canoe from the south shore of Lake Mackay, where I had left her in the beginning of last October. Many little hunting-canoes had been picked up along the track from Fond du Lac, and now every sleigh carried a canoe athwart-ships; these proved useful enough in crossing the small lake in the course of Lockhart's River, as on arriving

at the far side we found open water between us and the
land, and had to use the canoes to ferry our cargo to the
shore, the dogs swimming with the empty sleigh in tow,
while some enterprising spirits, who conceived the idea of
floating ashore on blocks of ice, came in for a ducking.[32]

After a successful muskox hunt, they launched the big canoe in the
Great Fish River on July 3, recalling sites and stories from Anderson and
Stewart's earlier travels. Capot Blanc, a storyteller, "gave us a long lecture
on the events that had taken place during this 1855 expedition, as he had
heard the story from his father."[33]

From the time they started downstream on the Great Fish River, the
relations between the white explorers and the Dene and Métis guides
and hunters became strained. First, there was a grim foretelling of their
journey by the Medicine Man, then a bad omen occurred in crossing a
creek when Pike and Capot Blanc were both swept off their feet, which
was attributed to "the Enemy" [Inuit] having made the water stronger.
Furthermore, the messy killing of a muskox by Mackinlay and Pike left the
meat discoloured, which prompted Saltatha to claim this as "an unfailing
sign of some great misfortune at hand."[34] Soon after, two campsites were
discovered that showed evidence, as campsites will, of axe marks, fires,
and at the second site, some seal skin. The seal skin proved to be the last
straw for the guides. These signs of Inuit presence stifled all desire and
willingness of Pike's crew to proceed any further — their fear of the Inuit
was strong and unwavering — and Pike's plans to hike overland with a
little canoe to Bathurst Inlet were dashed. However, the guides and hunters
had great enthusiasm for the upstream paddle back to Aylmer Lake.

While the campsites might have been that of Dogrib or even Anderson
and Stewart, and other events easily explained, the Back River initiative
was really thwarted from the beginning. Pike sums up his observations:
"they [Dene and Métis guides and hunters] have no courage outside
their own country."[35] As a practical point from a guide's perspective, it is
easy to understand why venturing beyond one's known environment in
this immense land was not the indigenous practice, particularly for the
hunter/family man with no obvious gains from exploration other than
prestige and white man's gifts.

Back at Sandhill Bay, sights were set for the August 1 rendezvous with the boat sent from Fort Resolution to meet them on the East Arm of Great Slave Lake. The familiar route via the Lockhart River, Aylmer, Clinton-Colden, and Artillery lakes proved easy travel with plenty of caribou in the country. Pike described Artillery Lake as a choice location to build boats with fine timber for any future trip down the Great Fish River. By now, Pike was well imbued with the indigenous ways of thinking and travel in the Barrens — travel light, hunt as needed, cache small canoes for long walks, build boats as needed, send parties in advance — all these practices allow a group to travel and live well. In addition, it is critical, when out of your familiar terrain in the rearguard of your enemies, to expect resistance from an Aboriginal crew.

Back in the home territory of his guides, they arrived at a family encampment on Artillery Lake where they were expected and caribou had been plentiful. Pike must have felt he was no longer a thorn in the hunters' side — forcing his agenda — as he had been on the remote Great Fish River. He was now a functional member of a well-oiled social travelling machine among the familiar hub of Great Slave Lake activities.

At the south end of Artillery Lake, the Dene migration from the edge of the Barrens plateau to Great Slave Lake began over *Ka a Ku*, the Chipewyan, or Denesoline name for Pike's Portage that means "place where you go up to the lake."[36] Pike enjoyed the portage and described it eloquently:

> [S]o we had to make use of a chain of lakes, eight in number, lying to the south of the stream. This is by far the prettiest part of the country that I saw in the North, and it was looking its best under the bright sunshine that continued till we reached the fort. Scattering timber, spruce and birch clothed the sloping banks down to the sandy shores of the lakes; berries of many kinds grew in profusion; the portages were short and down hill; and caribou were walking the ridges and swimming the lakes in every direction. A perfect northern fairyland it was, and it seemed hard to believe that winter and want could ever penetrate here; but on the shore of a lovely blue lake Pierre the Fool pointed out a spot where the

last horrors of death and cannibalism had been enacted within his memory.[37]

At the south end of Harry Lake, the last small lake before the final portage of three miles finds its end on a long curving sandy beach on the edge of Great Slave Lake, the canoes were abandoned. Pike understood that this trail held a special quality — that it was a distinguished trail:

> With loads on our backs [we] followed the well-worn trail that Indians have used from time immemorial as a route to their hunting-grounds. A natural pass with a steep descent led between the rough broken hills on each side, and a three-mile walk brought us within the sight of the waters of the big lake.[38]

Like Pike, Mackinlay, Saltatha, King Beaulieu (and his many sons and their many wives and children, and the many ancestors before), and the many white hunters, trappers, explorers, and surveyors soon to follow Pike's lead, we will never forget the view of Great Slave Lake from various places along that final "well-worn, time-immemorial trail" to and from the Barrens — as Pike said, it "is useless for me to attempt to describe."[39]

After two days of trading with the Indians at the foot of the portage that would one day bear his name, Pike boarded a Hudson's Bay York boat and hoisted sail for Fort Resolution. However, before pushing from shore, they "went through the ceremony of cutting a lop-stick, as is the fashion of the North, to commemorate our expedition."[40] As one man was up the tree cutting the lower branches, Pike and Mackinlay carved their names in the tree's trunk and guns were fired in unison to end the ceremony. They arrived at Fort Resolution on August 24, and Pike, always the fine northern student, observed from a "glance at the faces that gathered round" to meet them, that "living had been none too good, and that a man is sometimes better off among the caribou than depending upon an uncertain fishery for a livelihood."[41] On August 26, Pike set off from the fort after sunset, hoping that he would see again the many people whose faces looked his way as he paddled off.

Warburton Pike's "ordinary shooting expedition" in 1889–90 marked

This celebration lobstick was cut by the Pike/Mackinlay party in 1890. Tyrrell took this picture ten years later.

a new era of travel in the North. Rather than coming north with a nationalistic or entrepreneurial purpose, as Hearne, Franklin, and Back had done, Pike came independently, seeking sport and "delight[ing] in the Barrens for their own sake."[42] In fact, "this little known wilderness with a formidable history was *tantalizing* [emphasis added]" for Pike.[43] While he came as a sport hunter, he was an amateur geographer, historian, and anthropologist, mapping and recording the land, history, and traditions as he travelled, and in this case, sharing them with a broad audience in his book *The Barren Ground of Northern Canada.* While his book was intended only for sportsmen, it became much more than that. It quickly became essential reading for all people heading north, not just sportsmen, and is an interdisciplinary introduction to the North. He had an ability to share stories and insights of the land and its peoples in a much less Eurocentric manner than others of his time — although not completely absent of these biases — perhaps because he was a self-funded recreational traveller without a company or national agenda, or perhaps because he was an astute observer who was ahead of his time. Nevertheless, Pike did reflect some of the trends of his time and was "enamoured by contemporary ideals of the sportsmanship"[44] as it was seen in the late 1800s in the wealthy elite and played into his travel and hunting motivations. These included the desire for immersive wilderness experiences and the hope that the associated hardships would result in masculine identity, and, of course, the drive to kill exotic species, such as the prehistoric muskox.

Pike was an adventurer throughout his life, first in travel and "no ordinary shooting expeditions," and later as a mining entrepreneur. In these roles he had tales to tell — of becoming sick when forced to eat his tanned moccasins for nourishment on the trail (only un-tanned moccasins can be chewed for nourishment), and attending elaborate functions with prominent well-to-do men of the time, such as Theodore Roosevelt. Pike also became known as a generous man, once paying for a rescue party to bring starving men out of northern British Columbia, and then giving money to a widowed Hudson's Bay Company employee's wife he had befriended.

Pike was also described by one historian as maintaining a lifelong "penchant for slumming" and as a man who "rarely carried any money with him, preferr[ing] to go barefoot whenever possible, and because of his ragged clothes and tatty rucksack was often mistaken for a tramp"[45] even though for most of his life he could afford fine clothes and dining. Perhaps he was so caught up in the identity of the northern hunter that he remained awkward all his adult life in the emerging urbanity of North America. It appears so. These are traits we tentatively admire in a man who beyond the page is not entirely clear in our thinking — and this is a good thing. Like others introduced in this book, there is a complexity to the travellers who stepped aside from the dominate herd — so to speak — and ended up on Pike's Portage. To succeed as a traveller at that time, it was essential to exist in two distinctively different worlds — the urban and the wild. Maybe Pike truly fit the wild more comfortably than most others. In any case, we appreciate the mystery in Pike, who, like Samuel Hearne (whom he admired), boldly followed in the established *ways* of the land and its people.

Bob Henderson
Uxbridge, Ontario
Morten Asfeldt
Camrose, Alberta

Chapter 4

George Back: An Unsung Arctic Explorer

On August 18, 1833, George Back was making his way east along the north shore of Great Slave Lake in search of an access route to the *Thlew-ee-choh*, or Great Fish River, when he and his party "launch[ed] past some rocks, which had shut out the land in their direction, [they] opened suddenly on a small bay, at the bottom of which was seen a splendid fall, upwards of sixty feet high, rushing in two white and misty volumes into the dark gulf below. It was the object of [their] search — the river they were to ascend."[1] The river was the Hoarfrost River. The falls Back named Beverly Falls.[2]

This was Back's third Arctic Land Expedition. After living in the shadow of Sir John Franklin on his previous two Arctic expeditions, Back relished the opportunity to be the commander of this voyage, which had been commissioned to provide aid for the British explorer Sir John Ross and to find the source of the Great Fish River. Ross had not been heard from for nearly three years. Ross's plans had included the possibility of wintering in Regent Inlet, near the wreck of the British ship *Fury*, which had been abandoned there by William Parry in 1825. "According to the testimony of Indians,"[3] it might be reached by descending the Great Fish

Courtesy of George Back/Library and Archives Canada/C-097305.

George Back was an accomplished artist; this is his drawing of Beverly Falls as he saw them in August 1833.

River, which was known to flow east from the region northeast of Great Slave Lake, yet its end point was unknown. While wintering at Fort Reliance, near the mouth of the Lockhart River at the most eastern reach of Great Slave Lake in 1833–34, Back received word that Sir John Ross had returned safely to England. Nevertheless, Back spent the summer of 1834 mapping the Great Fish River, and a second winter at Fort Reliance, before making way for England in the spring of 1835. The expedition was a grand success and an extraordinary journey of exploration and mapping in remote and unknown territory along a river filled with boat-crushing rapids and waterfalls. The expedition was a feather in Back's hat that should have solidified him as a bona fide Arctic explorer; the river is now rightfully named the Back River.

George Back was born in England in 1796. In September 1808, he joined the British Navy, and just "two months shy of his twelfth birthday, [he] bade a tearful farewell to his mother and father."[4] It would be five years before he saw them again. He spent most of those five years in France as a prisoner during the Napoleonic War, where he became fluent in French and an able artist, both of which served him well in his later Arctic expeditions.

Shortly after Back's return to England, he was once again at sea. Following two stints as midshipmen, he again returned to England and passed his lieutenant exams with "flying colours"[5] before being appointed admiralty midshipmen under the command of Lieutenant John Franklin. This expedition provided Back with his first Arctic experience as they attempted to find a route to the Orient by sailing between Greenland and Spitsbergen and over the North Pole. While the expedition was unsuccessful in its ultimate goal, Back made a favourable impression on Lieutenant John Franklin.

In 1819, Back once again joined Franklin for a second foray into the Arctic — the first of three Arctic Land Expeditions. This time, their mission was to descend the Coppermine River and map the coastline to the east in an effort to fill in the blanks remaining on the map of Arctic Canada at that time. After a long journey across the country, they established Fort Enterprise near Winter Lake, in the central Barrens north of Great Slave Lake, where they wintered before heading down the Coppermine River in early June 1821. The party spent the summer mapping the Arctic coast, but with winter once more on the horizon, they retreated up the Hood River and overland back to Fort Enterprise rather than returning up the Coppermine River as originally planned.

The overland journey was a gruelling experience of starvation, cold, murder, and cannibalism. Before it was all over, nine of eleven voyagers and one Inuk interpreter had died, and officer Robert Hood had been murdered — eleven of the original twenty expedition members never returned. Despite the loss of life, for Back this was an important expedition; he had learned the value of Aboriginal knowledge and had demonstrated his ability to perform under the most demanding circumstances imaginable. In spite of a frequently strained relationship with Franklin, due to Back's abrasive personal style and overbearing conceit, Back was instrumental in reducing the human loss of the expedition. Near the end of the expedition, Franklin "congratulate[d] [Back] on his toughness, resilience and courage in pushing ahead and dispatching supplies that saved [their] lives."[6]

Back and Franklin were again united on a second Arctic Land Expedition in 1824. This time they headed down the Mackenzie River from Great Slave Lake and wintered at Fort Franklin on Great Bear Lake.

The task of this voyage was to map the Arctic coast east and west of the Mackenzie River. In the spring of 1825, one group mapped the coast east to the Coppermine River while Back and Franklin led a group west of the Mackenzie River into the then Russian-controlled Alaska. Both parties successfully returned to Fort Franklin for another winter after a combined mapping of 1,700 miles of coastline — with no loss of life. Once again, Franklin praised Back for his service, and even recommended him for promotion. The expedition had been a success.

For the next six years, while Back found himself ashore in England trying to advance his career, he embarked on a one-and-a-half-year retreat to the cultural centres of Europe. While he was in Italy in 1832, rumours reached him of an expedition in search of the missing Sir John Ross. The prospect of commanding such an expedition saw Back return to London in short order. By the fall of 1832, he had been appointed the commander of the Expedition to the Polar Sea to gather information on the status of the Ross Expedition, find the mouth of the Great Fish River, and continue mapping the Canadian Arctic. It was with these goals in mind that Back found himself at the mouth of the Hoarfrost River on August 18, 1833.

Morning on August 19, 1833, came early as Back and his crew embarked on their ascent of the Hoarfrost River, described by his Métis guides as a "series of appalling cascades and rapids."[7] Yet Maufelly, one of Back's guides, insisted that it was the "only practicable route."[8] Before departing, Back left a message for Alexander McLeod,[9] who had joined the expedition as directed by Hudson's Bay Company governor George Simpson in return for a promotion and increased pay, who was following a few days behind to "begin building an establishment, as soon as he should reach the east end of the lake"[10] and prepare for the return of Back and his crew sometime in September.[11]

The journey up the Hoarfrost River was punishing. They had to climb over fallen trees, find their way through thick and tangled forest, struggle across swamps, and navigate endless moss-covered rocks. Back describes how, adding to their toil, they had to endure the "combined attack of myriads of sand-flies and mosquitos, which made [their] faces stream with blood. There is certainly no form of wretchedness, among those to which the chequered life of a voyageur is exposed, at once so great and

Another of George Back's drawings depicts the punishing portage up the Hoarfrost River.

so humiliating; as the torture inflicted by these puny blood-suckers."[12] Remarkably, after two long days of backbreaking labour, they reached Cook Lake, twenty-five miles up the Hoarfrost River. As homesteader Dave Olesen says, "Those fellows could travel."[13]

After ascending the Hoarfrost River, Back was guided through a series of lakes and over many portages to the headwaters of the Great Fish River, which he first saw from the top of a sandhill at the north end of Aylmer Lake. However, finding the sandhill was no routine task for his guide, Maufelly. On August 24, somewhere beyond Walmsley Lake, while travelling through a bewildering maze of islands and bays, Maufelly "remark[ed] that many winters had glided away since he had visited the Thlew-ee-choh, as a boy, with his old father; but that he remembered his saying that there were numerous sand hills in its vicinity; and he felt some confidence now, that we should, sooner or later, find it."[14] Three days later, Maufelly found the hills of his memory.

When a map of that region is placed on a flat surface today, it is quickly observed that lakes, rivers, and long snake-like eskers of sand dominate the landscape with no obvious route across the terrain. Just imagine Maufelly guiding Back to those *specific* sandhills using only the map etched in his mind from his childhood journey. His talent for way-finding is almost beyond belief and highlights the critical role Aboriginal people have played in the exploration of northern Canada.

After finding the sandhills on August 27, Back sent Maufelly and three men in search of the first trickles of water that form the Great Fish River. Three days later they returned to Back, having "fallen on the river … and described it as being large enough for boats."[15] After waiting out a storm until August 30, Back and his crew made a brief scouting trip of the upper reaches of the river before heading for the winter establishment that McLeod was building at the mouth of the Lockhart River on Great Slave Lake. The return route took them through Aylmer, Clinton-Colden, and Artillery lakes.

As they were paddling south on Artillery Lake, so named by Back "out of respect to the distinguished"[16] artillerymen in his crew, Maufelly told the story of Beaver's Lodge and Rat's Lodge.

They first passed Beaver's Lodge on the eastern shore, a rock with a cone-like summit, and then Rat's Lodge on the western shore, which is a distinctive round-shaped mound on the tip of a long sandy finger reaching out from shore. The story goes that there once lived a beaver — the size of a buffalo — in this lodge (Beaver's Lodge), who roamed the neighbouring countryside, committing acts of nuisance and disturbance against the local people, often in partnership with his ally, the rat, who lived on the opposite shore in Rat's Lodge. However, wanting to put an end to the beaver's harassment, the local Aboriginal people set out to slay the beast. The beaver escaped, seeking refuge in the rat's lodge but was turned away by his collaborator who told him to swim "to some rocks to the south, where he would be safe from his enemies."[17] Angry over the rat's lack of hospitality, the beaver began to pummel the rat, but quickly abandoned the fight as the local people continued their pursuit. The beaver turned and fled south "down the cataracts and rapids"[18] of the Lockhart River and into Great Slave Lake, where the "exhausted animal yielded its life."[19] Nevertheless, says Maufelly, "its spirit ... still lingers about its old haunt, the waters of which obey its will; and ill fares the person who attempts to pass it in his canoe, without muttering a prayer for safety: many have perished; some bold men have escaped; but none have been found so rash as to venture a second time within its power."[20] As was Maufelly's practice of muttering a prayer, today the Dene continue to leave "an offering of thanks for safe passage on the land"[21] as they pass Beaver's Lodge.[22]

On September 6, Back and crew were nearing the south end of Artillery Lake. At this point, Back chose to descend the Lockhart River to Great Slave Lake rather than follow the age-old route over Pike's Portage.[23] After reaching Fort Reliance, McLeod expressed surprise at Back's route choice from Artillery Lake and had been expecting him to use "the lowest and most favourable route to the Barren Lands, [which] was preferred, it seems, to those by which [Back] had passed."[24] McLeod was no doubt referring to a traditional route that leaves Pike's Portage at Acres Lake and descends along a creek into the bay a half mile southeast of Fort Reliance;[25] however, Back claims to have been unaware of this route (see Map 2).

This choice is somewhat difficult to understand, given the route's long history of use by Aboriginal people, and Back's awareness of Maufelly's concern over descending the Lockhart. In the first hours of their descent

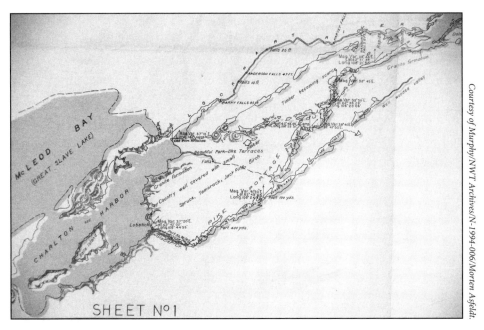

Courtesy of Murphy/NWT Archives/N-1994-006/Morten Asfeldt.

J.W. Tyrrell's map shows the alternate portage route from Acres Lake to Great Slave Lake that Alexander McLeod expected George Back to use in 1833.

of the Lockhart River, Back learned "that for days past Maufelly had been talking about the dangers he did know, and the dangers he did not know, in the Ah-hel-dessy [Lockhart]. The Indians, he said, never attempted it in any manner, either up or down; and, as he was not in a hurry to die, though he was willing to walk on the rocks, he would not, on any account, run it in the canoe."[26]

While it is somewhat intuitive to travel from one lake to the next along a river that joins the two, the trip from Artillery Lake to Great Slave Lake is not well-served by this practice.[27] Based on Back's experience in 1820, walking with an Aboriginal guide from Point Lake to Fort Enterprise, we would expect him to embrace local knowledge. In his journal from 1820, Back writes: "in passing through a strange country it is a saving of time to trust to the local knowledge of your guide in preference to your own — though his way will not be so direct yet it will be more convenient and without any risque."[28] Partway down the Lockhart River, Back abandoned his canoe and walked the remaining distance to Fort Reliance, struggling over broken rocks, up and down hills, through gullies, and over creeks. It was anything but the fine trail of Pike's Portage.

Photo by Morten Asfeldt.

The view west over Charlton Bay from Old Fort Reliance.

It is likely that Maufelly suggested the Pike's Portage route and that Back dismissed his suggestion, thinking that he knew better. Although Back had a good deal of respect and regard for his guides, his respect was guarded. At times, Back's view of the local people was the common British view of the time, seeing them as savages. In fact, earlier, on September 6, before reaching the Lockhart River, Back comments in his journal as they paddled by Timber Bay that "it was this spot that the Indians had recommended, as possessing all the requisites for building and supporting a new establishment; and a stronger example of their incapacity for judging, and the necessity of receiving their suggestions with caution, could scarcely be brought forward."[29] Nevertheless, on September 7, Back arrived at Fort Reliance, guided the final steps by the sound of working axes and the sight of trees stripped of their branches and lying in the forest waiting transport to the fort site where they would be used to build their winter quarters.

Fort Reliance sits above a sandy beach, overlooking Charlton Bay, about half a mile from the mouth of the Lockhart River. Today, the restored stone chimneys, storage pits, and outlines of the building are

Photo by Margot Peck.

Bob Henderson examines the restored chimneys of Old Fort Reliance in August 2006.

all that remain in the now park-like setting of tall trees, along with some primitive walkways bordered with logs and a commemorative plaque. Most of the trees would have been cut for building and firewood when it was inhabited by Back, but the trees have now had more than 165 years to grow and the spot likely resembles what McLeod first saw when he first arrived there in August 1833.

The winter of 1833–34 was not an easy one for the residents of Fort Reliance, as Back named it on November 5, the day they moved indoors. Back comments that "as every post in the country is distinguished by a name, I gave ours that of Fort Reliance, in token of our trust in that merciful Providence, whose protection we humbly hoped would be extended to us in the many difficulties and dangers to which these services are exposed."[30] Nevertheless, the winter was one of cold and starvation.

The house itself was quite large, measuring fifty-two feet long and thirty-two feet wide with an attached kitchen which was hardly a shelter at all. There were four separate rooms, each with their own fireplace, and a large reception area that was filled most of the winter with local Dene and Métis people who came seeking food, shelter, and cures for the sick. However, the supplies from outside were thin and the hunting and fishing poor and so there was little food for them to find, though they were provided with paltry medical care.

The shortage of food began in October. From time to time the locals would arrive with meat, seeking trade for tobacco and other goods, which were also in short supply. Akaitcho, a Yellowknife and Back's friend from previous Arctic Land Expeditions, was meant to supply the fort with meat throughout the winter. However, the caribou were not to be found nearby as normally expected, and some Dene and Métis claimed their disappearance was caused by the mysterious activities taking place in the observatory that Back had constructed in order to make regular meteorological and scientific measurements. The observatory was a forty-three-square-foot building surrounded by a fence enclosure. Its access was strictly regulated for only Back and Richard King, the expedition's surgeon and naturalist. At one point, while Back and King were concealed inside the observatory taking measurements, "two voyageurs listened, and hearing only a word at intervals, such as Now! Stop! always succeeded by a perfect silence, they looked at each other, and with significant shrugs, turning hastily away from the railing, reported to their companions that they verily believed I was 'raising the devil.'"[31]

As winter continued, the starvation worsened. Before moving into the fort in November, Back had reduced the rations to the men and stopped feeding the dogs altogether. Later, groups were sent to different fisheries throughout the surrounding country to try to increase the food supply and lessen the burden of feeding people at the fort. In an attempt to have the local people leave the fort, Back reduced the already meagre food allowance he afforded them in order to reduce the pleasure of remaining at the fort. While Back reduced the rations given the adults, "often did [he] share [his] own plate with the children, whose helpless state and piteous cries were particularly distressing."[32]

Regardless of the suffering state of his men, Back began to make preparations for the summer's journey down the Great Fish River. Near the end of February, he sent two carpenters and a helper to begin to make planking for boats from the woods that were discovered along the Lockhart River in the fall. On March 13, King and a group of men dragged the boat-building planking and hardware to Timber Bay on Artillery Lake —

about twenty-five miles as the crow flies from Fort Reliance — where the carpenters built the boats. On April 25, Back learned of Sir John Ross's safe return to England, at which point he and Mr. King, who "seldom, indeed … indulge[d] in libation,"[33] saw fit to raise their glasses in celebration. As the days lengthened and spring approached, their food situation improved, and on June 7 they boarded up the last of the fort's parchment windows, shouldered their heavy loads, and began the rugged trek along the Lockhart River to Timber Bay where the boats awaited them.

Once at Timber Bay, the finishing touches were made to the boats before Back headed off. Knowing that Ross was safely back in England, Back's mission was now to map the Great Fish River and as much of the coastline as possible while leaving himself enough time to return to Fort Reliance before being trapped in the Barrens by the Arctic winter. Therefore, he chose to take only one crew and one boat, leaving the second boat for McLeod to travel to Sandhill Bay where he was to meet Back in September and assist him on his return to Fort Reliance. Meanwhile, Back sent McLeod and a party of men ahead of him with stores of pemmican to cache at Sandhill Bay, which lightened their already heavy boat, and to make caches of caribou meat so they could prolong the need to eat the precious pemmican needed to sustain them on their Great Fish River journey.

On June 10, 1834, Back and his men began to drag their heavy thirty-foot boat over the ice-covered lakes to Aylmer Lake. On June 27, they arrived at Sandhill Bay, where they met McLeod and his crew and then portaged the boat overland to the headwaters of the Great Fish River. For the next seven days, McLeod and his crew assisted with the many portages and continued to set out food caches. On July 4, Back said farewell to McLeod and left him with instructions outlining his summer duties: to be waiting with the second boat at Sandhill Bay by mid-September, to make a trip to Fort Resolution for stores, and to build a house at a permanent fishery of his choosing. McLeod and his men then began their long trek back to Fort Reliance before beginning their summer tasks, which were arduous in their own rite, yet delivered routinely by Back.

On July 29, thirty-one days after leaving the headwaters of the Great Fish River, Back reached the Polar Sea — a journey of nearly six hundred miles. The journey had not been easy, with more than eighty rapids and waterfalls, many portages, and challenging navigation. Once again, Back and his crew demonstrated their remarkable ability to travel quickly through this remote and unknown land while mapping the country as they went. After exploring the coast for eighteen days, Back turned the boat around on August 16 and began the backbreaking upstream voyage back to Sandhill Bay — they arrived at Sandhill Bay thirty-three days later, on September 17, and met McLeod "who with four men and two Indians had already been [there] several days."[34] On September 24 they reached the Lockhart River and once again attempted to descend the river by boat. After navigating a number of rapids in the upper section, they abandoned the boat at Anderson Falls and walked to Fort Reliance after an "absence of nearly four months; tired indeed, but well in health, and truly grateful for the manifold mercies [they] had experienced in the course of [their] long and perilous journey."[35]

Knowing that the food supply at Fort Reliance would be meagre, Back sent all but six men with McLeod to the fisheries for the winter. After repairing the fort, which they found "standing, but that was all,"[36] Back and his men set into their winter routine. The local Dene and Métis people brought them meat from time to time but they otherwise lived on the stores that had remained in the storage pits during the summer.

Back left Fort Reliance on March 21, 1835, for the last time. He stopped at the fishery to say goodbye to McLeod, who had served him without fail, and then once again made his way to England where he was recognized by His Majesty, who "express[ed] his approbation of [his] humble efforts, first in the cause of humanity, and next in that of geographical and scientific research."[37] Back's first expedition under his full command had been a resounding success.

Less than a year after returning to England, Back found himself as commander aboard the HMS *Terror*, headed for the Canadian Arctic where he hoped to complete the route through the North West Passage. The ship became locked in ice for the winter near Southampton Island in the mouth of Hudson Bay, where it took a severe beating. His men suffered from scurvy, and a number of them died and were committed to the sea. The *Terror* was freed from the ice in July, and, due to the poor condition of the ship and its crew, Back steered the ship for England. The expedition had been a failure.

Back was forty-one years old when he returned from the ill-fated *Terror* expedition. He spent the remainder of his life on shore, where he rose to the rank of admiral and received many awards for his naval service, included being knighted in 1839. He served in a number of different capacities with the navy, including as a member of the Arctic Council, which co-ordinated the many searches for Franklin's lost expedition. He died peacefully in 1878 at the age of eighty-two.

Peter Steele, Back biographer and author of *The Man Who Mapped the Arctic*, finds it strange that it has taken so long for Back to be recognized for his many contributions and achievements "as one of the great Arctic Explorers."[38] While some criticized Back for "sloth, poor discipline, and lack of enterprise,"[39] as Mr. King did, he was also a man "of courage, of endurance, and of resource in calamity"[40] who made three extraordinary overland expeditions in the unknown lands of the Canadian Arctic under often difficult circumstances. Steele speculates that "[h]ad he died on *Terror* he might — since the public have an insatiable appetite for high drama — have been beatified and passed into Arctic mythology, as his former boss, John Franklin, was to be. Explorers who return safely, however awful the experiences they survive, take second place to those who die tragically."[41] Such was the case for George Back.

Morten Asfeldt
Camrose, Alberta

Chapter 5

Anderson and Stewart: The Byways to the Barrens

Canoeists paddling through McLeod Bay of Great Slave Lake, bound for the Barrens to the north and east, have always faced a challenge. Whether Dene hunters, Barrenland trappers, eccentric wanderers, or modern recreationists, they all had a stiff climb ahead of them. The report of a 1932 party from the Geological Survey of Canada stated the problem succinctly: "The country north of McLeod Bay is difficult to reach on account of a steep rise in the land from the north shore of the Bay."[1] In that direction "rock hills rise, within distances of from one to four miles from the shore, to an upland which continues north to Lac de Gras ... the tops of the hills at McLeod Bay stand at 900 feet above Great Slave Lake."[2] The best-known route from Great Slave to the Barrenlands is undoubtedly Pike's Portage — the subject of the other chapters of this book. But if Pike's route was the highway to the Barrens, there were many byways as well. In 1855, James Anderson and James Green Stewart — of whom, more later — had portaged north out of McLeod Bay en route to the Back River. Pike himself had used routes near the McKinlay and Mountain rivers, some sixty miles west of the trail that bears his name, to access the Barrens. Maufelly guided George Back

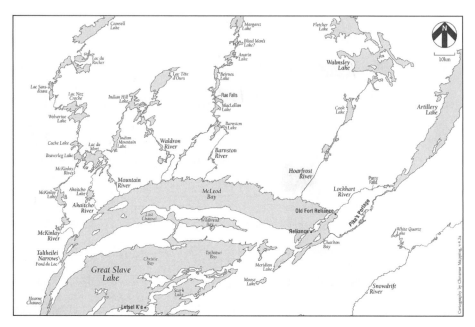

Map 4. Byways to the Barrens.

to Artillery Lake via the Hoarfrost River. Caspar Whitney, later Leonidas Hubbard's editor at *Outing* magazine, and Henry Toke Munn launched their pursuits of the muskox from the far west end of McLeod Bay.[3] The Geological Survey party mentioned above, heading south from MacKay Lake, worked their way down the Waldron River to McLeod Bay, and Guy Blanchet's 1924 field notes mention a route following the Akaitcho River to the Barrens. Why such a variety of routes?

Part of the answer is geography. Wherever one leaves McLeod Bay, one faces essentially the same problem — a steep climb, of some 820 feet in three miles, to reach the plateau above Great Slave Lake. Surmounting this challenge, one emerges on a mostly barren tableland, thickly strewn with lakes, where one can paddle and portage in almost any direction with no great difficulty. There are many feasible routes to the Barrens, if no easy ones, and for most white explorers or hunters it was likely just a matter of following the route their guide was most familiar with. The other part of the answer is ice. McLeod Bay breaks up from west to east in the spring — often its western reaches are open to canoe passage while its eastern tip near Pike's Portage is still icebound. A more westerly route to the North could enable a canoe party to save time and avoid the risks of ice-filled waters.

94

Photo by John McInnes.

There are many rapids found on the Barnston River.

This was a key reason behind Anderson's choice of his 1855 portage route.

My interest in the area north of McLeod Bay, and potential travel routes between the MacKay Lake area and Great Slave Lake, had been awakened by reading the books of sport hunters Warburton Pike, Caspar Whitney, and Henry Toke Munn. But these authors provided little in the way of detailed route information. Pike is the best of them, and he confessed to being no geographer. While many of the lake names from his map remain on modern topographic maps, it is not clear, in many cases, if they are still applied to those lakes Pike gave them to. Whitney's map is even more inaccurate, and less detailed, and Munn is no help at all. I was interested in exploring this area, but didn't know exactly how or where to start.

The first accurate canoe route description I found for this area was included in the 1932 "Annual Report of the Geological Survey of Canada." In the summer of that year, a party led by geologist Dr. C.H. Stockwell had completed its summer's travels by crossing from MacKay Lake to McLeod Bay, and had documented their route. They remarked on the uncertain routes of Pike, and Anderson and Stewart, and noted the only *accurately* mapped route was the one they had followed along the Barnston River.

Trying to follow their accurately mapped route on modern maps was initially puzzling — until I realized my problem. They hadn't been on the Barnston River after all, but rather on the Waldron River, the next significant stream to the west. The lake they had identified as Barnston Lake was, in fact, Lac Tête d'Ours — another name from Pike's map — which drains southward via the Waldron River to McLeod Bay. Once their route details were transposed to the Waldron River, they fit perfectly.

Armed with this information, I planned a canoe route to begin my explorations of this area. I flew into Beniah Lake, on the Beaulieu River near the treeline, and headed up the Beaulieu through Fat Lake and Lac du Rocher to Lac Sans-disant in its headwaters. From there, a series of short portages and small ponds took me to Lac Nez Croche, at the headwaters of the McKinlay River. I descended this stream through Wolverine and Cache lakes to Beaverleg Lake, then turned northeast through Lac du Mort, Indian Mountain, and Indian Hill lakes to reach the Waldron River at Benjamin Lake. From there, I followed the 1932 survey route south to Great Slave Lake. Travel was straightforward at first, through small lakes connected by rapids that could be run or bypassed by short portages. But this easy progress ended after a portage around an impressive falls put me in a narrow, unnamed lake about four miles long — the "seventh lake" of the survey report. Below here, they wrote, "the river is almost a continuous rapid and fall to its mouth at McLeod Bay, and was avoided, the route followed being through a chain of small lakes south of the seventh lake and west of the river."[4]

Travel through this chain of lakes was, on the first day, not too difficult and quite attractive: part of the route followed a chain of ponds on a small creek in a "hanging valley" with a fine view out over Great Slave Lake. On the second day, only two portages remained: the first "slightly over one mile long, was along a high ridge and down a steep slope with a drop of 380 feet;"[5] the second "about one-half mile long with a drop of 150 feet."[6] Downhill — how hard could they be? Pretty damn hard, actually, and not helped by the fact that they had to be done on a hot, sunny, windless day that brought several million of the local fauna out of their hiding places in the moss to accompany me. At the end, Great Slave Lake looked great, and tasted even better — especially when mixed with rum. I had learned two things: you can get down the north

Travelling by dog team on the Barrens in fine April weather is an idyllic experience.

Roger Catling holds a wolf hide ready for auction.

Toura Lake near the eastern end of Pike's Portage.

Muskox were the object of the early sport hunters' desire just as they are today for sport hunters from around the world.

The Northern Lights dominate the night sky over McLeod Bay.

Caribou travelling in a small group near Walmsley Lake in April 2009.

This white wolf was raising four pups in the hills behind the Hornby cabin at Hornby Point in August 1995.

The Kahochella Peninsula stretches along the south shore of McLeod Bay.

Photo by John McInnes.

The McKinlay River, like most rivers falling from the Barrens into Great Slave Lake, is dominated by rapids.

shore of McLeod Bay; and Geological Survey portage descriptions tend toward understatement.

Having survived this initial foray, I explored a few more canoe routes linking the barren plain north of Great Slave Lake with McLeod Bay. One route began in Lac du Rocher, arced north through Camsell and King lakes, and then swung southeast to the (real) Barnston River, which I followed south to Great Slave Lake. Another trail led east from MacLellan Lake on the Barnston, and required paddling and portaging along the edge of the plateau to reach the Hoarfrost River. I ascended that river to Walmsley Lake, went southeast via twenty portages linking small lakes and ponds to Artillery Lake, and then descended Pike's route to Great Slave. Another year I went south from Beniah Lake and through Rolfe Lake to reach the McKinlay River. I descended the river, past McKinlay Lake, to the start of its steep plunge to McLeod Bay, before swinging north through small ponds and Akaitcho Lake to reach the headwaters of the Mountain River, which I descended — well, portaged in the vicinity of — to Great Slave Lake.

Throughout this period, I had always been curious as to the exact route the Anderson and Stewart expedition had followed north from McLeod Bay in 1855. Finally I came across, in a 1940 edition of *The Canadian Field-Naturalist*, James Anderson's journal from that trip and a sketch map of the party's route.[7] I resolved to follow the fifty-mile portion of his route between McLeod Bay and the headwaters of the Barnston River at Anarin Lake at the end of my next trip in that area. I was curious how this route would compare, in relative difficulty, with the others I had travelled. And I wondered how closely Anderson's route description would agree with modern maps. The experience would answer a few of my questions, raise some new ones, and renew my admiration for the rate of travel of nineteenth-century voyageurs over rugged terrain.

But before focusing on just this portage route, it is worthwhile to appreciate Anderson's overall achievement. With James Stewart,[8] a Hudson's Bay (HBC) man who had spent most of his career in the Yukon and his second in command, as well as a hand-picked crew of voyageurs, Anderson was dispatched at the request of the British Admiralty to investigate the area near the mouth of the Great Fish (now the Back) River in Chantrey Inlet, and follow up on John Rae's discovery that men of the Franklin expedition had perished in that vicinity.

Anderson's party left Fort Simpson on May 28, 1855. They travelled up the Mackenzie River and east on Great Slave Lake, struggling through ice in McLeod Bay. Just west of the Barnston River, they portaged north out of Great Slave, heading for the Barrens. Reaching Aylmer Lake on the Lockhart River, they portaged into the headwaters of the Back, and descended it to the Arctic Ocean. Then, with autumn closing in, they retraced their route up the Back and over to Aylmer Lake. After descending the Lockhart River to Artillery Lake, they followed a portion of Pike's Portage route and then a small stream to reach the site of Fort Reliance.[9] On September 16, they were back at the Hudson's Bay Company post of Fort Resolution on Great Slave Lake. To any canoeist, especially one who has paddled in the Barrens, the magnitude of this achievement is obvious. Yet Anderson's expedition remains almost unknown. The Hudson's Bay Company clearly lacked the Royal Navy's aptitude for creating heroes.

Photo by John McInnes.

James Anderson named Rae Falls after Sir John Rae, the Arctic explorer. In his journal, Anderson recorded their height at fifty-four feet, but John McInnes estimates that they are only ten to thirteen feet high.

I joined Anderson's route in what is now Anarin Lake, identified as "David's Lake" in the sketch map provided in the *Field-Naturalist*. Joseph Anarin was an Iroquois canoeman with Anderson's expedition. "David's Lake" is taken from Pike's map — David was a young Inuk, an interpreter at the Fort Resolution mission, who accompanied Pike and HBC man James Mackinlay on their 1890 trip to the Back River.

I set out down the Barnston from a campsite on a fine sandy rise at the west end of Anarin on a grey, showery morning, one hundred and forty-three years and five days after Anderson had passed here heading north. I was planning to set a gentler pace. Anderson's voyageurs had, on the day they passed through Anarin, "began to load at 3 a.m. … made six portages … and about 47 miles through lakes. Encamped at 9:30 p.m., men rather tired."[10] Who could blame them? I paddled to the outlet of the lake and portaged the shallow exit rapids over a barren hill. I made good time through the shallow, rocky lake expansions below, then ran two small rapids into the north end of Beirnes Lake ("Ross Lake" on the *Field-Naturalist* sketch map). I paddled to the south end of this eight-mile-long lake and portaged its steep, shallow outlet rapids across a flat rock outcrop. According to his journal, Anderson had camped nearby, not far above Rae Falls, on July 4, 1855.

I crossed a small lake expansion, then portaged Rae Falls — named by Anderson after Sir John Rae — a short steep carry over bare rock. Anderson's description — "a fine fall ... passes through a door like cut in the rocks"[11] is accurate. The river rushes through a narrow gap in a rock dike. But his height estimate — fifty-four feet — is off by a factor of three at least. I estimated the drop at ten to twelve feet. Was Anderson's estimate a slip of the pen? Or were nineteenth-century canoeists, even eminently respectable chief factors of the Hudson's Bay Company, occasionally subject to the same temptation to exaggerate, a temptation that sometimes afflicts their present-day counterparts?

Contemplating this riddle, I paddled down MacLellan Lake ("Campbell Lake" on the sketch map) and camped in another fine sandy site on an island about three miles below the falls. It would be nice to think the lake was named after Murdo McLellan, an Orkneyman in Anderson's party. Anderson described the lake as "a large body of water, broad and 10 miles in length."[12] It is a fine lake, although pinched by a couple of narrows, and probably closer to six miles in length. On one point, though, Mr. Anderson and I were in exact agreement — with the skies clearing in the afternoon, the "weather is very warm and mosquitoes and sand flies dreadful."[13]

Next morning brought a fine, sunny day with just a light breeze — perfect weather except for a haze of smoke. I paddled to where the Barnston River left the lake, and portaged a steep rapid there, making an easy carry over bare rock beside a small overflow falls. With time in hand, I stopped to fish below the rapids. Anderson and his men had reached this point from Great Slave Lake in two-and-a-half days of hard travelling. I had the luxury of five days, going downhill, to reach the lake for my float plane pickup. While better-endowed with time than Anderson, I had no more luck — he complained that although the lakes "are said to abound in fine trout and W. [white] Fish; we ... have caught none."[14] I had the same experience.

From this unnamed lake below the rapids, Anderson's route leaves the Barnston River and heads southwest. For me, travel would become more difficult. Conversely, Anderson was at this point beginning to find progress easier after his steep climb from McLeod Bay. He joined the Barnston in this lake "which empties itself into Slave Lake by a very rapid river (unnavigable)"[15] and remarked that the country was becoming less arduous to travel. "The lakes are getting larger and the height of the mountains is diminished."[16] And of the eight portages his men had traversed that day, he could thankfully say "most of them short."[17]

Paddling to the end of a narrow bay, I soon reached the first portage. Just 1,600 feet in length, it nevertheless looked unpromising, as steep bedrock hills on both sides would force me to portage along the rocky bed of the creek that trickled down from the next lake. To my relief, the carry went quite well. The rocks in the streambed were quite flat and well consolidated, further up there were stretches of turf and an easy climb over a sandy knoll to the lake. This lake begins as a narrow gash between high rock hills, under a looming cliff, and extends about three miles to the southwest. Past the first narrows, however, its shores flatten out and a considerable amount of sand is in evidence. I camped on a sandy rise near the end of the lake. It had been an easy day, just twelve miles of travel and two portages — far below Anderson's standards, but an appropriate pace for a modern vacation.

The next morning was again warm, sunny, and smoky. I paddled to the end of the lake, and made a short carry over a sandy isthmus into the lake above. After paddling half a mile or so along its south shore, I portaged south into the headwaters of the creek that Anderson's route had followed north from Great Slave Lake. Again the portage was between steep bedrock hills, but the carry itself was good — downhill, open, and only 820 feet long. I appreciated this good fortune, without expecting it to last. After a quarter-mile paddle, I reached the next portage. It was more difficult, a half-mile combination of bog, outcrop, boulders, and brush. While carrying, I noticed a small rock cairn — just a couple of small stones balanced on a boulder — and wondered who had left such an inconspicuous marker behind.

This portage took me to a good-sized lake, almost four miles long, running to the southwest. I had intended to camp here, but couldn't find a good site on its steep rocky shores. I did find, atop a ridge on the large island in this lake, a larger version of the rock cairn I passed on the portage. At the end of the lake, I made a 160-foot portage over bare rock to a tiny pond. Here I saw evidence of chopping in a grove of stunted spruce — but no sign of a fire or camp. I wondered, again, who my predecessors might have been, but practical matters had to take precedence over speculation. I still needed a campsite, and the afternoon was wearing on. I paddled 325 feet to the end of the pond, and then portaged a quarter mile to the next lake. This carry began badly, over steep outcrops and through willows, but then emerged onto a fine sand ridge leading to the lake. I was tempted to camp here, but the tent would have been right on a major game trail — wolf, bear, and moose prints were all obvious, and recent. To ensure a restful sleep, I paddled a half mile to a flat rock shelf on a small island. Some small and incredibly gaunt spruce here bore eloquent witness to the power of the winter winds.

By my reading of his notes, I knew Anderson had camped in this lake at the end of his second day out of Great Slave Lake, after completing a portage "of about ¾ mile, which, tho' it had some steep ascents, was less rugged than the others."[18] Here he gave his men a bit of a break: "we encamped at 7:00 p.m. as the men tho' in good spirits seem pretty well done up with their last two days exertions."[19] They left camp at 3:00 a.m. the next morning, so as not to fall into any slothful habits. I did not intend to emulate their zeal.

Although it was well after 3:00 a.m., I did hurry out of camp in the morning. The day dawned cool and grey, with a strong wind from the northeast and a rising sea. I packed and ate quickly, loaded the canoe with some difficulty in the waves, and shot down the lake with about as much of a tailwind as I could handle. It was a relief to swing into the lake's sheltered southern bay. Here I elected to break Anderson's "less rugged" portage southwest to a narrow pond into three short carries by making use of a couple of tiny ponds. It still proved rough enough for this modern traveller, with rugged outcrops, boulders, and willows all in evidence.

I loaded up and launched in this pond, heading south and pushed by the strong wind. At its end, in Anderson's words, I "made two short portages and crossed two small tarns"[20] to reach a larger lake, nearly two and a half miles long. These two portages were short, but rugged.

Photo by John McInnes.

John McInnes discovered this paddle.

Meanwhile, the wind was still rising, making travel dangerous — the small poplars and birch on the ridges were whipping furiously in the gale. Just past the first island in this lake, I landed on the east shore, tied the canoe firmly in the willows, and spent the afternoon windbound, reading and sipping Earl Grey tea.

After supper, the wind dropped a bit and the sky cleared, so I set out in search of a decent campsite. Just south of the larger island in the lake, I pulled in behind a small point on the east shore. I found a good tent site behind a low outcrop, and was setting up camp when something caught my attention. Lying on a large boulder just a few feet away was an ancient paddle. Obviously handmade, it had been there for many years — it was weathered to silver-grey, and overgrown by lichen. Yet it was in quite good condition, since the rock it lay on was not only sloped, to shed moisture, but also slightly dished so only the tip and grip of the paddle contacted the rock: a fascinating artifact. It would have been a highly improbable — but tempting — assumption to attribute this paddle to Anderson's expedition, 143 years before. But it did show this had been a canoe route once. And now it was again.

I was now only five miles from Great Slave Lake. With luck, I thought I might be able to paddle two of the five. There was little solace in Anderson's journal tonight. He described the country ahead as "inconceivably rugged and desolate. The mountains are riven in every shape. Only a few dwarf spruce and birch are to be seen, and scarcely even a bird to enliven the scene."[21]

The next morning was fine and sunny. I was excited and a little apprehensive about working down the steep portage route ahead. Anderson had made three portages from Great Slave to reach this lake. In succession, he described them as: "about ½ mile … to a pond of about a mile in length;"[22] "about 3 miles to a small lake … (about ½ mile across);"[23] and a final carry of "a mile in length, and, of course, from the steep ascents and the ruggedness of the country, very fatiguing."[24]

My goal for the day was just to reach the last lake before Great Slave Lake — Anderson's nearly one-mile-long pond. Rather than follow Anderson's route exactly, I decided to follow the creek more closely, making use of three tiny ponds along it to break up the portaging. It wouldn't reduce the total carrying distance, but I reasoned that with a natural feature to follow, the time required for route scouting and marking would be reduced.

I had to drag through a rocky shallow to reach the end of the lake, thwarting my ambition to portage in dry boots. But my spirits rose when the first carry to a small pond went very well, about a third of a mile through open forest. About six-hundred feet of paddling brought me to the next portage. From here on, Anderson's description of the country would prove very accurate. The portage started well, on flat and open ground, but soon began to deteriorate. I was squeezed between the willows and boulders of the creek bed and a steep hill thickly clothed in small spruce. I climbed the hill to scout, and was rewarded with a tremendous view out over Great Slave Lake, my first sight of the big lake on this trip. Anderson must have found a similar viewpoint nearby. "From the top of one of the highest mountains perhaps 1,000 feet above the level of Slave Lake, I had a fine view of that body of water … and counted no less than fifteen small lakes or tarns."[25]

I didn't count tarns, but I did spot a reasonable portage route, and carried on to the next pond. It was a disappointment. I had to wade one rocky shallow, and portage two more, to reach its southern tip, where the creek slid over a low ledge and tumbled down a wide boulder bed toward Great Slave Lake. From here, I headed for a tiny pond just above Anderson's first lake, perhaps three quarters of a "straight-line" mile away. It wasn't easy — the forest was quite thick on this sheltered south-facing slope, and any clearings were floored with irregular boulders. My progress was far from a straight line.

After some tough-going, including a short stretch of very thick spruce through which I had to drag the canoe, I broke out of the bush at the top of a steep bank above the creek, about 650 feet from my tiny pond. Carefully working down to the creek, I followed it to the pond. Despite a few willows, the going was fairly open and dry. Then, with the portage only a few steps from completion, it took a final turn for the worse, when I broke through a section of floating bog and found myself hip deep in icy, soggy peat with the canoe on my head. My familiarity with this position has not reduced my contempt for it. I climbed out, scraped off most of the peat, waved ineffectually at a large cloud of insects, swung my paddle at an aggressive gull, and pushed out into the tiny pond. Anderson had remarked on the spirit of his men after their long portage: "The whole of the loadings with the canoes were rendered by 10 p.m. and the men are now laughing over their day's work!"[26] My mood was notably less cheerful.

After I paddled to the end of the pond, life began to improve. I found a good tent site among small birch, and put on dry shoes and clean pants. Supper, a wash, and a double rum ration restored my equanimity. Anderson would have approved. I was even able to appreciate another fine view of Great Slave Lake from the ridge behind camp. The long portage was over. Tomorrow, a short carry to the next lake and another to Great Slave Lake would end the trip.

Next morning I awoke to the strong smell of smoke. A thick grey pall had drifted in overnight from the forest fires raging east of Yellowknife. Great Slave Lake had vanished, and visibility was less than a half mile. But to find the lake, I just had to go downhill. After breakfast and a few limbering-up exercises to overcome the effects of yesterday's exertions, I was off on my second-last portage. After about a half mile of generally open going, and a steep descent on a serendipitously located moose path, I was on the last lake above Great Slave Lake. Just one carry to go! Scouting, I found a good portage route west of the stream. Landing on a flat rock shelf, I followed a moose path through a fringe of bush. Ahead was a few hundred feet of easy-going across a flat rock outcrop, then a steep but manageable descent through open forest. When I dropped the canoe into the marshy bay at the creek mouth, a sleepy mallard shot up in alarm. I guess he didn't see a lot of traffic coming through this way.

A couple of hours later I was camped across the bay, washed, dressed in clean clothes, and sipping the last of the rum. Looking back up the steep hills of the portage route, I thought about what Anderson and his voyageurs had done. In one way, it was hard to relate to. Going uphill — no maps, no Royalite, no nylon. No no-see-um screens, no DEET, no waterproof packs. No Twin Otter to pick you up if something went wrong. But in another way it was easy, for if the equipment has changed, the country remains as wild as it was in Anderson's day. With wisdom, and luck, it may stay that way for another hundred and forty-three years.

John McInnes
Edmonton, Alberta

Chapter 6

Ernest Thompson Seton: On the Portage

By 1907, Ernest Thompson Seton (1869-1946) was, at age forty-seven, a wealthy man. An immigrant to Canada at the age of six, he grew up in Lindsay, Ontario. There he first encountered the Aboriginal people who informed his autobiographical novel, *Two Little Savages,* published in 1903, and his Woodcraft Indians, precursors to the Boy Scouts of America, of which he became the first chief scout in 1910. Although his only academic credential was a diploma (and Gold Medal) from the Ontario College of Art in Toronto, he had more than made up for his lack of formal scientific training by years in the field. He had studied art in Paris with some of the great French academic masters of the late nineteenth century and he had published a major volume, *Studies in the Art Anatomy of Animals*, in 1896, as a service to art and science.

Beginning in Manitoba, where he homesteaded with his brother Arthur in the 1880s, he had become acquainted with many of the leading naturalists in the United States Biological Survey, at the American Museum of Natural History, at the Smithsonian Institution, and in Canada at the Geological Survey, initially as an illustrator of scientific monographs, by which he made his living. Beginning in 1881, he diligently maintained a field journal, which, at the time of his death in 1946, numbered almost fifty volumes, rich in careful observation and detailed hand-drawn images. He read voraciously in the emerging disciplines of biology and anthropology, and studied the original works of all the explorers to northern North America. He travelled extensively in the interior of the United States and Canada, sometimes in the field, sometimes on extended lecture tours with friends like Pauline Johnson, the celebrated Mohawk poet, who called Seton her "Wolf Cousin."

Officially appointed government naturalist to the Province of Manitoba in 1892, Seton had published several scientific articles and monographs on mammals and birds. He began writing articles for various popular magazines in the 1880s, and by the late 1890s, following the publication of his classic *Wild Animals I Have Known* (1898), quickly became famous throughout the world as an outspoken defender of wildlife. Seton's realistic animal "biographies" were composites assembled from his journal observations of species in the field. Today they are recognized as pioneering contributions to the science of ethology, or animal behaviour, but in 1903 their credibility was challenged by American naturalist John Burroughs in the famous "nature-faker" controversy, which dragged on well into 1907. Burroughs's arguments were subsequently demolished, but literary scholars today frequently refer to them as if they constitute legitimate authority. Certainly Seton was seriously wounded by Burroughs's charges. He needed a dramatic demonstration of his acumen in the field to recover his reputation and to prove that he knew what he was talking about.

On May 5, 1907, accompanied by thirty-six-year-old Edward A. Preble of the United States Biological Survey, Ernest Thompson Seton left Winnipeg on the Canadian Pacific Railway, commencing a self-funded, seven-month journey that would take them to what Seton, in his published account of the expedition, called "the Arctic prairies."[2] At Calgary, the two friends took the train to Edmonton, from there travelling the ninety-three miles to Athabasca Landing by "livery rig." On May 18, they set out in their Peterborough canoe, travelling in tandem with a convoy of thirteen Hudson's Bay Company freight scows captained by John MacDonald, the chief pilot on the leading scow, and crewed by Métis boatmen.

Chapter 6

On May 28 they reached Fort McMurray. Discovering that the steamboat *Grahame*, which they had hoped to board for passage to Fort Chipewyan, had been delayed, Seton purchased a thirty-foot sturgeon-head boat and sailed, drifted, and rowed the distance, arriving on June 5. This ambitious project could not have been accomplished without thirty-year-old William C. Loutit, an Orkney Métis from Fort Chipewyan, who signed on as Seton's guide and cook and who remained with him for the duration of the *Arctic Prairies* expedition.[3] Seton, Preble, and "Billy" Loutit were joined, as crew, by Royal North-West Mounted Police inspector A.M. Jarvis, whom Seton had known in Toronto, and who, by pure coincidence, had been aboard the convoy. Jarvis was travelling to Fort Smith, having been commissioned to undertake a formal investigation into the apparent decline in neighbouring wood bison populations. This unlikely quartet made it to Smith Landing on June 7.

For much of the next month, Seton accompanied Jarvis, at the latter's invitation, on three separate reconnaissance missions inland from Fort Smith in search of the bison — the first two on horseback, the third by canoe. Seton's primary interest lay in obtaining photographs of wood bison. He was an excellent photographer and aspired to obtain images from the field to illustrate both his account of the expedition and his analytical studies of wildlife. Each of these side trips was guided by a different individual, the first by the legendary Métis, Sousi Beaulieu:

> Unlike the founder of the family, Sousi has no children of his own. But he has reared a dozen waifs under prompting of his own kind heart. He is quite a character — does not drink or smoke, and I never heard him swear. This is not because he does not know how, for he is conversant with the vigor of all five languages of the country and the garment of his thought is like Joseph's coat. Ethnologically speaking, its breadth and substance are French, but it bears patches of English, with flowers and frills and strophs, and classical allusions of Cree and Chipewyan.... He was forever considering his horse. Whenever the trail was very bad, and half of it was, Sousi dismounted and walked — the horse usually

following freely, for the pair were close friends.… [H]e
was kind, cheerful, and courteous throughout.… Speak
as you find. If ever I revisit that country I shall be glad
indeed to secure the services of good old Sousi …[4]

The second guide was Pierre Squirrel, first chief of the Slave River
Chipewyan, who had signed Treaty 8 in 1899, and whom Seton describes
as "a pleasant and intelligent companion."[5] Visiting Squirrel's community
at Fort Smith, Seton observes "dreadful, hopeless, devastating diseases,
mostly of the white man's importation. It made me feel like a murderer
to tell one after another, who came to me with cankerous, bone-eating
sores, 'I can do nothing.'" At one point Squirrel says to him, "You see how
unhappy we are, how miserable and sick. When I made this treaty with
your government, I stipulated that we should have here a policeman and
a doctor; instead of that you have sent nothing but missionaries."[6]

The third to guide Seton and his entourage into bison country was
the Chipewyan François Bescaya (spelled by Seton, "Bezkya"). Bescaya
led Seton, Preble, Jarvis, Corporal Stafford, E.A. Selig (another RNWMP
officer who joined Jarvis in Fort Smith and who served with the force
from 1880 until his death on Herschel Island in 1911), and Billy Loutit.
Bescaya had been recommended to Seton as a good man and a moose
hunter. "At Fort Smith are two or three scores of hunters, and yet I am told
there are *only three moose-hunters*. The phrase is not usually qualified; he
is, or *is not*, a moose-hunter. Just as a man is, or is not, an Oxford M.A."[7]

As mentioned earlier, Jarvis's objective on each of the three side trips
was to ascertain the health of the bison. As it happened, they actually saw
animals on the first trip only. Not being terribly sophisticated in these
matters, and with a conservative tendency to respect authority, Seton
was uncritical of the Mounty's estimation of the circumstances resulting
in declining populations. If one reads Jarvis's subsequent reports to his
superiors carefully, one cannot help but deduce that he had cynically made
up his mind, before even entering their territory, that the Chipewyan
and Métis — led by Pierre Squirrel and Sousi Beaulieu — were solely
responsible for killing off the bison.[8] Keep in mind that Seton and Preble
were guests of Jarvis. Nevertheless, Seton was a founding member of
the American Bison Society in 1905, so was well aware of the declining

numbers long before arriving. Seton records Pierre Squirrel's argument that "When our people made this treaty, there was nothing said about reserving the Buffalo. If you are going to take that hunting from us, we want a better treaty, more compensation, for that is part of our living." Seton draws his own conclusions from this conversation:

> There were about 300 Buffalo left in 1907; they are not increasing, partly because the Wolves kill a few calves every winter, and chiefly because the Indians pursue them regularly for food.
>
> There are, I think, two things needed to enforce the existing law and save the remnants of Buffalo.
>
> 1st. Admit the justice of the Indians' plea and compensate them to let the Buffalo alone. On their own evidence, the value of the hunting is small.
>
> 2nd. Have a Police Station on or near the Buffalo range. A Policeman 100 miles away cannot protect the Buffalo from poachers on the spot, especially when those poachers have in their favour the sentiment of the whole community.[9]

Seton's primary concern was always the animals. Despite his racialized language, he was not hostile to First Nations people. He did not understand what he regarded as unnecessary killing in any context, by any human being. He sincerely believed that the bison were endangered, but he did not believe that their rescue should come at the expense of the people. Of course, his proposed solutions, including the creation of a new national park, were all born of his own culture.

On July 9, Jarvis and Selig left their colleagues on the Nyarling River and raced ahead, down the Little Buffalo to Great Slave Lake and east to Fort Resolution to catch the steamer *Wrigley* back to Fort Smith. Seton, Preble, Bescaya, and Billy Loutit followed a few days later in Seton's canoe.[10]

At Resolution, Seton borrowed a Hudson's Bay Company York boat, filled it full of provisions that he had arranged to have sent by steamer from Fort Smith, loaded in his canoe, and, on July 16, set off north and eastward across Great Slave Lake with Preble, Loutit, and a hired crew of Métis and Chipewyan. Among the crew of seven was another of the Beaulieu clan, François Jr., an independent spirit for whom Seton had no time — apparently because he knew his own mind and could speak for his fellows. Beaulieu effectively led a mutiny against Seton for the provisions he had brought. All the way up Great Slave Lake, the refrain "Grub, no good" resonated among the men. Seton was gradually, and grudgingly, made to understand that country food was deemed superior, and also that country food required a lot of time, for a lot of killing. "I have trouble enough in matters that *are* my business and this they consider solely their own. It is nothing but kill, kill, kill every living thing they meet. One cannot blame them … since they live by hunting and in this case they certainly did eat every bit …"[11] Also on board was the Métis Louison d'Noire, or as he was known in the country, "Weeso." "He was a nice kind, simple old rabbit, not much use and not over-strong, but he did his best, never murmuring.… He alone did not ask for rations for his wife during his absence; he said 'It didn't matter about her, as they had been married for a long time now.' "[12] On July 27, the crew reached the lobstick marking the beginning of Pike's Portage and, as contracted, carried Seton's canoe and gear over the first long stretch to Harry Lake. Before releasing the crew, Seton hired Weeso to remain as his guide into the Barrens.

> There were two peculiarities of the old man that should make him a good guide for the next party going northward. First, he never forgot a place once he had been there, and could afterward go to it direct from any other place. Second, he had the most wonderful nose for firewood; no keen-eyed raven or starving wolf could go more surely to a marrow-bone in cache, than could Weeso to the little sticks in far away hollows or granite clefts.[13]

Following J.W. Tyrrell's 1900 map of the portage, the four men navigated the thirty-mile journey from Charlton Harbour to Artillery Lake in three-and-a-half days; all but Seton able to shoulder 220 to 275 pounds on the trail.[14] Seton noted that two of the smallest lakes on the portage had not previously been named. "I therefore exercised my privilege and named them, respectively, 'Loutit' and 'Weeso' in honour of my men."[15]

112

Courtesy of the Seton Family.

Billy Loutit, axe in hand, about to chop down a 250-year-old dwarf spruce near Artillery Lake.

On August 1, as they paddled Artillery Lake, Seton observed:

> There is something inspiring about the profundity of
> transparency in these lakes, where they are 15 feet deep
> their bottoms are no more obscured than in an ordinary
> eastern brook at six inches. On looking down into the
> far-below world, one gets the sensation of flight as one
> skims overhead in the swift canoe.... As we spun along
> the south-east coast of the lake, the country grew less
> rugged; the continuous steep granite hills were replaced
> by lower buttes with long grassy plains between; and as
> I took them in, I marveled at their name — *the Barrens*;
> bare of trees, yes, but the plains were covered with rich,
> rank grass, more like New England meadows.[16]

A few days later, Seton made a project of counting and registering in
his journal the rings on various trees at the Last Woods campsite, marked

on Tyrrell's map on the east shore of Artillery Lake. He photographed Billy Loutit, axe in hand, poised to take down a specimen dwarf spruce, about 250 years old, "the first dendrochronological sampling at the arctic treeline in North America." Seton's accompanying analysis, "anticipating the positive correlation that has been found between ring widths and summer conditions," is reckoned the first of its kind in central Canada, of vital importance in ascertaining climate change.[17] Seton and Preble also took great care in assembling a rare plant collection from this region. From Great Slave Lake, especially on Kah-d'nouay, Caribou, and Et-then islands, from Pike's Portage, and from Artillery Lake, they recorded numerous species in appendix E of *The Arctic Prairies*. Their specimens were donated to the herbarium of the Geological Survey in 1910, inspiring the director R.W. Brock to write, "This is much the finest lot of plants we have ever had from the region, in fact I doubt if such fine specimens from there are in any herbarium, and several species were not before represented in our collection."[18]

The Last Woods campsite represented Seton's entrée to the world of the caribou, the real destination of his long journey. On July 22, in the narrows between the Pethei Peninsula and the mainland on Great Slave Lake, he had encountered a band of Dogrib and inquired if they had seen any caribou: "When one is in Texas the topic of conversation is, 'How are the cattle?' in the Klondike, 'How is your claim panning out?' and in New York, 'How are you getting on with your novel?' On Great Slave Lake you say, 'Where are the Caribou?'"[19] The Dogrib had seen none. But here, on Artillery Lake, and north toward Ptarmigan Lake, caribou were in abundance. Seton recounts stories about "shooting" them, much to Weeso's dismay, with his camera. "A young buck now came trotting and grunting toward us till within sixteen paces, which proved too much for Weeso, who then and there, in spite of repeated recent orders, started him on the first step to my museum collection."[20] On August 7, Seton is overwhelmed by the number of caribou crossing their path:

> In the morning Billy complained that he could not sleep
> all night for Caribou travelling by his tent and stumbling
> over the guy ropes.... One had the feeling that the whole
> land was like this, on and on and on, unlimited space

114

with unlimited wild herds.... Other travellers have gone, relying on the abundant Caribou, yet saw none, so starved.... I took plenty of groceries, and because I was independent, the Caribou walked into camp nearly every day, and we lived largely on their meat ...[21]

By the time they reach Ptarmigan Lake, Seton has wholly committed to country food: "Caribou meat fresh, and well prepared, has no superior ...[22]

By August 9, the travellers had reached the southern extremity of Clinton-Colden Lake, relying now for direction on "the small chart drawn by Sir George Back in 1834, but it was hastily made under great difficulties, and, with a few exceptions, it seemed impossible to recognize his landscape features."[23] Intent upon remedying the dearth of knowledge about the region immediately north and west of Artillery Lake, and no doubt anticipating the imprimatur of the Royal Geographical Society to which he planned to report the results of his expedition, Seton naively set about the task of exploring, surveying, and mapping Clinton-Colden and Aylmer lakes — armed with virtually no technical skills for the enterprise. He claims, for example, "in the east arm of Clinton-Colden," to have "discovered the tributary that I have called 'Laurier River,' and near its mouth made a cairn enclosing a Caribou antler with inscription 'E.T. Seton, 10 Aug., 1907.'" One searches in vain for this river today.[24]

By now the four canoeists were in extraordinarily good condition, able to paddle thirty to thirty-five miles a day even against strong headwinds. The Thanakoie Narrows opened out on to Aylmer Lake on August 12, and they continued journeying west, "seeking the open sea" illustrated on Back's map: "On the morning of the 15th we ran into the final end of the farthest bay we could discover and camped at the mouth of a large river entering in."[25] Seton is almost overjoyed to have proved Back's map inaccurate: "The great open sea of Aylmer was a myth. Back never saw it; he passed in a fog, and put down with a query the vague information given him by the Indians." Seton left a monument at the mouth of the Lockhart River, a simple stone cairn with a cross on top, marked SETON EXPEDITION, 1907.[26] On August 16, shortly after having been aggressively confronted by a nine-hundred-pound bull muskox —

Courtesy of the Seton Family.

Weeso, with a nine-hundred-pound muskox; the head and hide were brought south by Seton and donated to the American Museum of Natural History.

shot in the event by Weeso, who probably saved his life — Seton "made the most important geographical discovery of the journey." This was the Thonokied River, which Seton promptly named for Earl Grey, then the governor general of Canada: "Then and there I built a cairn, with a record of my visit, and sitting on a hill with the new river below me, I felt there was no longer any question of the expedition's success."[27] Seton may have been correct — that he was the first white man to see this river. It is not marked on Pike's nor Whitney's map. It is marked, but not named, on Blanchet's detailed 1926 map.[28] But today, as it should, it keeps its Dene name. After exploring and taking further specimen collections at the western extremity of Aylmer, the crew paddled to the northernmost reaches of Sandhill Bay where Seton installed yet another cairn at the portage leading to Sussex Lake, leaving his mark beside those of Back, Anderson and Stewart, and Pike, all of whom had preceded him.[29]

After several days of exploring, surveying, collecting, and waiting out storms on the adjacent Barrens of Aylmer and Clinton-Colden, Seton turned his canoe homeward, exulting in the strength of the crew as they covered between thirty to forty miles each day, reaching the campsite at Last Woods on the east shore of Artillery Lake on September 2. On

(Left to right): Seton, E.A. Preble, Billy Loutit, and Weeso pause for a standard shore lunch on Aylmer Lake.

their way north they had cached provisions here and were thrilled to find them untouched by wolverines:

> How shall I set forth the feelings it stirred? None but the shipwrecked sailor, long drifting on the open sea, but come at last to land, can fully know the thrill it gave us. We were like starving Indians suddenly surrounded by Caribou. Wood — timber — fuel — galore! It was hard to realize — but there it was, all about us, and in the morning we were awakened by the sweet, sweet home-like song of the Robins, singing … just as they do it in Ontario…. We now had unlimited food as well as unlimited firewood; what more could one ask…? These were the happy halcyon days of the trip, and we stayed a week to rest and revel in the joys about us.[30]

At Artillery Lake, Seton makes many interesting observations of caribou behaviour, most of which turn up again much later, and in greater detail, in *Lives of Game Animals*.[31] He deeply regretted that they could not stay longer, his "one unfulfilled desire" being that he could not see the caribou returning to their winter range.[32] In *The Arctic Prairies*, Seton demonstrates convincingly that he had done his homework in preparation for the expedition and in the research that followed it.[33] Nevertheless, drawing upon observations made by Pike, H.T. Munn, Buffalo Jones, and others, he calculated, preposterously, a population of thirty million caribou ("and maybe double of that") between the Mackenzie River and Hudson Bay. "In which case they must indeed outnumber the Buffalo in their palmiest epoch."[34] In response to unsubstantiated charges of overhunting, Seton assures his reader that Native hunters "do not average 20 Caribou each in a year … and there is no reason to fear in any degree a repetition of the [white man's] Buffalo slaughter that disgraced the plains …"[35]

On September 9, the party covered five of Pike's portages, reaching Harry Lake — the same distance it had taken two days to cover going out. After being windbound on Great Slave Lake for three days, they finally made it to Fort Reliance on September 14, taking refuge from a brutal storm for three days in the cabin built by Buffalo Jones ten years earlier. In McLeod Bay they encountered two separate Chipewyan bands, both running out of food. Because of Billy Loutit's exceptional hunting skills, Seton's crew had been able to eat caribou and spare most of their provisions, so "we supplied them, and these were among the unexpected emergencies for which our carefully guarded supplies came in [sic]."[36] On the return voyage down Great Slave Lake "our gallant boat went spinning … covering in one day the journeys of four during our outgoing, in the supposedly far speedier York boat. Faster and faster we seemed to fly … in and out of the larger islands … and when we should have stopped for the night no man said 'Stop,' but harder we paddled."[37] Weeso left the crew at Fort Resolution on September 27, but Billy Loutit accompanied Seton and Preble upstream, tracking the canoe most of the way to Fort Smith, then taking the steamer *Ariel* to Fort Chipewyan where they arrived on October 9.

As they poled, lined, and paddled south, Seton wrote:

> When we had embarked on the leaping, boiling, muddy
> Athabaska, in this frail canoe, it had seemed a foolhardy

enterprise. How could such a craft ride such a stream for 2,000 miles? It was like a mouse mounting a monstrous, untamed, plunging and rearing horse. Now we set out each morning, familiar with stream and our boat, having no thought of danger, and viewing the water, the same turbid flood, as our servant.[38]

This self-assured tone is dashed in the canyon south of Fort McMurray on October 20 when the canoe upsets. Seton's graphic description of the ensuing crisis is riveting, capturing both his own sense of panic at the loss of his journals, specimen collections, compass surveys, and drawings and at his concern for Preble, who is drifting back downstream, hanging on to the badly damaged, overturned canoe. Billy Loutit and Elzéar Robillard, a Métis who had joined on as crew at Fort McKay,[39] save the situation almost entirely on their own, Seton leaving the reader in no doubt about his own frailty. While he plucks easily visible floating food and bedding objects from the eddies, and lights a fire on the shore, it is the two Métis who race seven miles back, clambering over the rocks and swimming through the raging torrent, eventually rescuing the canvas bag containing the journals, "the most precious of all my things."[40] It is Billy Loutit and Robillard who repair the canoe and who develop a strategy for retrieving the Winchester and the shotgun from the frigid waters. Without Seton's journals we would not have this story, which, fittingly, he concludes on his arrival at Athabasca Landing on November 1, with the observation that if he can go back again to the Arctic prairies, "Grant only this, that I gather again the same brave men that manned my frail canoe …"[41]

As contemporary scholarship in environmental history and ecocriticism makes clear, it is impossible to extract Ernest Thompson Seton from the racist discourse of his time.[42] This is especially the case in *The Arctic Prairies* where at times he could be a poster boy for Carl Berger's thesis in *The Sense of Power*.[43] But he was not a one-dimensional figure and it would be a mistake to conclude that he was insensitive to First Nations people, that his knowledge of wildlife was superficial, or that he was wedded to some notion that collecting specimens for science trumped the legitimacy of Aboriginal hunting. Unlike his detractors, he was wholly self-taught. He had no university credentials, no theoretical equipment, but merely his observer's eye, undermined by the myriad prejudices, platitudes, and assumptions in which he was immersed by the culture in which he had been nurtured. Indeed, he was — like most of us — a human brew of inconsistencies, ambiguities, and contradictions about whom it is quite impossible to make definitive generalizations. Seton was an immigrant to Canada, a settler in a settler society, deeply confused about his own identity. He was born Ernest Evan Thompson but he changed his name several times — settling finally on "Seton" in 1901 after persuading himself that he was descended from Scottish nobility. He loved to rub shoulders with the powerful and numbered among his closest friends the pillars of the New York and Washington intelligentsia. But we must juxtapose this with the fact that he was also a founder and first chief scout of the Boy Scouts of America, an organization he fought tirelessly to model after First Nations cultures, in opposition to the militarism of Robert Baden-Powell and Theodore Roosevelt — a principled position that resulted in his being unceremoniously turfed from the organization in 1915. He was a complex person.

We have to look at the racialized language of *The Arctic Prairies* in the context of Seton's ambiguities. Seton lived his life on a metaphorical portage, in a condition of liminality. Because the portage was not always well-marked, or because he could not read the signs, Seton frequently became lost. He was saddled with cultural baggage, yet actively engaged in an intellectual and spiritual voyage of discovery, constantly moving, and torn, between where he had come from, and where he was. His formal science was governed by the Linnaean preoccupations of government agencies in Canada and the United States. Taxonomy was all about inventorying, ordering, and naming, and for that reason must be seen as part of the same colonization process that created the Commission of Conservation in 1909, Wood Buffalo National Park in 1922, and the Thelon Game Sanctuary in 1927. Institutionalizing nature in managerial units was then an uncompromising process that wholly ignored power differentials, placing the nobility of science above the lived experience of the Aboriginal peoples whose lives it marginalized.

The Arctic Prairies reveals that Seton was indeed infected by this logic. Throughout his report of the expedition he is at pains to tell us about his plant, insect, mammal, and bird collections, each of which is laboriously recorded in systematic detail in a separate appendix, verified, and legitimated by E.A. Preble, the government expert. But Seton is also mesmerized by the vagaries of animal behaviour, particularly of the bison, caribou, and muskox he encounters. Behavioural observations are explored in the text, not in the appendices. The analyses are often flawed, as we now know, but they also constitute attempts to get beyond mere history, description, location, and measurement. Animals are also observed and discussed in relationship to the cultures of the Chipewyan, Cree, and Métis. In 1909, Seton published *Life Histories of Northern Animals*, revised and expanded some years later as *Lives of Game Animals*.[44] These two works, the second of which incorporates a great deal of material from his 1907 journals, cemented Seton's reputation as a naturalist of acute perception and laid to rest the charges of John Burroughs. (Indeed, in a nice twist of irony, for *Lives* he was awarded the John Burroughs Medal in 1927 and the Daniel Giraud Elliot Medal of the National Academy of Sciences in 1928.) He opens each chapter by identifying the species under discussion with the Aboriginal names by which it is known among different linguistic groups. First Nations observers are frequently cited in the works as authorities or as trusted observers.

On the *Arctic Prairies* expedition, Seton first named lakes on Pike's Portage after Billy Loutit and Weeso, his Métis partners on the expedition. Then, in contradistinction, he named rivers after the prime minister and the governor general. Yet none of these names remains on government maps, despite the fact that all were formally registered. There are many beautiful prose passages in *The Arctic Prairies* that demonstrate Seton's nascent ecological understanding and deep love of the land. These are interlarded with sometimes outrageously disparaging comments about Dene and Métis people, which seem completely out of place when set beside his obvious affection for Billy Loutit and Weeso, Sousi Beaulieu, Pierre Squirrel, François Bescaya, and others he encountered along the way. A year after the publication of *The Arctic Prairies*, Seton wrote, "I never yet knew a man who studied the Indians or lived among them, without becoming their warm friend and ardent admirer."[45]

When the work and ideas of an individual are brought to the support of generalizations, it is always important to leave room for more questions. In Seton's case we might, for example, consider the trajectory on which he had embarked rather than merely dismissing him as a culprit in the process of colonization. Instead of looking backward at him, from the comfort of our visionary hindsight, perhaps we could bring him forward into our own time. He would, I believe, be the first to applaud the creation of a new national park in the East Arm of Great Slave Lake, especially as it is now the shared project of the Lutsel K'e Dene and the Government of Canada. Thaidene Nene, unlike Wood Buffalo, carries the name and conservation objectives of its people — to save the land and its traditional resources from the rapacious poachers of late capitalism: diamond mining, uranium exploration, oil pipelines, and tourism.

John Wadland
Peterborough, Ontario

Chapter 7

Buffalo Jones: God's Work, But Whose God?

After having captured and conquered every species of animal on the North American continent, like Alexander the Great, except as to the greatness, I longed for other worlds to conquer. Having had so much experience with wild creatures, I could read their very thoughts; I thought no more of roping a grizzly than of going into my corral and roping a domestic steer.[1]

— from *Lord of Beasts: The Saga of Buffalo Jones*, 1961

I remember the first time I saw a list of the names of those who had crossed Pike's Portage in the exploration and early trapper period (1890s–1920s)[2]: Warburton Pike, David Hanbury, Ernest Thompson Seton, Guy Blanchet, John Hornby, Charles Jesse "Buffalo" Jones. Wait a minute! Who is Buffalo Jones? With thirty years of reading northern literature, how did I miss this guy? Now, having pondered the content of three books: *Lord of Beasts: The Saga of Buffalo Jones*; *Buffalo Jones' Forty Years of Adventure*; and *The Last of the Plainsmen*, the question still remains; who is this guy? Of course, one can know

This classic Buffalo Jones portrait was taken during his years in Africa, where he was known as a much-celebrated hunter.

the basic story, but the facts get sketchy when you probe into them, and the embellishments (certainly from Jones's own telling) at times are just plain twisted. Certainly there is a classic American frontier story to be told here, cowboys and Indians stuff, even Indiana Jones stuff. But, if you consider the Aboriginal involvement and in particular the story they might tell, it suggests a very different account. It would be, for example, a story that is *not* a classic to the Canadian North. Buffalo Jones seems more displaced than others concerning his time in the North. He is idiosyncratic, yes, but more like an aberration to the Canadian North. One shouldn't overly generalize. These are complex people. But as much as Warburton Pike was toward the extreme of the "sporting gentleman" and Tyrrell and Blanchet were government surveyors, Charles Jesse Jones was toward another end of a continuum as an American frontiersman. He didn't fit. His departure was likely much celebrated.[3]

In the end, it is not easy to know what really happen with Buffalo Jones's time in the North. He was three seasons in the Arctic east of Great Slave Lake from the time he left the Indian Council held at Fort Smith concerning his presence in the North to his final departure north on the Mackenzie River and over the Rat and Peel rivers into Alaska. His biographers do wisely remind us: "… if we note his foolishness, we note the foolery of an epoch. If we see his manhood, we see the manhood of a frontier that a softer age has relegated to the paperback and the viewing screen."[4] Through Buffalo Jones's own telling, these biographers offer us much foolery, but also much to be respected. Adventure and resilience come to mind as dominant attributes, I surmise. Biographers give us a cowboy movie telling of the American frontier transferred to the Canadian North. From celebrated Western frontier author Zane Grey, we do get one popular western paperback with *The Last of the Plainsmen*. These are a good sell, too — fine stories. Trouble is, they just don't always add up. They are, I believe, too much of a "larger-than-life" account at times. Indeed, in many ways, this is what makes the story particularly interesting. I'll try to unpack it here.

First, the basic story: Charles Jesse Jones (1844–1919) was an American frontiersman. He was cut from the same cloth as the Jesse Jameses and Buffalo Bills, but he advanced the American frontier mentality of staunch individualism farther afield. He lived at a time between two wars, the American Civil War and the First World War. He might have been a great war hero, but instead he was a *Lord of Beasts*, or *The Last of the Plainsmen* — both titles of books describing his life. The *Kansas City Star* in 1914 called him "King of the Cowboys, conqueror of the animal kingdom, boy among boys, man among men, master of the chase, dauntless and more courageous than the greatest chief in his war paint."[5] In the waning American frontier he was easily romanticized, but again, this romance does not fit in the North.

Jones was inspired by the biblical injunction to have dominion over every living thing. In the Genesis proclamation, the frontier became everyman's playground. Certainly, it was God's will to "celebrate" wild animals by bringing them into captivity, domestication, and finally hybridization projects — a mission of religious zeal. The time (the foolery of the epoch) warranted it. Also called "The Saviour of the American Bison," Jones had a hand in the bison's demise and a bigger hand in their recovery from extinction, similar to Grey Owl's 1930s work toward conservation of the beaver, but with one obvious exception: hybridization projects were not a part of Grey Owl's mission.[6] In their day, hunter- and trapper-turned-conservationist was a noble shift with a bit of insight, though that's easy to say in hindsight. In 1889, Jones distinguished himself by purchasing nearly all the buffalo left in Canada — eighty-three head for $50,000 — an unthinkable sum of money in today's dollars. He took a shipment of buffalo to England (a follow-up to the successful Buffalo Bill's Wild West Show) for viewing and sale to breeders and zoos.

His Arctic trip in 1897, at age fifty-three, to capture muskox and return south with them (along with fox, marten, and other valuable fur-bearing animals to propagate on an island in the Pacific Ocean) for study, zoo display, and cross-breeding purposes was his greatest adventure at the time. In his senior years he was off to Africa with his famous lasso to capture lions and gorillas with varying success. At age sixty-five (1909) the *New York Globe* ran the following headline: JONES ROPES RHINOS ALIVE — FAMOUS WESTERN COWBOY MAKES GOOD WITH LARIAT IN AFRICA.[7] At the time of his death, at age seventy-five, he was writing a book of his adventures and concocting a scheme to cross domestic sheep with Rocky Mountain bighorns. Always a "think big or go home" adventurer and entrepreneur (economic incentives should not be ignored — a muskox calf sold in New York in the early 1900s for $1,600), Jones believed he had the backing of God's will and God's science. From his home base in Kansas, this American frontiersman's travels and projects made him a giant among men in America. The same cannot be said of his Arctic reputation, which might explain one reason why he is not well-known in the Arctic today.

Charles Jesse Jones likely felt his buffalo restoration work on the frontier was well-established and that it was time to move on to new frontiers as the world was opening up for global travel of high adventure. At the same time, the mighty muskox remained among the world's most remote and elusive animals — the North was a logical next step. Hunting was only a part of it for Jones; there was also the missionary zeal to bring this animal into captivity for southern exposure and a "greater" purpose. There were big game hunters before and after Jones, but none had developed a mission to fulfill the biblical mandate to subdue and dominate and domesticate as Jones had.[8] Jones was to be a stand-alone story in the region — in more ways than one.

Jones left home in the Midwest on June 12, 1897 — he would return 495 days later. Travelling what was already the usual way, he followed the railway to Calgary and north via Edmonton to Athabasca Landing, and then by stagecoach and river steamer to Fort Smith where he had troubles securing rivermen to help him with the portages at the Slave Rapids — a little foreshadowing here. On August 3, at Fort Smith, Jones was invited to a Council of Great Chiefs where he was warned not to take any animals out of the country alive. The fear was that if he took a muskox away, all other animals would follow, and the people would surely perish. As Jones would later learn, but never understand, the muskox and caribou were revered by the Dene and Métis people. At the time, the Chipewyan talked to the muskox as if they were human and sought permission in various ways before killing any. Jones's reply was that they — the Indian Council — should domesticate all the animals to improve the quality of their lives as ordained by the "White Man's God." I'll suggest here that this was the wrong response. Jones soon realized that since leaving Edmonton, messengers had forwarded the intention of his plan. Indeed, he'd been told orders were sent to "refuse [him] any assistance whatsoever, and to place all the obstacles in [his] way as possible even to killing the animals [he] might capture, rather than permitting them to leave the country."[9]

Seen here is the cabin that Buffalo Jones built around one of George Back's chimneys at Old Fort Reliance.

Needless to say, with such a message accompanying him, co-operation from the local Aboriginal people was difficult to secure, and his progress slow. For example, a boat for travelling the distance of Great Slave Lake could not be obtained, so he and his competent partner John Rea, an independent trapper and trader whom he had met along the way, had to build their own at Fort Resolution. Eventually, Jones and Rea and three local men hired as pilots left Fort Resolution on September 6, bound for Fort Reliance. Upon their arrival, Old Chief Siena learned of Jones's mission and refused to help any further. Jones and Rea built a cabin around the remains of one of Back's chimneys at Fort Reliance. With winter setting in, their plan of returning with their prize by December was unrealistic.

Their survival now depended on hunting and carefully hording their supplies from the "miserable creatures"— as they called the local people who regularly attempted to get whatever they could from the two lone white hunters. Jones often voiced his preference for the "noble" Plains Indian over the "miserable" Chipewyan, who, in the past, had shown at least some form of co-operation and mutual regard from white visitors. Before leaving on a hunting trip, Jones once set up a booby trap for any would-be intruders — a loaded gun pointed directly at the door with a string set to fire the gun when the door opened. Jones claims this was necessary to prevent burglary — perhaps he was right. Jones also claims that the local people had attempted to burn down the cabin unless tobacco and tea were shared — in this case Jones relented. Later, a fist fight broke out in the cabin and Jones and Rea claim they subdued a gang of invaders…hmm? There is no doubt Jones and Rea had developed an adversarial relationship with the local people, but who knows how much of Jones's stories of bravado are true.

During this time — December to February — Rea spent twenty-three days exploring the Barrens to the east, reaching as far as Clinton-Colden Lake, about one hundred miles northeast. The two men had drawn straws to see who would go exploring; Rea won and Jones stayed behind to protect their "fort." For both men the hunting had been successful, and although they had hoped to see muskox, tracks were all they saw.

With Yellowknife guide Joseph "Sousie" Barromie, the two men set out on February 25, 1898. With a team of dogs, they headed northeast of Reliance, but not via Pike's Portage. Instead, they followed a creek from Fort Reliance to Acres Lake and from here they joined Pike's Portage (see Map 2).[10] Barromie, however, appears to have been more of an inter-tribal watchdog than a guide. Nevertheless, Jones and Rea needed him to help access the headwaters of the Back River — muskox country. Jones was clear on his opinion of the Yellowknife people generally, and of Barromie specifically, stating: "the Yellowknives were extra-ordinarily inept at getting a living and totally lacking in the charm and dignity which often characterized the Plains Indians."[11] Jones accused Barromie of being lost on their return from the Back River headwaters and claimed that his own "sense of direction held true." At the same time, Barromie's "superstitions and rituals for the hunt" confounded the two white hunters. Jones's ridicule of his guide didn't help bridge any ideological gaps or superstitions between the three of them. Nevertheless, Barromie did lead the men to a successful early hunt. Jones, referring to the muskox as "black monsters," had anticipated "great sport" in the hunt but was disappointed as he felt it was the equivalent of "slaughtering cattle in a corral."[12] It seems to have been unclear to Jones that Sousie Barromie had likely hoped a successful hunt would be the end of it, but when the more elaborate plan to capture live muskox was not abated, Barromie deserted them at the north end of Artillery Lake. I, for one, doubt he was ever *lost*. Rather, Barromie was forced to bide his time waiting to see what would happen with the next muskox hunt. This speculation is the Native voice that is a between-the-lines exercise here.

From here, Jones and Rea headed east in a blinding storm for two days, claiming to reach a tributary of the Dubawnt River (likely they mean the Thelon River because the Dubawnt is about 155 miles to the east — an impossible distance to travel in two days in the blinding storm). They met Inuit people here for tea, but Jones was distracted, fearing supplies would be stolen. Remarkably little was offered by way of description. Okay, I'll be honest. Both the distance of travel suggested and his Inuit meeting is suspect in my mind. Also suspect is the later wolf attack where "they killed twelve [wolves] outright and twice as many more, wounded, had gone off to be devoured by their companions."[13] This reads like a classic Wild West "circle the wagons" shoot-up.

The heart of this story, and an aspect likely free of embellishment, is the actual capture of five yearling muskox by lasso. The technique used involved shooting the males, then shooting the hind legs of the cows which caused the animals to buckle. The yearlings then cowered around the cows ready to be lassoed. It wasn't "easy pickings" but it is certainly possible. As Jones himself notes, "true, this was cruel, but such acts are always pardonable in the interests of science."[14] One need not wonder what the Fort Smith Council of Chiefs was thinking.

Now, with live young muskox hobbled, a twenty-four-hour guard was required to protect them from the wolves that might kill them and the local people who might let them loose. While the initial fear was wolves, the true threat to the plan — as clearly stated to Jones at the outset — was the Dene and Métis determination to not have the animals leave the region alive. Not surprisingly, they awoke soon after the capture to discover all the yearling muskox had been killed by a cut to their throats. In Jones words, "the marauders left a peculiar-looking knife on the snow."[15] The special knife was likely symbolic of a ritual killing. Clearly, it was meant for Jones and Rea to see and learn from.

The men returned to Fort Reliance on April 10, 1898. They had been out forty-four days, claiming "not less than 25 miles per day" and "975 miles" "on snowshoes and dog team.[16] Waiting for open water, they departed Fort Reliance on June 20. Aside from the yearlings, they had also lost all their trophy muskox heads to the wolves. They abandoned their captive marten and foxes at Fort Resolution and decided to return south via the Mackenzie and Yukon rivers.

I will end the story of Buffalo Jones's Arctic travels here. Impressive? Certainly. Factual? Questionable in many places. Driven by God's will and a humanitarian mission? Yes, but whose God? Misguided as northern travel? I think so.

But one might be reminded of nineteen-year-old Mary Shelley's 1818 *Frankenstein* and the force of science that pervaded that century: power over nature made one a true child of the enlightenment.[17] Buffalo Jones, the western American frontiersman, was one such "child." He represents the foolery of the time that is still with us and is still a barrier to white travellers and their relationships to both Aboriginal people and nature. In addition, he represents the noble adventurer and the hard-nosed resilience of his time. Rudy Wiebe wisely asks all readers of literature, "Where is the voice coming from?" To understand the stories of Buffalo Jones, we must continually remind ourselves of this question.[18]

Jones, as a storyteller and biographer, offers a western frontier paperback or movie script transplanted to the Arctic with the waggery of a modernist raconteur. However, as cultural historian Theodore Roszak tells us, "We have, as a culture, been talked into the proposition that our security as a species depends upon our power over nature, and in turn, we have been persuaded that our power over nature requires us to screen the personhood of nature out of our lives — even as a professional torturer must begin by denying the personhood of his victims in order to gain total control over them."[19] Jones understood it to be God's will to derive power over nature and in the process deny the "personhood" of the land, the animals, and the local people — it is a cold and stark perspective but sadly not so uncommon, even today. Finally, to further the point, George Grinnell, a fine northern traveller who for decades taught History of Science courses at McMaster University in Hamilton, Ontario, captures a central distinction of the Buffalo Jones story and his relationship to land and people when he talks about Art Moffat, the leader of a 1955 Dubawnt River canoe trip: "What Art had understood, and we had not (his five younger travel companions) is that God is not he who kills and eats, but that which is killed and eaten."[20] This belief was appreciated and perhaps even embraced by the sporting gentlemen (Pike, Seton, Hornby) and government surveyors (Tyrrell and Blanchet) suggesting that they respected the Dene and Métis reverence for wildlife as expressed by the Fort Smith Council of Chiefs and Sousie Barromie.

There are lessons in the much-exaggerated Buffalo Jones story beyond "don't try to bring home the wild animals." One lesson might be to look for the sacred in nature, to meet nature without an agenda, and to observe an unfolding of nature while finding reverence — or God if you prefer — in the "ceaseless creativity" of nature.[21] I can't help thinking that Jones missed so much (or perhaps he just told the story that would sell.) It is a great story, but I find myself sympathetic to Sousie Barromie and his countrymen and grateful for the departure of Buffalo Jones.

Bob Henderson
Uxbridge, Ontario

Chapter 8

J.W. Tyrrell: The Man Who Named Pike's Portage

James Williams Tyrrell, the lesser-known but equally competent younger brother of Joseph Burr Tyrrell, began his inauspicious account of a most auspicious journey with these words:

> Herewith I have the honour to submit the report of my exploratory survey of 1900, extending from Great Slave lake and Hudson bay, in the districts of Mackenzie and Keewatin ... In all, seventeen hundred and twenty-nine miles of survey were accomplished, and in the performance of this, four thousand six hundred miles were travelled with sleds and canoes.[1]

Tyrrell must be credited with assigning the name to the now-famous link between Great Slave Lake and Artillery Lake, which he crossed in the process of his remarkable "exploratory survey." Well into his report, he states unequivocally that "This route first described by Warburton Pike, is by far the best canoe or boat route leading from Great Slave lake to Artillery lake."[2] Of course, this assertion necessarily omits the inevitable

J.W. Tyrrell in Reliance in 1900.

certainty that Pike was, in fact, shown the route by his Indian guides, whose people must have been using it for generations. Nonetheless, his point is taken. George Back, his most famous non-Native predecessor in these parts, had not used the route when he traversed from Great Slave to Artillery, fifty-six years before Warburton Pike.

Pike wondered why exploration of the Barrenlands had all but ceased after Back's passage. The Tyrrells responded, in the service of the Geological Survey, so that J.W. could claim "that the unexplored territory of over two hundred thousand square miles west of Hudson Bay was in those two years [1893 and 1894] reduced by more than one-half."[3] As he set out in 1900, he noted that "The country lying to the west of the Doobaunt, and comprising an area of about ninety thousand [square] miles, remained shrouded in mystery."[4] It was this mystery that J.W. Tyrrell was determined to unravel.

Tyrrell was a surveyor. He had accompanied his brother J.B., the geologist, on descents of both the Dubawnt and the Kazan a few years earlier. But the principal purpose this time was strictly to explore and map, so the surveyor-general in Ottawa called upon J.W. At the time he received the request, "in the hands of an Indian courier," the younger Tyrrell was working on a survey of timberlands in northern Ontario. He lost no time in complying.

The party consisted of nine men. In Winnipeg, on the way west, Tyrrell engaged "two half-breed voyageurs from the St. Peter's reserve,"[5] Robert Bear and John Kipling. In Edmonton he added Percy Acres as cook, and two expert Iroquois canoemen he knew from the earlier Barrenland expeditions, Pierre French and Harry Monette. Later, in Fort Chipewyan, another voyageur was hired, a Dene (Chipewyan) man named Toura. A surveyor from Ontario, C.C. Fairchild, came along to assist with the fieldwork, and Archdeacon Joseph Lofthouse, whom Tyrrell had met in Churchill, completed the team.

Their wilderness quest began literally at the end of the road 180 miles north of Edmonton. On February 26, 1900, five heavily laden dog teams pulled away from the Hudson's Bay Company post, to begin a journey by sled and canoe of 4,573 miles. By early May, after a difficult but ordinary — for the time — trip north, the nine men and about three tons of equipment reached Pike's Portage at the eastern extremity of Great Slave Lake. As Tyrrell wrote, "the last of our outfit was safely landed on 'Pike's Portage' [it is noteworthy that he felt compelled to put the name in quotation marks] at the extremity of the lake on May 9, by a lot of starving but faithful dogs."[6] Henceforth, the party advanced strictly under its own power. There was no snow on the portage trail, so even if the dogs had had sufficient strength remaining, they would have been of little use, but the reality was that "the dogs were played out and we had nothing with which to feed them."[7] The dogs' work was finished. Those that had survived were sent back to Fort Resolution.

Tyrrell provides us with the earliest (and perhaps the most) detailed description of the portage route in the account of his travels across it in May 1900:

> By adopting Pike's route, advantage is taken of a chain of small lakes — eight in number — which cover more than three-fourths of the twenty-four miles of travel.
>
> For convenience of reference the larger of these lakes have been given the following names in the order of our advance: 1, Harry; 2, French; 3, Acres; 4, Kipling; 5, Burr; and 6, Toura, after the names of our voyageurs.
>
> The only difficult portage on the route is the first in ascending order, viz., that from Charlton harbour [Great Slave Lake] to Lake Harry. It is 3¼ miles long, and from end to end has an ascent of 570 feet, besides several ascents and descents on the way. Lake Harry is three miles long and is separated from French lake, which is ten feet lower in elevation, by a portage of four hundred yards.
>
> French lake is over four miles in length, and discharges to the northeastward into Acres lake, which is six feet lower. A short portage of one hundred yards is necessary between the lakes. Acres lake, which is of very irregular shape, is the largest of the chain, though its length is only about four miles. It has an elevation of 1,074 feet, and discharges from one of its westerly bays by a stream, which I believe to be the one entering Charlton harbour, about a mile southeasterly from Fort Reliance.

Kipling lake — the fourth link in the chain — discharges into Acres lake with which it is connected by a narrow, winding, sluggish creek, navigable for canoes. It is only two and one half miles in length, but is one of the prettiest lakes of the series, its beautifully wooded shores and sandy beaches sloping down gradually to the water's edge in many places. Thus far the country passed through was found to be fairly well wooded with small white spruce and tamarack; whilst on the first long portage a grove of jack pines — the last seen by us — was passed. Some small white birch trees were also noticed at various points. By May 19 we had our outfit of about three tons weight, in cache at the north end of Kipling lake. The body of the lakes was still covered by ice, but around the shores and for half a mile or so near the inlets and outlets, open water had already formed, and this was causing our voyageurs much care and trouble, for the ice near the edges of the open water was for some distance treacherous and rotten. Canoes and sleds had to be used alternately in crossing the lakes, and much care and difficulty were often necessary in making the transfer from one conveyance to the other.

From lake to lake, the ground being bare, all goods had of course to be portaged on the men's backs.

Many old Indian camps were to be seen along our route, indicating that it is a much frequented way, but up to this time we had seen no deer [caribou]. Their tracks were, however, to be seen everywhere, as well as many scattered bones and antlers.

One party of Indians, "Pierre Fort Smith" and several others, had passed us on their way to Artillery lake, whence they were going to hunt deer [caribou], and later in the season, musk oxen.

From the north end of Kipling lake, a portage of one thousand yards easterly, took us to a pond which is separated only by a narrow neck from Burr lake, the fifth of the series. This lake is in a straight line not more than twelve miles distant from Old Fort Reliance, with which it is connected by a natural pass having a gradual descent to the westward. It does not afford a favourable canoe route, since it contains few lakes of any size, and too small a stream to be of any service, but as a route for a highway, steam, or electric railway it appears to be the most advantageous, and since the elevation of Burr lake is 1,131 feet, the mean gradient from the lower terrace at Reliance would be fifty feet to the mile.

At the north end of Burr lake there is situated a nice grove of white spruce timber, containing trees of ten and twelve inches diameter. A photograph of this was fortunately obtained, as it proved to be the last timber of any consequence met with before entering the barren lands, excepting some on the west shore of Artillery lake near Timber bay.

The portage from the north end of Burr lake to Toura lake is three-quarters of a mile long, and may be made either in one or two parts, by avoiding or taking advantage of a little lake lying to the east of the straight course. The seventh lake of the chain, which is nearly a mile in length, is reached by a very short portage from Toura lake, and is at an elevation of twelve hundred and eighty-two feet, being at the summit of the divide between Great Slave and Artillery lakes. From it a portage of seven hundred yards to the eastward takes one to the eighth and last lake, which is less than half a mile in length, and one more down hill portage of a quarter of a mile in length lands one at the southern extremity of Artillery lake, so named, though but crudely surveyed, by Sir George Back, after some British artillery men of his party. In addition to the portage route above described, which was followed by our voyageurs, several others were discovered by myself and Mr. Fairchild, and are shown on my accompanying maps, but will not require further description. The district is composed of granite and dolomitic rocky hills, some of which attain elevations of from nine hundred to one thousand feet above the level of Great Slave lake.

The distance from Reliance to the southern extremity of Artillery lake in a straight line is about sixteen miles. The elevation of Artillery lake is 1,188 feet, or 688 feet above Slave lake, which would make a mean gradient of about forty-two feet per mile.[8]

Less than a gripping read in places, but finely detailed and telling in so many ways, Tyrrell's report stands today as a most valuable description of the historical route he named "Pike's Portage." He saw it as much more than a future portage route, though he offers all the detail needed for this purpose. He assessed its value in timber. He considered its potential for a highway or railway. He named its lakes. He measured it with a surveyor's eye.

Once over the portage and camped on the shores of Artillery Lake, Tyrrell had his mind set on the Thelon River, the principal object of his explorations. By June 18 there was enough open water to allow their advance up Artillery Lake, and they retraced David Hanbury's[9] route in reverse, though there is no evidence to suggest that they had any mapped information from him. Hanbury was a well-educated British adventurer who travelled up the Thelon and Hanbury rivers and over Pike's Portage in 1899 in pursuit of sport and wilderness travel. Tyrrell apparently relied on the sixty-six-year-old sketch map that a Native guide had drawn for George Back. And, fortunately, he also met a Dene hunter, Pierre Fort Smith, familiar enough with the country to draw his own version, not substantially different from the earlier one.

Once over the height of land and into the Thelon system, Tyrrell's party moved as quickly as the mapping duties permitted. This branch of the river he named after Hanbury, perhaps begrudgingly acknowledging "the first white man to ascend it," in what proves to be Tyrrell's only reference to his predecessor on the river. The three canoes reached the junction with the main branch of the Thelon on the morning of July 7. Along the way, he documented the remnants of former Indian camps,

Courtesy of J.W. Tyrrell/Library and Archives Canada/PA – 019564.

The first Inuit that J.W. Tyrrell met on the Thelon River.

including at least one standing tipi frame. He also remarked that nearly all the muskox sighted were found on the north bank of the river, a suggestion consistent with most modern-day experience, although over the past decade the numbers of muskox sighted along this stretch of the river have dropped dramatically.

Just where the river exits sharply out of the widening around what is now known as Ursus Islands, and heads straight east toward Beverly Lake, Tyrrell encountered people for the first time:

> The encampment consisted of three or four lodges, and thirty-three souls in all, chief amongst whom was an old coast Eskimo, named Ping-a-wa-look, commonly known by the traders at Fort Churchill as "Cheesecloth." With him, as well as with one or two others our archdeacon was acquainted, and one of them had met me in 1893, so we found ourselves amongst warm friends.[10]

On Beverly Lake, waiting out a ferocious Barrenlands storm, Tyrrell made a decision to split the party, knowing that he had very nearly reached the point where the Dubawnt River — which he had paddled in 1893 — joins the Thelon. Fairchild, Lofthouse, and four of the voyageurs were to continue the mapping on down to Chesterfield Inlet, concentrating on those sides of the larger lakes that Tyrrell had not surveyed in 1893. Then, as his instructions read, they were to return upstream by the same route, making sure to arrive back at Fort Reliance by September 15. Tyrrell, together with the remaining voyageurs, Robert Bear and Toura, headed back upstream determined to explore the uncharted main branch of the Thelon, upstream of the Hanbury–Thelon junction. The two groups parted company on July 16.

At Pingawalook's camp, Tyrrell traded for some moccasins: "They were much needed before we got out of the country, for as my men tracked the canoe up stream, the sharp rocks and stones over which they had to walk, cut through two or three pairs of shoes a day."[11] Nevertheless, on the 28th they reached the Hanbury–Thelon junction, and three days later headed upriver into unknown country, on the main branch of the Thelon.

On August 9, the upstream march, "obstructed in several places by shallow rapids,"[12] reached the confluence with the Elk River. (It should be noted that it took Tyrrell's party as many days to go upstream, against an often strong current, as it would take most modern-day canoeists — this writer included — to run the same distance downstream.) Neither fork appealed to Tyrrell, with "both branches rapid and shallow."[13] And so, "judging from my progress during the last two weeks, and the prospect of increased difficulties ahead, I came to the conclusion that it would be unwise to attempt to push through to Lake Athabasca."[14] Instead, he returned back downstream about halfway to the Hanbury junction, where he remembered seeing a stream joining from the west. (This small tributary Tyrrell named the Mary Frances River, after his wife.) That, he thought, might provide a route over the divide, back toward Great Slave via Artillery, where they had begun paddling two months before. The stream, however, was too small; only a few miles up it, there was not enough water to float the canoe. Tyrrell, as ever, was decisive:

I decided to send my two men with the canoe, around by the way we had come, to Artillery lake, and that I would walk across alone.

It seemed that there could be no great difficulty in doing so, for the distance in a straight line I knew to be only about eighty miles [from his own surveying]; the season was still early and there were now plenty of deer roving over the country. Thus viewing the problem, I sent my men back with the canoe and its contents, and having selected my necessary outfit for the tramp, bundled it up into a neat pack of about fifty pounds and started off. It did not feel heavy at first, and the weather being fine I made fair progress, but as the day wore on, my pack became burdensome and by evening I was quite ready to lay it down and creep into my sleeping bag. This first day's march, which covered thirteen miles, was along the course of the stream, [and] took me to the shore of a small lake, which of itself formed no serious obstruction to travel. Because of the irregularities of the shore and the impossibility of seeing any great distance ahead, it required a twelve mile tramp to get free from this lake, and that represented my second day's journey. My rations were obtained from the carcass of a deer which I had shot, and some biscuits which I had brought in my pack.

On the morning of my third day, only three miles from my "camp" I came upon a large lake — to which I have taken the liberty of attaching my own name — since I am sure it has never been, and perhaps never will be, of as much interest to any one else as it proved to me.[15]

It was far from an easy trek. He was impeded by large lakes — the largest named after himself — and streams too cold and swift to swim across. He tramped through muskeg up to the ankles. His moccasins, from Pingawalook's camp, were soon worn out; he resorted to removing the sleeves from his jacket and wrapping them around his feet. After five days he had moved west only sixteen miles. There remained, by his own calculation, more than sixty miles ahead to the shores of Artillery Lake. Then the weather turned sour and his real trouble began:

> The morning of my sixth day set in with a chilling northeast wind and pelting rain, which not only saturated my clothing, but also the moss, so that I could make no fire. Having a small flask of brandy with me, I refreshed myself with a little of it, in water, and a biscuit, and tramped on, making thirteen miles during the day. The night being dark at this season, it was not possible to travel continuously, so, wet and shivering as I was, I lay down on the rocks in the pelting rain to try and sleep, but this was not to be, for my bed soon became a puddle of water, and I was uncomfortable indeed. I earnestly longed for the daylight, so that I might get up and travel, and at length it came, but still the cold rain came down, so that I could only wring out my single blanket and start on without breakfast. A deer skin which I carried in addition to my blanket had become so water-soaked as to be too heavy to carry and was left behind.[16]

The next day, the sun came out at mid-day and Tyrrell managed to shoot a caribou, so his circumstances improved dramatically. However, he still had a long walk ahead. And by late August in the Barrenlands, the weather can be very unstable. Tyrrell knew this well enough; he and his brother only just escaped with their lives from their first Barrenlands expedition seven years earlier, in 1893, when they were caught by the onset of early winter weather. Now, on his lonely trek west across unmapped country, he kept a watchful eye on the sky:

> Observing the approach of a heavy storm, I proceeded to fortify myself as well as my blanket and canvas wrapper would admit of, and so fairly well weathered out a bad night. But the next day was intolerable. I endeavoured to push on, but so cold and drenching was the rain that

I shivered even as I travelled, under my watersoaked burden. Later in the day the weather became so thick, that I was as one walking in the dark — not knowing what was before me — and soon found myself almost entirely surrounded by water. I was now forced to await an improvement in the weather, and so, partaking of a wet biscuit, for I had nothing dry, and a drink of brandy, I lay down on the sand.

All night the cold rain came down in torrents, so that I was perfectly saturated with it. As the morning dawned conditions were not improved, for the rain had changed to snow and clothed the landscape in her chilling garment of white. It left me in an extremely uncomfortable condition, to say the least, being without shelter, fire or cooked food, but the worst seemed to have passed, for at eleven o'clock the next day the sunlight broke forth again and brought me much needed relief.[17]

It was now August 22, and Tyrrell found himself retracing his steps back up a long peninsula and working his way slowly around a large lake. Through all this, despite the conditions and his own miserable state, he somehow managed to keep a careful and detailed account of the land, and produced sketches from which he could ultimately draw the first maps of this territory with remarkable accuracy. The next day brought another storm:

A gale from the northeast, with driving rain and sleet — so severe that I was forced to seek shelter, which to some extent I found on the lee side of a rock. Here I spread my canvas and, wrapping my wet blanket about me, remained for two days until the storm of wind, rain and snow had spent its fury. My biscuits were now all gone, and the only available stimulant I had at this camp was the remainder of my flask of brandy, of which I gladly availed myself.

My condition had become decidedly serious. I had not slept a night since I had left my canoe, and

144

this wretched weather and lack of food was already telling seriously upon me. The barren ground is a most inhospitable place in bad weather, but having exposed myself to its inhospitality there was only one thing for me to do, and that was to get out again as best I could, and this I was quite resolved to do.[18]

At the end of August, nearly spent himself, Tyrrell reached the shore of Artillery Lake, and found a cache he had left there in June. Of the comforts that implies, he says only that he made "a snug camp in the spruce grove,"[19] and leaves to the imagination the pleasures of once again being warm, dry, and nourished.

Two days later, Robert Bear and Toura, his two voyageurs, paddled into camp, having completed their ascent of the Hanbury River. Only a few days after that, Fairchild and his party arrived in Artillery Lake, having been all the way out to Hudson Bay and back. Reunited, the expedition headed back over Pike's Portage and on south. It took another three months to reach Edmonton by canoe, steamer, and dog team.

Tyrrell's mapping of the territory east of Great Slave Lake — in all he set down 1,719 miles of new survey — became the basis for the official maps of Canada for many years to follow, until the job was taken over by aerial surveying. It is as an explorer and a map-maker, therefore, that he is remembered. But equally noteworthy is a single paragraph in his final report to Ottawa, in which he joined David Hanbury in advising that "for the preservation of the musk-oxen — which may be so easily slaughtered — and are already rapidly diminishing in numbers, I would suggest that the territory between the Thelon and Back rivers be set apart by the Government as a game preserve."[20] His was one of the early voices, added to later by John Hornby, pressing government to create the preserve we now know as the Thelon Wildlife Sanctuary, Canada's oldest fully protected wilderness area.

David Pelly
Ottawa, Ontario

Part III

On the Trail in the Early 1900s

Before the advent of air travel in the Far North of Canada, the east arm of Great Slave Lake served as a key gateway to the tundra regions of the Northwest Territories. Beginning in the late nineteenth century, an assortment of hunters, naturalists, and geologists — most of whom travelled north via the Peace, Athabasca, and Slave River waterways — used this narrow eastern section of Great Slave Lake to reach the treeless Arctic prairies either by crossing over to its north shore or travelling to its farthest eastern extremity and traversing the portage to Artillery Lake. The place names on the modern map or nautical charts of the area show the traces of these men. Seton Island, Blanchet Island, Preble Island, Hornby Channel: much of the geography of the region is named for the naturalists who first came to record, identify, and catalogue its flora and fauna.[1]

— John Sandlos, *Hunters at the Margin: Native People and Wildlife Conservation in the Northwest Territories*, 2007

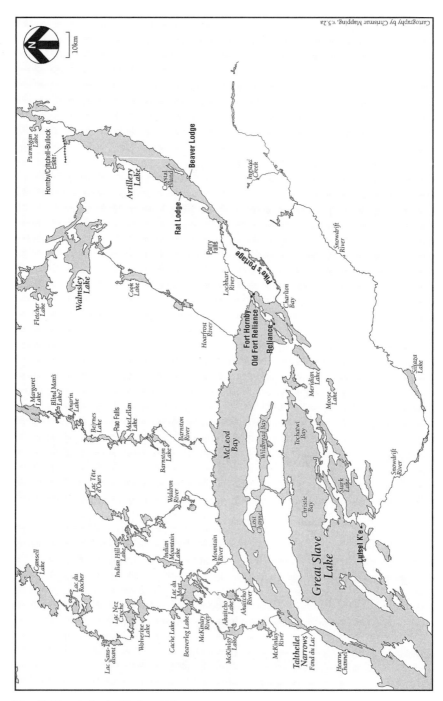

Map 5. Travels in the Early 1900s.

Chapter 9

The Beaulieu Clan: "Unlettered People"

In the Northwest Territories, perhaps someday we'll finally get it right, historically speaking. We've all been told that Samuel Hearne "discovered" Great Slave Lake in 1772. Everyone learned in school that in 1789 Sir Alexander Mackenzie — following through on "discoveries" made in the late 1770s and early 1780s by the American-born fur trader Peter Pond — was the first to float down the river that still carries his name. Yet, after all these years, we've still got it wrong.

And it's not just the obvious problem of justifying a claim to discovering a lake or a river while people wave at you from shore. Even the early explorers knew that the Dene (literally "person" or "people" — a term used for most Athapascan-speaking people) had lived in the North for thousands of years. And by the way, they universally take exception to claims of outsiders *discovering* their lands.

No, our history problem is one of perception and perhaps of prejudice. We've got our facts wrong concerning who were the first non-indigenous people to stand on the shore of Great Slave Lake or to paddle the mighty Mackenzie.

Oblate missionary Émile Petitot knew it wasn't Hearne, Pond, or Mackenzie. He told of this glaring northern historical error way back in the 1860s when he wrote:

> The presence in these subarctic regions of very old French Métis born in this very country, such as Beaulieu, Poitras, his brother-in-law Cayen, Le Camarade, Lafleur, de Charlois, the Touranjeau brothers, and others, is proof that our [French] compatriots arrived in the North Country before our good neighbours from across the English Channel. Sadly, poor adventurers, obscure *coureurs de bois*, unlettered people without any declared goal, they never bothered to claim the honour and the glory of having been the first to discover and live in these remote and inhospitable regions.[1]

It was in 1760, give or take a few years, that these French Métis families floated down the Athabasca and Slave rivers to settle in what is today's Northwest Territories. That's twelve years before Hearne and almost twenty years before Pond. When Sir Alexander Mackenzie hired François Beaulieu to guide and paddle his canoe down the Mackenzie River — presumably because Beaulieu had been on the river before — French Métis families had been living in the North for close to thirty years.

How we missed these historical discrepancies is easy to understand. What we know of the history of these very early Métis families comes to us through a combination of sources. Family lore has, for generations, been kept within these families and as these stories now emerge they often conflict with the much better known written observations of fur traders, explorers, and adventures who made little distinction between the Dene and Métis they interacted with. It's clear they saw these people, while useful as guides and trappers, as socially inferior because they were indigenous.

Sifting through 250 years of lore and prejudice to reveal the true story of the North is not an easy task. Take for example the Beaulieu family. Danny Beaulieu, the family's historian and genealogist, has spent years trying to sort out all the connections and to try to understand generations of marriage between his family, other early French Métis families, and his numerous Denesoline (Chipewyan), Tatsanottine (Yellowknife), and Tłįcho (Dogrib) relatives.[2] It may never be possible to know the full story behind these early Métis families but what we do know of the story of the Beaulieus is likely similar to the stories of other early Métis.

The first Beaulieus, part of that early French-Cree Métis migration north, were brothers François and Jacques. They were employed by La Compagnie des Sioux in what is present-day northern Saskatchewan. The government of New France closed these northwest fur-trading posts in 1760[3] and these coureurs de bois "were reluctant to go back either because of the new English regime or because they already had families in the northwest."[4]

The Beaulieus, Poitras, Cayens, Lafleurs, Charlois, Touranjeaus, and others had made their way across the Methy Portage onto the Clearwater River and down the Athabasca and Slave rivers to Great Slave Lake. These are all family names that are still common in the North, and this seems especially true for the Beaulieu clan.

In fact, if it were possible to bring together all the people of the Northwest Territories — estimated by Statistics Canada in 2008 to be 42,514 — and then throw a stone into their midst, your chances of hitting a member of the Beaulieu clan would be much, much higher than winning the lottery. In 1889, Warburton Pike warned this might happen. Pike, writing of his hunting trip onto the Barrens northeast of Great Slave Lake, claimed the Beaulieus were such a big family "that it makes one tremble for the future of the Great Slave Lake country"[5] as these were "the biggest scoundrels I ever had to travel with."[6]

Casting slings and arrows in the direction of the North's Métis and Dene people seemed a favourite pastime of Victorian sporting gentlemen. Well-educated and well-off, Pike believed he occupied the pinnacle of the civilized world, yet he wasn't immune to its critical eye. His friends, acquaintances, and enemies eventually came to know him as "Dirty Pike," "One-Shirt Pike," and "Crazy Pike." Unfortunately, our impression of what the Beaulieus and other Métis families were like more than a hundred years ago is tainted by the myopic vision of travellers like Pike.[7]

So, how did the Beaulieus in particular become so numerous that they drew the ire of self-important northern visitors? Again, according to Warburton Pike, they were the offspring of François Beaulieu who "settled at Salt River [near present-day Fort Smith] … and by an indefinite number of wives raised a large family which is threatening gradually to inundate the North."[8] Pike at least got this one fact about the Beaulieu family right; they are a very big family. But it's only when we peel back the prejudice that we can begin to understand that they are, in fact, one of the North's greatest founding families.

Pike was referring to *the* François Beaulieu, who, born about 1771, was one of the first generation of northern Beaulieus. He was the most famous and perhaps most influential of all the Beaulieus, and, in a family where the name François is common, has been designated François Beaulieu (II) to differentiate him from other Françoises. A great deal of confusion over who is who in the Beaulieu family, and what their accomplishments were, still lingers.

François (II) was the son of François Beaulieu (I). His mother was a Chipewyan woman named Ethiba. Apparently François (I) didn't stick around to help raise his son, and Ethiba then married a Chipewyan hunter known as "The Rat." François (II)'s early years were spent with Tatsanottine and Tłįcho relatives north of Great Slave Lake.

We don't know how long François Beaulieu (I) stayed in the North but it's been suggested that he and his brother Jacques did have some part in the tail end of the Chipewyan-based trade between the Great Slave/Lake Athabasca regions and Fort Churchill, the Hudson's Bay Company's trading post on Hudson Bay. Shortly after the establishment of Fort Churchill in 1717, the Chipewyan began to make annual journeys to the post to trade their furs for European manufactured goods. These goods were then hauled back to the Great Slave Lake region and the Chipewyan middlemen traded them to local Dene.

This was a significant part of Chipewyan history and Dominion land surveyor Guy Blanchet[9] claimed to have discovered, in 1925, evidence of the old trade route used by the Chipewyan in their travels to Hudson Bay. Using the traditional knowledge of an old Chipewyan woman living at Fond du Lac on Lake Athabasca, Blanchet travelled to a height of land south of the East Arm of Great Slave Lake. The height divides waters that run south to Lake Athabasca, north into Great Slave Lake, and east to Hudson Bay. According to Blanchet, this was a major junction in the Chipewyan trail to Hudson Bay: the more southerly branch led to the

Souci King Beaulieu is shown with a small caribou. Guy Blanchet took this photograph in August 1923.

rich fur country south of Great Slave Lake while the northern branch led to the Barrenlands and the Coppermine River. Blanchet called this route a "highway" that was still visible after more than 130 years, when it was last used by the Chipewyan.

The Beaulieu family, while part of this long-distance trade, may also have played a role in its demise. A family story, told by François Beaulieu (II) and recounted by Émile Petitot, tells of the arrival of North West Company fur traders in the Great Slave Lake region during the mid-1780s. These traders, led by Peter Pond, were trying to circumvent the Chipewyan trade with Hudson's Bay and "had barely arrived when they came to the cabin of my uncle, Jacques Beaulieu. 'Among you, is there anyone who understands French?' they asked us. 'Without a doubt,' we responded. 'All of us here are French or the sons of Frenchmen.'"[10]

François (II) was a teenager when this first meeting between these fur traders and his uncle Jacques took place. He said the meeting was at Jacques' cabin on Big Island at the head of the Mackenzie River, near the outlet of Great Slave Lake. As the story goes, in this face-to-face meeting between Jacques Beaulieu and Peter Pond, Jacques was asked to use his considerable influence and family ties among the Dene of the region to smooth trade with the newly arrived fur traders.

Use of the old Chipewyan trade trail to bring goods from Hudson Bay was quickly abandoned in favour of the more easily obtained goods brought from Montreal by the North West Company. While the bosses of the North West Company spoke English, the workers — Métis coureurs de bois of the old system — communicated in French, which must have been very appealing to the Beaulieu family.

As a strong young man who spoke French, and who had family ties among the Dene, François Beaulieu (II) was drawn into that trade. After Alexander Mackenzie's brief trip down the Mackenzie River in 1789, the North West Company began to build trading posts along the river, and, by 1799, they had one on Great Bear Lake. It was there the twenty-eight-year-old François Beaulieu found himself in charge of a group of Dene supplying meat for the post the North West Company called "The Castle." It was during this time that it's been suggested François began "establishing himself as a middleman in the Great Bear Lake trade … [and this] … may have been the start of Beaulieu's career as a trading chief."[11]

Trading chiefs were influential Métis or Dene who both negotiated fur prices for their people while also conducting their own trade as middlemen. Through this system, trading chiefs became powerful men who, it's said, ruled with near absolute authority. That authority seems to have been maintained through loyal soldiers, though it's also likely that their followers didn't need much convincing because they received better prices for their furs at the trading posts and were likely cared for during hard times.

While this makes trading chiefs sound like benevolent dictators, François Beaulieu (II) distinguished himself as one who may have maintained his power through other means. According to François Mandeville, François Beaulieu (II) "made a habit of seizing beautiful and powerful women from their husbands and killing anyone who attempted to stop him."[12] A different perspective was given by Métis elder Frank Laviolette: "it was François Beaulieu's willingness to take care of the weak as well as the strong that made him a great leader."[13]

Regardless of how he got there, by the early 1800s, François Beaulieu was one of the three most powerful trading chiefs controlling the fur trade around Great Slave Lake. Beaulieu ruled the area from Big Island north along the west shore of Great Slave Lake to Great Bear Lake. Camarade de Mandeville had the East Arm of Great Slave Lake and northeast to the Thelon and Lockhart rivers while Akaitcho was firmly established between the two along the Yellowknife River and out onto the Barrens.[14]

The amalgamation of the Hudson's Bay Company and the North West Company in 1821 resulted in trading-post closures, and this in turn caused a collapse of this system, destabilizing the entire region. The Tatsanottine and Tłįcho battled over territory and settled old scores. François Beaulieu was part of this conflict, though we're not sure which side he was on. He claimed to have killed twelve enemy.[15]

It was more than ten years before an uneasy peace returned to the Great Slave Lake region. And yet, while the Hudson's Bay Company was beginning to reap the rewards of its fur-trade monopoly, they still had one major thorn in their side. By manipulating the system, pitting one Hudson's Bay Company trading post against another and continuing to act as a middleman with his Dene kin, François Beaulieu (II)'s power and influence continued to grow.

François' relationship with the HBC was constantly changing. One year he'd be working for them, the next, against them. For example, in 1848, when François Beaulieu was seventy-seven years old and still getting in the way, the Hudson's Bay Company put him in charge of their Fort Resolution post. His family ties helped open up trade with the Tłı̨chǫ northwest of Great Slave Lake, which in turn led to the establishment of Fort Rae on the North Arm of the lake.

François Beaulieu (I) and his family have also had a long association with the Salt River, a connection that may have begun through François Beaulieu (II)'s step-father, The Rat. As early as the 1820s, the family gathered salt from shallow evaporation pits along the river and traded it throughout the North. As they firmed up their control over the salt trade, the family also got into the meat trade. François Beaulieu (II) recognized that for the Hudson's Bay Company to conduct a profitable fur trade in the Mackenzie Valley they required a reliable source of food. By the early 1840s, he and his family had pioneered new routes and re-established a few old ones, from the East Arm of Great Slave Lake onto the Barrens. Each year the meat from thousand of caribou was dried, packaged, transported, and eventually used to feed the fur brigades travelling the Mackenzie.

François' sons and grandsons were a large part of this trade. François Beaulieu (II)'s son, François Beaulieu (III) worked on the Mackenzie River York boats, while another son, Joseph "King" Beaulieu, was hired by the Hudson's Bay Company to manage their post on the East Arm of Great Slave Lake and worked as a guide for Warburton Pike and E.T. Seton.

This is where the family's long association with the East Arm was born. The East Arm trading post was referred to as either Fond du Lac (and often confused with Fond du Lac on Lake Athabasca), King Post, Snowdrift, or even Fort Beaulieu.[16] Use of the name Fond du Lac suggests an origin within the Beaulieu family, as many of the French names for geographical features north of the East Arm of Great Slave Lake can be traced back to the Beaulieus. Lac du Mort, Lac du Rocher, Lac au Sauvage, Lac Tête d'Ours, Lac Capot Blanc, Lac de Gras, and many others read like a road map of the traditional caribou hunting routes used by the Beaulieus as part of their meat trade.[17]

These names can also be considered as indicators of close family ties between the Beaulieus and the Dene. Take Lac de Gras for example.

In recent years this area has become famous as the location of Canada's first diamond mine. The mine is named Ekati, the Dene name for Lac de Gras. *Ekati* translates as "Fat Lake," and is a description of white rocks along the south shore that are the colour of caribou fat. And because third- and fourth-generation Beaulieus of a hundred years ago still spoke French, it was their translation of Dene names that made it onto official government maps.

It was, in part, the publication of these maps that meant travellers to the East Arm and north onto the Barrens no longer required the geographic knowledge of members of the Beaulieu clan. By the 1920s, the North had changed. Free traders, independent trappers, prospectors, and miners had flooded the North, marginalizing both Dene and Métis, while urbanization and residential schools of the mid-decades of the last century left their ugly scars.

It's only in recent years, with an emergence of Métis pride, that "to trace one's ancestry to François Beaulieu is much like a Scot tracing his ancestry to Robert the Bruce. You descend from a founding father."[18]

It's a start, and a long time coming, but recognition of the achievements of northern Métis, and in particular François Beaulieu (II) and the Beaulieu family, was made by Canada's Historic Sites and Monuments Board in 2000. They recognized François Beaulieu (II) as a "National Historic Person" for his role as a "founding father of Northwest Territories Métis [and a] pre-eminent Métis leader."[19] His name was added to an exclusive list of important Canadians, which includes former prime ministers Pierre Elliott Trudeau and Lester B. Pearson.

While Warburton Pike didn't make the list, it's ironic that Samuel Hearne and Peter Pond did, and that Alexander Mackenzie's "discovery" of the Mackenzie River received designation as a National Historic Event. It may take generations for northern Métis, these "poor adventurers, obscure *coureurs de bois*, unlettered people without any declared goal"[20] to receive the full recognition they deserve.

Randy Freeman
Yellowknife, Northwest Territories

Chapter 10

Guy Blanchet: A Northern Surveyor on Pike's Portage

I took advantage of a pause in other activities to make a short trip to the plateau which lay beyond the valley hills. Indians in the remote past had found a route following a chain of small lakes by which they could reach their hunting ground on the plateau. Warburton Pike had used this in 1889 and it had been given his name, "Pike's Portage." Even when he travelled it, moccasined feet had worn a trail from lake to lake for twenty-five miles to Artillery Lake from which Lockhart River discharges.[1]

These words were written by Guy Blanchet while working as a government surveyor for the Department of the Interior, and in charge of three parties of surveyors assigned to map Great Slave Lake in 1922.

For more than a dozen years Blanchet had been one of the Dominion land surveyors employed in mapping all of western Canada onto a grid system defined by north–south meridians and east–west base lines. Beginning in 1906, he had worked in the northern areas of Alberta and Saskatchewan, with one foray into Manitoba on the Berens River. The grid was nearly complete when oil was discovered near Fort Norman on the Mackenzie River in 1920, and, anticipating a rush of prospectors to the area, the government ordered a survey of both banks of the river to be done the following year. Three surveyors were given the task, with Blanchet put in charge of the section that stretched from the start of the river to Fort Simpson. It was his first time north of 60° and, while he did not find the Mackenzie an interesting river, Great Slave Lake had for him an air of remoteness and romantic links with the past that epitomized his idea of the North.

Guy Blanchet, a graduate engineer, precise and scientific in his work, had strong feelings for the land, and through his reading could identify closely with the historic past. Always, in mapping new areas, he preferred to have Native guides wherever possible and was attentive to their ways and their traditional knowledge. Early in his surveying career he had picked up a working knowledge of the Cree language.

In beginning the survey of Great Slave Lake, Blanchet chose to start in the East Arm, the area in most urgent need of correction on existing maps, both for the position of the shoreline and for its confusing mass of islands. In Ottawa, he prepared by studying all available information as well as the mapping done by earlier travellers. Great Slave Lake, the eighth-largest body of fresh water in the world, did not appear on any map until after 1772 when Samuel Hearne published the account of his epic overland journey from Churchill to the mouth of the Coppermine River. Hearne, having seen only a part of the lake in winter, sketched his map from the description given him by his Native companions, and although the shape was approximately correct, it was far from its true position. In 1789, Alexander Mackenzie traversed the western end of the lake, mapping it in detail and giving its true location. Franklin added details of the North Arm as far as present-day Yellowknife in 1819, and traders had completed that area as far as Marian Lake. George Back, in 1834, made a track survey following the Indian route through the one hundred miles of massed islands known as the Inconnu or "Cony" Channel, and his sketch of Christie Bay gave shape to the east end of the lake. In 1890, Father Émile Petitot made a track survey from Great Bear Lake to the North Arm and from there traced the north shore easterly to McLeod Bay. While details were added by others, the cartographers drawing the map in current use had ignored Petitot's survey and continued to produce maps containing serious errors.

*Guy Blanchet
with pilot
Souci King
Beaulieu on
board the
Ptarmigan.*

Photo by Richard Blanchet.

Blanchet, with his three parties of surveyors, reached Fort Resolution at the mouth of the Slave River in late June 1922, and transferred to a schooner, *Ptarmigan*, which would be used as the base for their operations. Blanchet hired the celebrated hunter of muskox and caribou, Souci Beaulieu, to be the pilot for the schooner, using his long experience of travelling the complicated waters of the East Arm. As he told Blanchet, "The father of my grandfather was a Frenchman of the Brigade. Once them camp at Fort Chipewyan. That was the start of my family."[2] François, a son of that original union, had paddled with Mackenzie on his journey to the Pacific and later was a hunter and guide for John Franklin. A son of François, known as King Beaulieu, was the chief guide for Warburton Pike on his hunting expedition in 1889. In his book *The Barren Ground of Northern Canada* Pike described him as a brilliant hunter but rapacious and quarrelsome, especially when accompanied by his large and greedy family.[3] Souci was a member of that family, and like his father, was seldom pleased and never grateful. According to Ernest Thompson Seton, the name Souci is the Chipewyan for Joseph, and Seton encountered him — referred to as "Souci King Beaulieu" — on only one occasion.[4] In Pike's book, he is called José, and Pike had nothing good to say about him. Despite Beaulieu's questionable nature, Blanchet enjoyed his company and found him a mine of information.

As they were crossing the lake to the area to be surveyed, towing seven canoes behind *Ptarmigan*, a lone canoeist appeared, paddling toward Fort Resolution. This was John Hornby, a dishevelled wraith of a man who had wintered alone near Fort Reliance and was nearly starving, an injury having prevented him from hunting. He was invited aboard the *Ptarmigan*, and, when he learned where they were headed, advised that there was a more sheltered route than the one they were planning to use. He took over as pilot of the schooner and spent several days on board during which he produced a rough sketch map of the area and its islands which turned out to be remarkably accurate. Hornby and Blanchet developed a lasting friendship, but when Blanchet invited him to join the survey party, he declined, being intent on returning south to Edmonton.

The three survey parties, with enough supplies to last each of them several weeks, were delivered to their respective areas: the south shore, the north shore, and the islands. Blanchet remained on the *Ptarmigan* to chart the numerous channels, large and small, that wove between the many islands. This involved spending many hours on the quarter-deck of the schooner while Beaulieu piloted the boat and told stories of the traditional life of his people. As they made a wide crossing, they passed two canoes using blankets for sails. Beaulieu told him that many people had been lost on this crossing, adding "If caught by a storm with a loaded canoe, the man would first throw the women overboard … then the dogs."[5]

Blanchet was more than a surveyor — he was an explorer at heart. Taking a break from charting the channels, he anchored the *Ptarmigan* in the harbour at Fort Reliance, and in a canoe with Beaulieu he set out to explore up the Lockhart River. They left the canoe at the first cascade and went on foot up to the first falls, which plunged a spectacular ninety feet into the canyon below. These were named the Tyrrell Falls for James W. Tyrrell who had made an extensive survey in 1900 from Great Slave Lake to Hudson Bay. To photograph the falls, Blanchet climbed down into the canyon, making his way over spray-swept ledges, all the time being warned to be careful by Beaulieu. Blanchet was touched by Beaulieu's obvious concern until he heard that Beaulieu was really concerned for his own reputation if Blanchet should meet with an accident.

It was during this time that Blanchet made his first trip up Pike's Portage with Beaulieu, which produced the quotation at the beginning of this piece. As they made their way up the roughly six hundred feet to the plateau, he watched the forest dwindle to scattered trees and saw the bare, rocky hills littered with boulders. At Artillery Lake they met a party of successful hunters returning from the hunt and stopped to boil a kettle with them. Standing on the shore of the lake, Blanchet saw band after band of barren ground caribou swimming across, and longed to go farther. The sight had stirred his soul, but his time was limited and he knew it would be another year before he could return — but return he must.

As soon as the ice was out in 1923, Blanchet, accompanied by one assistant, was back on Great Slave Lake, with two objectives: to mark navigational hazards at various points around the lake, and to complete the survey of the North Arm as far north as Fort Rae. After completing the work at the fort, he left his assistant to continue north through Marian Lake, knowing he had time for an exploratory trip to the Barrens. Blanchet returned in the *Ptarmigan* to Fort Resolution to find two young Native men to accompany him, but at the trading post was told that the young men no longer knew the country and preferred to loaf in the summer. However, his old pilot, Beaulieu, now close to seventy, expressed a wish to see the Barrens again and "to fill his belly once more with the meat of the caribou." He in turn persuaded Black Basile, a man close to his own age, to come along. As Blanchet was laying out supplies for their month-long trip, Beaulieu said, "What for — we carry store food to country where meat abounds? In my country I can always find meat," and Blanchet left behind most of the intended provisions.[6]

The three men were a study in contrasts. Blanchet, the engineer, quiet and observant, was accustomed to being in charge of expeditions, but he also knew how to blend into his surroundings. Souci Beaulieu had inherited his father's traits — both his ability as a hunter and his domineering nature. In his talk he was always the big man who could find game and bring meat to starving people, and who knew how to find his way in the land. Basile was a Yellowknife, whose people had controlled the area in the time of Samuel Hearne, but after suffering a crushing defeat from the Dogrib in the 1800s, their spirits never truly recovered. When Basile was very young he had travelled into the Barrens

Photo by Richard Blanchet.

Black Basile with a great find — a caribou shank — while Souci King Beaulieu holds an equally precious bundle of willow for fuel.

on foot with the women while the men hunted using canoes, but even as a youngster the features of the land were firmly planted in his memory.

In a letter to George Douglas, written in 1958, Blanchet described the climb up Pike's Portage: "Pike's Portage is a very ancient 'Indian

Road' which makes the climb of a thousand feet in 25 miles by small lakes and portages (the usual Indian road). Black Basile the Yellowknife Indian guide with me in 1923 showed me where his father had killed two muskox and ... there were the horns ..."[7]

Beaulieu dominated Basile in every respect. Basile did the heavy carrying up Pike's Portage, and when they reached the lakes, Basile paddled while Beaulieu rested on his paddle and talked. The two men talked volubly in Chipewyan, a language Blanchet could not understand. Blanchet wrote many years later in an article in *The Beaver*: "I told Beaulieu to ask Basile if the country became flatter after we climbed 'the mountain.' There was much talk and no answer. Finally I asked, 'What did Basile say?' Souci replied, 'Basile say nothing, just laugh.' He had said a great deal and had not laughed — he never did."[8]

When they reached Artillery Lake and were still in wooded country they sighted a band of caribou, shot two, and the feasting began at once. The men gorged on boiled meat, roasted meat, and marrow. Blanchet's last view of his two companions that night was of each tearing at a caribou head that had been resting at the edge of the fire. The next morning both men complained of an attack of the "misery."

Blanchet was familiar with the literature; he had read the accounts by Hearne, Franklin, and Back, all of whom stressed the remoteness and rugged character of the land. He had also read Ernest Thompson Seton and Warburton Pike; both had described the beautiful lakes, grassy valleys, and rolling hillsides clad in shrubs, moss, and lichens, and the unbroken silence. Blanchet watched the forests dwindle from "the strong woods" through "the land of little sticks" to the treeless barrens, where, in a few favourable spots, pockets of small trees developed from seedlings, surviving almost as Japanese miniatures, natural bonsai — ancient, tough, and tiny. Beaulieu was careful not to cut down such trees, using only dead branches from them, and he showed Blanchet the way to cook using heather or the black moss that grows in thick clumps on sandy hillsides.

Both Beaulieu and Basile had been taught by the missionaries, but being on the Barrens revived the old beliefs of their childhood. At one place there was an isolated dome-shaped hill on each side of the lake, and Beaulieu identified the larger one as the home of the giant Beaver, the small one as the home of his slave, a huge Muskrat. He declared that they must pay for permission to pass or the Beaver would be angry. Beaulieu did not consider the plug of tobacco that Blanchet dropped in the lake big enough, and said the Beaver would be angry. He was. A sudden squall blew up that threatened to swamp their canoe and for once Beaulieu put real muscle into his paddling. When they reached the windward shore he could be heard saying, "Thank you, thank you," without explaining who he was thanking.

Basile's great fear was of the "terrible Natives of the North" — the Inuit — and he seldom ventured away from camp alone and always carried a rifle. When asked if he had ever seen an Inuk, he replied, "Once, far off and very big." After further questioning, he admitted it might have been a caribou. But when he found a ring of tent stones almost buried in the moss and a bit of fur that Blanchet identified as seal skin, his fears resurfaced, greater than ever.

When they reached Clinton-Colden Lake, Beaulieu was confused by its many bays, points, and islands, his hunting expeditions having been mainly in winter. Basile became the hero of the hour, climbing to the highest point of an island to study the country and, remembering his childhood trips with the women, he picked out the blue ridge that marked the Arctic divide, the famous caribou crossing at the Strait of Thanakoia, between Clinton-Colden and Aylmer lakes.

On reaching that landmark, Blanchet saw the great Arctic Barrens stretching to the horizon and longed to continue exploring. Reluctantly he made the decision to turn back before the winds of late summer made their little canoe unseaworthy. During a stormy night, Basile spotted a dark smudge in the distance and they paddled hard into the gathering dark to reach the first stand of dwarf trees and build a fire. Beaulieu almost embraced the leaping red flames. "Fire is like a father to me," he said, "I was glad to see the Barren Grounds and the caribou, but never again will I leave the woods." The two men were happy to return to Fort Resolution where Beaulieu could brag about where they had been and what they had seen, and Basile, relieved of his fears, could resume his humble life on the outskirts of the village.

Blanchet returned south to the office in Ottawa, knowing that he would return the following year, 1924, to survey and map the lakes north of Great

Courtesy of Russell/NWT Archives/N-1979-073-1017.

Guy Blanchet poses at the headwaters of the Coppermine River in 1924.[9]

Slave Lake and to search out the headwaters of the Coppermine River. Before embarking on this exploration, Blanchet and his wife had a spring holiday in England where they arranged to meet with John Hornby and his mother. Hornby's mother asked Blanchet to persuade her son to stay in England where he was needed, and by the time Blanchet and his wife sailed back to Canada, he thought he had been successful in that mission.

In late June 1924, Blanchet and his team of surveyors arrived at the eastern end of Great Slave Lake and put the schooner *Ptarmigan* into a safe anchorage at Fort Reliance. Even with a set of wheels, it took six trips up Pike's Portage before they had all their gear assembled at Artillery Lake. Here they split into three groups, each with an assigned area. Blanchet headed north to the Strait of Thanakoia, his turning point of the previous year, and on into Aylmer Lake. At the north end of Aylmer Lake he found a caribou antler inscribed E.T. SETON, 10 AUG. 1907. Blanchet's group continued north and west, surveying the perimeters of the lakes and mapping the outlines in the correct locations. At the far end of Lac de Gras, Blanchet finally saw the Coppermine River flowing out through a gap in the hills and was satisfied he had found the source of the river before turning south.

Blanchet and his two companions were the first to arrive at the bottom of Pike's Portage and canoed around to Fort Reliance to get the *Ptarmigan* ready to collect the other teams of surveyors. As their canoes touched the shore, they were greeted by John Hornby who had just finished building a cache for his supplies before heading up the portage with a group of trappers, planning to winter somewhere in the vicinity of Artillery Lake. Blanchet and Hornby, similar in size and sharing a deep love of the North, were pleased to see each other, and Blanchet supplied Hornby with surplus equipment from their expedition, transporting it to the base of the portage. This was the beginning of a year-long episode for Hornby and Critchell-Bullock, wintering in a cave excavated from an esker, trapping, and eking out a meagre existence. They would meet again in Ottawa after Hornby and Critchell-Bullock had survived the winter and made their trip down the Thelon River.

The surveyor had the right to name geographical features, and while Blanchet always tried to use traditional names, the name Basile can be found on a bay, and a lake near the channel is named for John Hornby. The names of members of Blanchet's team of surveyors are given to other features, and a large island in the Hearne Channel on Great Slave Lake is named for Blanchet.

Blanchet had made his last trip over Pike's Portage, although he would continue to work and travel in the North for the rest of his working life. The North was in his blood and he would always feel it pulling him back. In a search for the headwaters of the Thelon River, he made two explorations of the land east of Great Slave Lake, mapping a large area and making the only known descent of the Snowdrift River by canoe. In the years 1928–29, while working for the Dominion Explorers Company, he established and took charge of their first aerial, prospecting camp, wintering on the shores of Hudson Bay. In the course of that work he made a three-hundred-mile late-winter trip south to Churchill by dog team and snowshoe. After a fallow period, which included being out of work during the Great Depression and going overseas as a soldier in the Second World War, Blanchet returned to the North. He was caught up in the building of CANOL — the first oil pipeline, a project of the United States Army. To determine the route the pipeline should follow from Norman Wells on the Mackenzie River to Whitehorse in the Yukon, he made a month-long winter trek by dog team across the mountains with Mountain Dene, which rekindled his love of the North and of travel with Native people. His pipeline experience led to work of a similar nature on the Trans Mountain pipeline, which supplies the west coast with petroleum, carrying oil from Edmonton to the refineries of Vancouver and area. He completed this work as he turned seventy.

In retirement in his gracious home in Victoria, his thoughts continued to turn to the North. There, surrounded by his collection of northern books, he wrote articles for *The Beaver* and the Victoria newspaper *The Daily Colonist*, and a book, *Search in the North*, an account of his year on the coast of Hudson Bay, including the successful aerial search he led for the missing planes of the mining executive for whom he worked. He also carried on a wide correspondence with friends, most of whom were associated with the North[10]

Pike's Portage had been his gateway into the world he loved.

Gwyneth Hoyle
Peterborough, Ontario

Chapter 11

John Hornby: An Uncommon Man

When writing about John Hornby, Pierre Berton points out that "The English had a special fondness for those adventurers who insisted on doing things the hard way, especially those who failed nobly."[1] Given this fondness, it is no surprise that John Hornby has become the legend that he has in England, Canada, and beyond.

He certainly did things the hard way, with what appeared to be an intentional martyr-like approach rather than one rooted purely in ignorance or simple bad luck. He loathed planning, organization, discipline, foresight, and, often, basic human civilities. It is easy to imagine that Hornby's infatuation with the Canadian North was an escape from the expectations of English wealth and an attempt to deny some inner struggle, conscious or unconscious, that he simply couldn't reconcile in civilization. This escape was perhaps the driving motivation for his repeated forays into the North rather than the romantic ideals associated with life on the Barrens, which included the many hardships and privations that were his constant companions.

Ultimately, he failed. After luring his blue-eyed eighteen-year-old nephew Edgar Christian on a journey into the harshness of the Barrens,

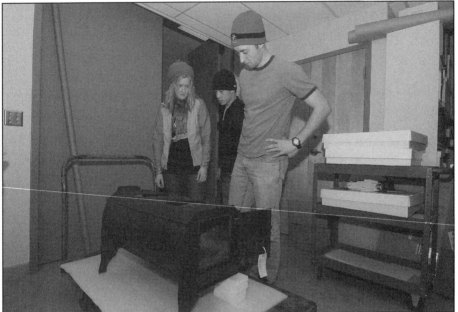

Photo by Morten Asfeldt.

Augustana students admire Hornby's stove, which was the vault that preserved Christian's diary and the legend of John Hornby.

they, together with their companion Harold Adlard, all starved to death — some claim it noble, others foolhardy. In either case, had it not been for the journal of Edgar Christian published in 1937 under the title *Unflinching*[2] and George Whalley's 1962 book *The Legend of John Hornby*[3] he would likely be a largely forgotten figure in the storied past of the Canadian North. Christian chronicled their demise in his diary which he wisely placed inside the cabin's stove before he struggled to lie down on his bunk and pull two red Hudson's Bay blankets over his head as his final living act. The diary was thus saved from exposure to the wind and rain that found their way through the deteriorating cabin roof and walls.

✳

Hornby was born into English affluence in 1880. He was educated at the prestigious Harrow School, as was his father, who was an internationally renowned cricket and rugby player. Hornby, the youngest of four brothers, did well at school and excelled in a number

170

of sports, particularly running and hurdling, but never achieved the athletic prowess of his father or eldest brother. After finishing school, Hornby spent some time in Germany, training for a diplomatic career. In 1904, he made his way to Canada and made a home with his cousin in Onoway, Alberta. For the next four years, Hornby was engaged in a variety of bush and homesteading jobs that began to prepare him for adventures farther afield. As a loner, he frequented hotel bars in Edmonton to pass the time.

It was in Edmonton's King Edward Hotel that Hornby met Cosmos Melvill,[4] which led to his first escapade into northern Canada and the start of his fixation with the Barrens and a lifetime of flirting with disaster and starvation. In the spring of 1908, Hornby made his way from Onoway to Athabasca Landing to rendezvous with the Melvill[5] party where they cast off for Great Bear Lake to trade, hunt, and trap. During this time, Hornby learned the ways of travel by canoe and York boat, cabin building, caribou and muskox hunting, trading, and trapping, as well as being mentored in the traditions of Barrenland travel. On a winter muskox-hunting jaunt to the Coppermine River with Melvill and a group of local Dene men, Melvill noted Hornby's remarkable ability to perform extraordinary acts of strength and endurance for which he became famous. He was a small man of five-feet-four-inches and only slightly more than one hundred pounds, yet he always made a point of carrying heavier loads and travelling longer distances than men twice his size. In fact, it is said that Hornby once ran from Edmonton to Athabasca Landing in twenty-four hours, a distance of one hundred miles. He was likely on his way to meet the Melvill party en route to Great Bear Lake when he accomplished this feat.

On first arrival at Great Bear Lake in 1908, the Melvill party built a trading post on Caribou Bay, which was later named Hornby Bay. In 1910, they relocated to Dease Bay. It was here that Hornby fell in love with Arimo, a Sahtuotine Dene woman, and built a cabin for her.

In the summer of 1911, Hornby met George Douglas in Fort Norman on the Mackenzie River where he was bidding farewell to Melvill who was going south. Douglas and Hornby would become lifelong friends. One would never have imagined it based on Douglas's first impression of Hornby. Whalley paints a picture of that first meeting:

John Hornby in Fort Resolution modelling a typical "larger man's load."

[S]mall, fidgety, voluble, "just like a monkey," he chattered, pouring out incoherent conversation. He gave facetious or misleading answers to Douglas's perfectly grave questions, and seemed to know nothing accurate or certain about the country he had spent nearly three years in. Worst of all he kept dipping filthy fingers into the sugar bowl to the growing annoyance of Captain Mills. Douglas, at first tempted to think that Hornby was bushed, soon realized that he was being evasive; but he can scarcely have guessed that Hornby's reason was that he resented other people getting into what he now regarded as *his* country, and that consciously or by neurotic compulsion Hornby was throwing up a screen of confusion, ambiguity, and vagueness to mislead or distract the Douglases from their announced purpose.[6]

In spite of Douglas's first impression, Hornby and Douglas's relationship developed throughout the fall and winter of 1911–12 and Hornby accompanied the Douglas brothers on a two-month mineralogical exploration to the Coppermine River that cemented their friendship.

Once the Douglas brothers left Great Bear Lake, Hornby returned to Dease Lake, northeast of Great Bear Lake, along with Father Rouvière, his friend and cabin mate of the previous winter, as well as the newly appointed Father Le Roux.[7] The priest, Le Roux, was a quick tempered and opinionated fellow who caused Hornby a great deal of frustration and drove him into isolation with his strong disapproved of the union between Hornby and Arimo. Le Roux did his best to drive them apart. Throughout the summer and fall of 1912 the tensions between Hornby and Le Roux continued to build until Hornby finally retreated to Fort Franklin[8] in January 1913, returning to Dease Lake in the summer. Hornby spent the winter of 1913–14 in Fort Franklin and Fort Norman — likely to escape the oppressive Le Roux — before departing on the *Mackenzie River* for points south in July 1914.

Before he departed from Fort Norman, he met D'Arcy Arden, who was headed for the country that Hornby had occupied for the past five years. Hornby offered little information to Arden and reacted much as he had when he first met George Douglas — as if he were jealous to have someone enter the country that he considered *his*.

On September 20, 1914, Hornby joined the Canadian Army but later resigned and joined the army of his homeland, the British Army. His years in the armed service were not happy ones, and he became further disillusioned with society and resented having been turned into a murderer of men. In July 1916, Hornby was wounded. One report describes his wounds as "superficial" while another indicates he had "seven machine gun bullets right through his body under his ribs."[9] In either case, he was hospitalized in England and then later deserted to Canada and vanished for the better part of a year. His desertion was a great source of embarrassment to his loyal and nationalistic friends and family. In September 1917, Hornby returned to Dease Bay in hopes of finding the idyllic life he once enjoyed there. It was not to be.

The social architecture of Dease Bay had changed dramatically in his absence. Father Le Roux and Hornby's friend Father Rouvière had been murdered, George Douglas had not returned, and D'Arcy Arden had assumed Hornby's role of importance with the Dene and Inuit and, even more devastating for Hornby, Arden had married his beloved Arimo. The changes overwhelmed Hornby. He retreated to the loneliness of Hornby Bay where he injured himself with an axe, severely limiting his ability to provide for himself, and he had his first experience of a cold, dark, and lonely winter of starvation. He spent one more winter of misery and hunger on Great Bear Lake before leaving in June 1914, never to return. He left a bitter man. The paradise and contentment he had experienced with Melvill, Douglas, and Rouvière could not be rekindled; it was lost forever. The combination of isolation inflicted by Father Le Roux, his war experience, and the disappointments that awaited him on his pilgrimage back to Great Bear Lake deepened "his conviction that civilization was evil and social man diseased."[10]

Hornby returned to Edmonton in the summer of 1919 but could not stay. "Edmonton was much grown in the fifteen years since he had first come there but that made it the more lonely and crazy place. 'The post-war flurry irked me,' he said, he had to go North again."[11] He devised a plan to set himself up as a trader and trapper on Artillery Lake east of Great Slave Lake, but, as with most of his plans, it was half-baked and ill-prepared. Leaving Edmonton late in the fall of 1919, winter stopped him near Fort Chipewyan and he spent the winter alone in an enlarged wolf den. "Those who saw him that winter had difficulty understanding his speech and thought he might be mad."[12]

Determined to follow through on his plan to set up on Artillery Lake, Hornby moved on in the spring to Fort Smith where he severely injured his leg, perhaps even broke it, playing football. But in his typical manner, no amount of pain, suffering, or privation was to slow him down, and a week later, in mid-May, he managed to manoeuvre himself into his canoe and began paddling his way to Old Fort Reliance where he arrived on September 1, 1920. He hoped he had arrived at his new Shangri-La.

Because of his leg injury and the absence of any Dene or Métis to help him when he arrived, he was unable to make his way over Pike's Portage, which now separated him from Artillery Lake. Turning his back on Artillery Lake for now, he built a small six by eight foot cabin at the mouth of the Lockhart River with a view across to Old Fort Reliance.[13] Out of a sense of bitterness and resentment toward the civilized world and his homeland, and perhaps also for humour's sake, he named his humble cabin Fort Hornby.

The winter 1920–21 just about killed Hornby; it was filled with a series of accidents and setbacks that caused his friend Guy Blanchet to comment that, "A normal man would not have got into such a situation but if he did neither could he have come through as Hornby did."[14] Once again, Hornby flirted with death and starvation but his uncanny resilience helped him to survive. Once Fort Hornby was finished in late October, Hornby became ill. He then fell against his stove and severely burned his leg, which put a halt to his critical fall bait-and-food gathering. He later injured his hand, which slowed his ability to do daily chores, and some people stole food and equipment from him, and by February, the lack of caribou and fish had starvation once again knocking on his door. With spring approaching, Hornby deemed his trip a complete failure "financially, physically and mentally"[15] and began to make "final preparations"[16] should starvation overcome him.

In May, he made an attempt to cross Pike's Portage in search of caribou but was turned back by ice at Harry Lake. He returned to Charlton Bay and set up his tent on Fairchild Point[17] waiting for the lake ice to clear so he could paddle to Fort Resolution. In the fall of 1921, Hornby returned to his tent site on Fairchild Point and built a cabin, and here he spent yet another winter of hardship, loneliness, and starvation. He went out to Edmonton in the summer of 1922, and did not return North again until the summer of 1924, when he came with Captain James Charles Critchell-Bullock whom he had met by chance at the King Edward Hotel in Edmonton, the same place where he had met Cosmos Melvill in 1907.

In the months leading up to the Hornby-Bullock expedition of 1924–25, and during the expedition itself, Hornby once again displayed his eccentric, erratic, and unpredictable behaviours that would be a continuous source of frustration and confusion for Bullock. After their chance meeting in the King Edward Hotel, Hornby and Bullock (also a prestigiously educated Englishman of wealth) began to stitch together a plan for an expedition to the Barrenlands where they would spend the winter trapping, taking photographs, and making films, as well as making daily scientific observations. For Hornby, it was another escape into *his* country and in Bullock he found a willing and able partner who could finance the affair. Bullock had come to Canada seeking a new life after being dismissed from the British Army as unfit due to illness from malaria. Sadly, his family's promised wealth was contingent on Bullock's remaining in the army. With an army life no longer possible, he was a broken man who "turned to Canada for forgetfulness."[18] In Hornby, Bullock found expertise and experience, or so he thought. However, as Whalley points out, "Bullock is an interesting phenomenon: he was the only person who ever proceeded on the assumption that Hornby was a competent northern traveler and survived that curious assumption."[19]

Bullock rented an apartment in Edmonton. He and Hornby both lived there, and it also served as their expedition office and headquarters. In early 1924, Hornby departed for Ottawa to meet his friends in the government and try to raise funds and support for the expedition. Meanwhile, Bullock was assembling the expedition equipment, which included a mass of expensive scientific equipment, all at his own expense. After making his rounds in Ottawa, Hornby sailed for England to visit family and continue his quest to drum-up funds and support. To Bullock's surprise, he received an unexpected seven-word cable from Hornby. It read, "Necessary I remain in England. Cancel expedition."[20] Bullock was flabbergasted. He considered many possible responses to Hornby's astonishing cable, including cancelling the expedition. However, in the end, he decided to continue without Hornby, and sent off an equally brief message, asking permission to use the Fort Hornby cabin. Hornby's response was immediate: "Returning by next steamer. Wait for me."[21] Bullock would later realize that Hornby's perception of the Barrenlands as *his* country was the source of his immediate turnaround.

Hornby and Bullock did proceed with their expedition, although not without continued tensions and disagreements. Bullock had only just begun to see the extent of Hornby's eccentric and unpredictable behaviour, which would be fully revealed during the long, cold winter they spent together in a dark, sandy hole they dug in an esker at the edge of the Barrens near the north end of Artillery Lake. Among the long list of Hornby's strange behaviours were his practices of keeping his dental plate in a tin can with dead mice, of ripping at his food with his one remaining tooth (he only wore his dental plate in civilization), and of skinning wolves and foxes on his bed with the same knife he used for every other imaginable task, yet never washed. During this winter, Bullock also learned that Hornby would only travel with people who had blue eyes (which Bullock did). And, for some strange reason, Hornby always carried his dinner suit and tie with him in the bottom of his bag, even on the Barrens.

While with Bullock, starvation lurked from time to time, especially on the journey down the Hanbury and Thelon rivers, but it wasn't their constant companion. When they finally reached Baker Lake in September 1925, the Hudson's Bay factor asked where they had come from. Hornby took a great deal of pride in saying, in the most matter of fact manner he could, "Edmonton." The factor was shocked and asked the question again. Hornby replied, "Yes, yes. Edmonton. We had a fine trip. Splendid. Couldn't be better."[22] It was a glorious moment for Hornby that he had long been waiting for.[23]

Once back in civilization, Bullock and Hornby went their separate ways. Hornby travelled to England where he gathered up his nephew Edgar Christian and planned his final and fatal expedition. Bullock also embarked on a fatal journey, though not a legendary one. He was unable to sell his meagre expedition film footage, he was unsuccessful in securing

Photo by Morten Asfeldt.

The graves of Hornby, Christian, and Adlard have been lying silently at Hornby Point for more than seventy-five years. This photo was taken in 1995.

funds for another Arctic expedition, he had two failed marriages, and his investment in a Kenyan mine drove him into bankruptcy. His final fatal act was to shoot himself in the head in 1953.[24]

Meanwhile, with Edgar Christian in tow and the blessing of Edgar's parents, Hornby and Christian arrived in Canada in the spring of 1926. "What Marguerite and Colonel Christian could not know — and there was probably nobody in England who could have told them — was that Hornby, for all his fabulous experience and rhapsodic talk, was an extremely dangerous man to travel with."[25] As Hornby and Christian travelled across Canada and onward to Fort Reliance, a number of people tried to convince Hornby not to take Christian into the Barrens, including George Douglas's father and Guy Blanchet in Ottawa, Hornby's one time girlfriend Olwen Newell in Winnipeg, and Guy Blanchet again in Edmonton and in Fort Chipewyan. In each case, their pleading was ignored. George Douglas would come to regret not meeting Hornby in person that summer, as he felt he may have been the only one able to stop him from his doomed journey.

In Onoway, about forty miles northwest of Edmonton, Hornby and Christian took on Harold Adlard, a friend whom Hornby had promised

This sled was used by Hornby, Christian, and Adlard on their last desperate trip to "the cache" from March 10–15, 1927.

to take on an expedition. Once again, supplies were quickly gathered in Edmonton before they boarded the train for Waterways and paddled their way to Fort Reliance where Pike's Portage awaited them. They arrived there on June 23, having made good time from Waterways. However, it was early October before they began to build their winter cabin at what is now called Hornby Point on the Thelon River. Hornby had discovered this site on his way down the river with Bullock in 1925. It was "on a high bank overlooking the river to the southward, with good building timber in a small thick tongue of spruce that had licked up the valley of the Thelon far beyond the general trend of the treeline."[26] Their winter here would be Hornby's last dance with starvation.

By November the trio was already short of food and there was little sign of caribou. Hornby had speculated that the caribou would winter here along the Thelon, but this was sheer guesswork, as neither Hornby nor any other white person had ever spent a winter in that region. The search for food occupied every moment of every day, and while there were intermittent successes through the fall and winter, it was not nearly enough to sustain them. At one point, the three men made a desperate trek to a cache they had established upstream only to return home empty-handed and find caribou tracks several feet from the cabin; this was a devastating blow.[27]

179

On Christmas day they had "that great Northern delicacy — caribou head"[28] and Christian wrote in his diary:

> Christmas Day & although it seems hardly credible I enjoyed the feast as much as any, although we had nothing in sight for tomorrow's breakfast. When we awoke today we had made up our minds to enjoy ourselves as best as the circumstances would permit. Our frugal meals of rich bannock [I] enjoyed as much as a turkey. During the day we put in the net successfully now we hope for the best. I went round martin trail & got 1 hare (breakfast). A Wolverine had upset 2 traps & got away but I reset everything & hope tomorrow he is in. Weather much warmer by 20°F. Only -28° at dusk. I hope everyone in England has enjoyed today, & at the same time hope to God we rustle enough grub for a month from now & not wish we had not feasted today.[29]

On April 17, 1927, Hornby died an agonizing death by starvation. He may have been the first to die because of his gallant efforts to find food that continually sucked the last life out of him. Christian and Adlard wrapped Hornby's body in an old tent and placed it outside the cabin. On May 4, 1927, Adlard too breathed his last breath. At the limits of his remaining strength, Christian wrapped Adlard's body and dragged it outside to lie beside Hornby's. Christian was now alone without food, without his dear Hornby, and without much hope of surviving his hungry state. However, Christian did live on for about a month after Adlard died, and made his last diary entry on June 2, 1927: "9 am. Weaker than ever. Have eaten all I can. Have food on hand but heart petering [out]? Sunshine is bright now. See if that does any good to me if I get out and bring in wood to make a fire tonight. Make preparations now."[30]

Sometime later, after the last fire in the stove had gone out and the ashes cooled, Christian buried in them his diary, letters, and other papers of Hornby's and Adlard's. After closing the stove door for one last time, he wrote on the stove WHO[EVER COMES HERE] LOOK IN STOVE.[31] It was a year before anyone discovered the bodies,[32] and two years before the RCMP came to bury them and found Christian's now famous diary.

Many people have written about Hornby and the writing and scholarship continues today. Christina Sawchuk[33] writes insightfully about Hornby, demonstrating how different groups responded to his death and how people write about him today. Reacting to his death, Sawchuk claims that southerners, including those in England, view his death as romantic and tend to see Hornby in heroic terms. Northerners, and particularly trappers, saw his death as less dramatic and more as a part of life in the North where they all faced starvation and accident from time to time. In contrast, many of Hornby's friends, such as Blanchet and Douglas, who didn't fit neatly into either of the northerner or southerner categories, as their lives were split between these two regions, subscribed to the view that Hornby was an incompetent fool who travelled and prepared recklessly, causing the unnecessary deaths of Christian and Adlard. Sawchuk also suggests that some of the anger displayed by this group, particularly Blanchet and Douglas, was out of a sense of guilt for not having been able to stop Hornby from taking Christian and Adlard into the Barrenlands in the first place.

Sawchuk also points out that most of the people who write about Hornby are not northerners themselves and largely ignore the perspective of northerners, and therefore tend to romanticize his story. For example, Waldron[34] portrays Hornby as an admirable and effusive gentlemen, Whalley[35] views Hornby as a tragic and romantic figure, while Berton, a northerner himself, mercilessly attacks Hornby for his incompetence and tries to destroy the Hornby myth, claiming he had a death wish. Similarly, Clarke, a biologist of note who spent considerable time in the Thelon Valley in the mid-1930s where he met many people who knew and had met Hornby,[36] says, "Much nonsense has been written about Hornby. He was not a well man, nor a strong man. He was opinionated, but his capacity for living off the land did not approach that of the natives and white trappers. They liked him, but pitied him. He made the cardinal error of not getting his meat when it was available. In spite of that, an Eskimo family could have lived where he starved."[37] What's more, Roger Catling expressed, with an element of disappointment, that his mentor Gus D'Aoust, who lived and trapped in the Barrens for over thirty years, is not well-known because he was competent and didn't kill himself. Yet, because of Hornby's stupidity and the survival of Christian's diary, Hornby became famous. Roger exclaims, "It's odd, but that's the way it is!"[38]

Regardless of one's perspective, even now, many years after his death, some elements of Hornby's life seem clear while others remain a mystery. It seems clear that his uncommon life in the North was an escape from civilization and a family tradition of wealth and privilege that he could not reconcile. However, there may also have been an inner struggle that remains a mystery. It is clear that Hornby's war experience changed him. As his good friend George Douglas commented, "he had been steady, albeit a bit erratic before the War, he was now unpredictable and unreliable, a man whose screws seemed to be working their way slowly loose."[39] Similarly, Bullock claimed, "the war [had] evidently unhinged his brain."[40] However, he displayed strange and mysterious behaviour prior to the war, as well. In spite of the evidence against him and the temptation to write Hornby off as some sort of "nut case," he did write a brief but influential report[41] following his 1924–25 expedition with Bullock that helped create the Thelon Game Sanctuary that continues to protect a large portion of the Barrenlands today. Sadly, Hornby would never know that the Thelon Game Sanctuary had been created, as an Order-in-Council to create the sanctuary was passed on June 15, 1927, only two months after he died and a year before his body was discovered.[42]

What is also clear is that many people have travelled, and continue to travel, the Thelon River by canoe on a pilgrimage to visit the Hornby cabin in order to embrace the mysteries of the story that continues to linger in that place. In August 1995, I found myself immersed in Hornby's enduring spirit as I sat at the edge of the cabin remains with a group of students, reading Christian's diary aloud from start to finish. It was a moving experience and we all sat spellbound for a timeless period as the story, which we all knew well by then, took on new meaning. The day before, we had travelled down the river and seen wildlife galore — moose, caribou, muskox, wolves, and grizzly bears — and caught a few fish. Surrounding the cabin were piles of mammal scat of all kinds; it was difficult to imagine that anyone could starve to death in the abundance of summer life that we were seeing. After reading the diary, we walked up the hill behind the cabin onto the Barrens as Hornby, Christian, and

Adlard had done countless times in their search of food. As we walked in silence, I wrestled with the story of their deaths; I struggled on the one hand with the angry urge to blame Hornby for his stupidity and arrogance that caused the death of Christian and Adlard, both innocent young men who fatally trusted him. On the other hand, I wanted to reach out to Hornby with a sliver of empathy by trying to convince myself that he may not have been as neurotically mad, eccentric, and reckless as it first appears. I wanted to believe the romantic version of the story, that he was a rightful hero and his death a noble one, but I couldn't. His many years of carefree flirting with death made it too difficult to believe and the hardships of his northern life seemed more than any person would knowingly inflict upon themselves. Today, however, empathy for Hornby is easier for me to come by. Nevertheless, in the end, the tensions and mysteries of Hornby's uncommon life remain suspended on a continuum somewhere between romance and madness.

Morten Asfeldt
Camrose, Alberta

Chapter 12

The Letter[1]

Guy Blanchet, who spent many years in the northwest making topographical surveys for the Dominion Government, knew John Hornby from 1922 onward, both in the Canadian North and in England. Later, he crossed trails with Hornby and Critchell-Bullock. He wrote this story soon after the 1924–25 expedition that the two men made from Slave Lake to Baker Lake, from what they told him of the trip and each other, and from Bullock's diary, which Mr. Blanchet then had. Each of the men, he says, had reported to the police a belief that the other was mad. Mr. Blanchet, now retired, lives in Victoria.[2]

It would be difficult to conceive of a more miserable habitation than the hole in the sandhill at the edge of the Barren Grounds where John Hornby and J.C. Critchell-Bullock had taken up their quarters in the winter of 1924–25.

Rarely, too, has such an absurd bargain been made as when, one night, following an argument as to whether or not one could spend a million pounds in a year, Hornby had said with one of his erratic changes of ideas: "See here, Bullock, you get many letters and no one writes to me. I'll give you five pounds, one fox skin, for one of your letters in the next mail."

Critchell-Bullock glared at him indignantly. "Don't be a silly ass. What possible interest could you have in one of my letters?" The very idea disgusted him. Reading another man's letter was bad enough, but to buy one! Hornby was in an obstinate mood and persisted. "I've made you a sporting offer. Who knows what I may get? That is my chance. What risk are you taking?"

Bullock considered for a moment. A fox skin was valuable and he needed money. "All right," he said shortly, "I'll take you up."

Just before Christmas, Hornby set out with the dogs for a caribou hunt and it was ten days before he returned. Bullock was left in the wretched little shelter, filthy with falling debris, drying skins, and haunches of caribou, the candlelight hardly relieving the glimmer of daylight through the one small window.

While the hours and days dragged by, his mind became more active, mulling over the past in a ragged fashion, dwelling on this, skipping over that. His brightest memories were of the army, the life of a crack cavalry regiment stationed in India, when cavalry still meant horses and army life had some permanency. Active service during the war had ended his army career and he had had to seek a different climate and find a job.

He had chosen Canada and there he met Hornby. Two men could scarcely be more different than Critchell-Bullock and Hornby. The former looked his part, a cavalry officer, six foot three, good looking, but there was no quickness of expression, no laughter in his eyes. He had looked down on the small, elderly man, carelessly dressed, almost shabby, nondescript, except for his eyes. These were startlingly blue, dancing with excitement when he was interested, at times filled with puckish glee and then suddenly taking on a quality of remoteness. Hornby could not be judged by ordinary standards.

Bullock recalled this meeting clearly. "What a queer old customer" had been his first impression but soon he realized that here was a romantic character, one who had to be reckoned with. Listening to Hornby's stories of the Far North, Bullock had thought, this may be what I am looking for, unknown country to explore, books to write about it and here is one who knows the North and how to live and travel there. He had asked, "Would there be opportunities for me in this country of yours?"

"Come with me if you like," Hornby had said, "but I promise you only hard travel and a life that will make or break you."

Bullock had met a number of Hornby's friends. They admitted that he was odd but claimed that he had fine qualities and that he was a famous northern traveller. He had come out thirty years before and drifted into the North. "He has had many narrow escapes," one said, "and one of these times it will be too close. He is the 'lone wolf' type, you know."

"Lone wolf! That should have warned me," wrote Bullock in his diary. "There was no suggestion of any serious purpose to his travels and how could I expect companionship from one who had gone native and preferred to live alone?"

Into the North they went, but their association did not develop into friendship, they differed too much in qualities that neither admired in the other. Hornby regarded life and people with amused tolerance while Bullock had neither a sense of humour, nor easy adaptability to new and strange situations. There was friction between them, both in big things, like the purpose of the expedition and in the most trivial matters of daily life, cleanliness and order. Bullock was fastidious and orderly, both by nature and army training. To Hornby, time meant nothing and he ignored conventional ways of life.

Hornby was the leader and set the order of travel. Meals and sleep took no set pattern. "We'll eat when we're hungry," he had said, "and we'll sleep when we're tired but our travel is more important than either."

In their intimate association in canoe and tent, Hornby's talk had become wilder and, to Bullock, more senseless. Even talk of the Old Country brought no common interests.

"You could see the changes in Hornby, almost from day to day as we left civilization behind us," noted Bullock with forebodings about the future. "Instead of being just odd, there was more than a touch of madness in his state of mind."

There were weeks of hard travel by canoe, by rivers and across back-breaking portages to waters that carried them in autumn past the last woods, out to the bleak Barren Grounds at the north end of Artillery

Lake, beyond Great Slave Lake. It depressed Bullock. "Where are we going?" he had asked. "What is there ahead?"

Hornby's eyes were glowing like sapphires as his glance swept the country, searching out familiar details. "We are going to do something that has never been done before. We'll den up in a hole in the ground like animals. The snow will make a blanket over us and the gales will sweep past. We'll see caribou and wolves and foxes, maybe musk-ox, as woodland trappers never dreamed of. We'll be famous because we'll have done one of the few things that has never been done before."

"Mad," thought George. "I should have known then. Sane men do not talk like that nor do they plan such fantastic things. I could not turn back. All my capital of hopes and money was invested in the expedition."

They reached the sandhill where they were to winter. Its bleakness was accentuated by the few dwarf shrubs that were to provide their fuel. The country stretched away in stony hills and tundra flats. Even the sky settled on them in low misty clouds. They dug a hole and roofed it with their tent, covering all with branches and sand. When this was completed, Hornby had said, "Now we'll know how bears and ground squirrels live in winter."

Life in the dug-out was even worse than travelling. There was scarcely room to move. Most of the time it was dark and cold. Worst of all, they were forced into too intimate association; two men who had scarcely a thought or a habit in common. The long, dark, cold winter stretched ahead of them.

Once, an Indian hunter had visited them and had brought mail, many letters from Bullock's scattered friends. In answering these, he had poured out his misery and disillusionment and then, in a mood of self-pity, he had written to the police at the nearest post to say that he thought that Hornby was insane and might become dangerous. "What a fool I was to put that on official record! Who knows who may see the letter and when it may be produced?"

When Hornby was away, the days dragged and Bullock knew he could not meet the arctic winter alone and unaided. After Hornby returned from a prolonged trip with the dogs a sense of relief swallowed up all other feelings and Bullock's introspection was swept away in the delight of a human companion, someone to talk to, a break in the deadly loneliness. Hornby gave Bullock a quick glance, noticing a break-down of his stolid front. He said, soothingly, "I'll soon straighten things out and here, this will cheer you, letters." He dumped a packet of twenty or more on the floor and glanced at the addresses. "None for me, not one, but remember our bargain?"

"What bargain?"

"Why, I am to have one of your letters for a fox skin. Here it is, one of my best." He laughed as he carelessly picked out a long official envelope with RCMP stamped on the flap. He shoved it in his pocket but Bullock had seen it. He remembered his letter to the police questioning Hornby's sanity. This must be the answer. "Not that one," he cried, "that's private business." Hornby had already lost interest as he proceeded to prepare supper. "What does it matter?" he said.

Bullock hesitated. There was nothing that he could do or say. The bargain had been made. What would have been no more than a silly joke between two normal men, living an everyday life became a matter of importance, something sinister and menacing. A nagging worry as to what was in the letter and what Hornby would do about it dug deeper and deeper as days and weeks went by.

Midwinter closed about them, reducing activities, enclosing the two men through long hours, often for days, in the dug-out. They slept as much as possible, sometimes they talked, often they just sat, each lost in his own thoughts. Hornby found an outlet in outdoor activities, hunting, searching for wood, just being out. He could endure solitude but often he found Bullock an intolerable companion. He thought that his brittle mind might break and, however lightly he had taken on the responsibility of looking after him, he had to see it through.

Bullock's interest was not action but observation and this took the form of his log book in which he recorded what he thought and saw and did. He noted the weather and the movement of animals. He even impressed his moods on the blank pages. "My great exploration into the Arctic has become a test of how much mental and physical misery a civilized man can endure. Life in this hole has convinced me that there is a limit. A man cannot live as an animal does, his mind is too active. It must have something to work on or it grinds itself to pieces. Just how does this happen?"

Chapter 12

In another mood, he wrote, "Just look at him, squatting on his bed skinning a fox ... blood and grease every where. Either he talks such rot with that diabolical grin on his face that I am convinced that he is mad or his mind is so far away that he doesn't even hear me speak. What is he planning? Why can't he say what is on his mind? Why can't I do something?"

Once when Hornby returned from a visit to his trapper friends he remarked casually, "Corporal Thorp was there on patrol."

Now it's coming, thought Bullock. "What was he after?"

Hornby ignored Bullock's confusion as he sat repairing his dog harness. "He didn't say much, asked me some questions, wanted to know how you were getting along. He was cursing greenhorns coming into the country and getting bushed and giving the police extra work."

Bullock waited for something definite, something that he could answer, but Hornby had lost interest or at any rate said nothing more. Once again, Bullock found himself completely in the dark as to what had been said and what Hornby thought or planned to do. In the disordered state of his mind, he set down the gleam he caught in the blue eyes to gloating over some secret.

Days went by with midwinter monotony, the long hours of enforced idleness heightening the friction of personalities. At last the mounting sun started the snow melting on southern slopes. The cave became uninhabitable and the time had come to set out, to use the last snow to cross the divide with the dogs, to reach waters flowing eastward.

The overland journey was a hard one on men and dogs. They reached a large lake where the ice was beginning to clear and presently they launched their canoe, crossing unknown lakes, following untravelled streams. The hard work shared had brought them together. For a time petty frictions had been forgotten; the letter, even, no longer seemed important. Then, suddenly, Bullock saw his situation revealed with stark reality.

Hornby was a skilful canoeman but he took long chances to avoid portaging. He took the canoe through rapids which were too dangerous. Once, running a particularly bad piece of water, Bullock watched helplessly while the canoe crashed against a rock. Hornby took the split-second action that saved them and swung into the eddy below, half swamped but safe. His eyes were shining as he shouted, "Not many men could do that."

During those seconds, Bullock had realized what his situation would be if anything happened to Hornby. How could he explain his loss? There was the letter. Hornby was well known and he was unknown, no one had seen him for six months. "No one else would be foolish enough to try," he replied bitterly. "Where would I be, canoe and gear lost with you who know the country?"

"What would you do?" asked Hornby, curiously.

"That is simple. I should travel as far as I could. I should do what hunting was possible with my few shells, but — with the last one I should blow my brains out. And you, what would you do if it happened the other way?"

Hornby did not answer at once. He was squatting on his heels sipping scalding tea, gazing into the fire, looking over the plains to the misty horizon. "I could easily find my way out and live off the country ... but I would not do that. The police ask too many questions, there would be your letters and what is in them. No. I would lose myself in the Eskimo country for a year or two. You would soon be forgotten."

Bullock leapt to his feet, his long hair and beard giving him the appearance of an ancient prophet. "I'm not dead or forgotten yet and I still plan to live through and write my books and tell my story. Look. Jack," Bullock had suddenly become tense, "See — caribou — our starving time is over." They raced across the plain after the caribou, two wild figures with streaming hair and ragged clothes and presently they squatted about a fire of willow roots, gorging on half-cooked meat.

The savagely exacting journey ended as the turbulent river broke from the hills to its quiet course across the plain. All the confusion of their winter life seemed to be ended too when they brought their canoe through the last stretch of the Thelon River to Baker Lake, the little settlement of missions, police, and traders, 107 days after leaving their cave near Artillery Lake.

The sudden emergence from the wilderness after a year affected the men differently. To Hornby, it was just another episode, a slightly different adventure, a pause before a new venture. He was in his element, squatting on his heels, telling of his beloved Barren Grounds and of their winter life, tales which Bullock listened to with astonishment. Fact and fiction were so woven together that it was hard to tell where one began and the other ended. Even Bullock was a hero in Hornby's stories.

It was not like that for Bullock. The events of the past year seemed tremendously important. There had been adventures, desperate situations, and long-drawn-out times of misery. In the confusion of the moment, he could not reckon up what the experience had given and taken. At least he had lived through it. Hornby was no madder than he had always been. Bullock seemed to recover his personality on meeting friendly people again and living a conventional life. The fantastic nightmare ended and he found himself in a world of familiar things in which he could indulge his ingrained love of order, in a life in which yesterday predicted tomorrow. Life was worth living again.

The letter … might the whole miserable affair of the letter have been a mistake? Nothing that Hornby had said or done could be definitely put down to it. Looking back, it all seemed so petty, and as he thought over the past year, the journey out especially, he realized what a fine chap Hornby was, unselfishly taking the brunt of the work, never complaining, always taking the big load, the serious risks. At last, he decided to speak out …

He chose an evening when they had been reminiscing, both in a cheerful mood. "I say, Jack," he tried to make it sound casual, "How about that letter?"

"Letter! What letter?" Hornby seemed to have no recollection of it.

"You know well enough. The letter you bought for a fox skin. The police letter. The cursed letter."

Hornby looked astonished, and then burst out laughing. "Oh, now I remember. Surely that did not worry you? Here, just a minute." He dumped the contents of his kit bag on the floor, wolf skulls, skins of mice and birds, an army medal not easily won, rags of clothing. From the pocket of an old pair of pants he produced a dirty, crumpled letter. It was unopened.

Bullock took it shamefacedly. I should have known, he thought. He is a gentleman. There are things he would not do. Bullock tore the envelope open and drew out a thin, official slip and read: RECEIVED FROM GEORGE CRITCHELL-BULLOCK — THE SUM OF THIRTY DOLLARS — FOR LICENCE TO TRAP FOXES IN THE NORTHWEST TERRITORIES. SIGNED CORP. THORP RCMP.

Guy Blanchet (1884–1966)
The Beaver, Spring 1963

Chapter 13

Helge Ingstad: Inspiration for a Life of Adventure in the Land of Feast and Famine

I barely escaped the city's shadow. Only in the wilderness did I feel I was free. There I became myself.[1]

— Helge Ingstad

Helge Ingstad, Norwegian author, adventurer, and explorer, led a remarkably long and full life. Born on December 30, 1899, in Meråker, Trøndelag, Ingstad's life spanned three centuries. Pivotal events in his life included a promising, albeit short, career as a lawyer in Norway in the early 1920s, stints as Norwegian governor of eastern Greenland from 1932–33 and of the Arctic archipelago Svalbard in the 1930s and 1940s, periods living with Aboriginal peoples in Canada, New Mexico, and Alaska, and involvement in the Norwegian resistance movement during the Second World War.

Ingstad is best known internationally for the role he played in the 1960s in locating and excavating the first authenticated Viking-Age site in North America at L'Anse aux Meadows, Newfoundland. The excavation work was led by archaeologist Anne Stine Ingstad, Ingstad's wife.[2] L'Anse aux Meadows is now a UNESCO World Heritage Site. At Ingstad's state funeral in April of 2001, a funeral at which the Norwegian king and queen were present, Norwegian prime minister Jens Stoltenberg stated in his eulogy that Ingstad "changed the understanding of world history while at the same time he changed the Norwegian self image"[3] — an indication of the iconic status Ingstad achieved in Norway and beyond during his lifetime.

Most Norwegians, unlike most North Americans, are aware that though Ingstad's years in northern Newfoundland led to widespread Canadian and international attention, this was not his first noteworthy Canadian experience. More than thirty years earlier, when Ingstad was a promising young lawyer in Norway, he sold his practice in order to pursue a dream of spending time in the Canadian wilderness. From 1926–30 he travelled, lived, and worked in the area northeast of Great Slave Lake, spending time with other trappers and hunters as well as alone on the Barrens, and living for a year with a group of Dene.[4] Ingstad's adventure convinced him that he wanted to make exploration and adventure a central part of his life, and one can speculate that Ingstad may never have embarked on his quest to locate a Viking site in North America if he hadn't had this earlier Canadian experience. Ingstad himself gave credit to his Dene hosts for teaching him skills and ways of thinking that aided him in his search for the remains of a Norse settlement on the eastern coast of North America decades later.[5]

In addition, Ingstad's account of these years, *Pelsjegerliv Blandt Nord-Kanadas Indianere*, published in 1931 and translated into English in 1933 as *The Land of Feast and Famine*,[6] gave him confidence as an author, and Ingstad went on to publish numerous books during his life.[7] In these accounts he not only documented his accomplishments, but he also shared his adventures with a broad audience. His books were akin to the published accounts of the famous Norwegian polar explorers Fridtjof Nansen and Roald Amundsen,[8] to whom Ingstad was at times compared. In addition to being translated into numerous languages and becoming one of the bestselling books of the twentieth century in Norway, *Pelsjegerliv* also inspired several generations of Norwegians to embark on their own adventures. Ingstad received mail from young people who had been influenced by this book throughout the rest of his

The tall man with the pipe in the middle of this group of trappers is believed to be Helge Ingstad.

life,[9] and his account has had a profound and lasting impact on the image of Canada in the Norwegian collective imagination, contributing to a fairly romanticized view.

Helge Ingstad grew up in Bergen, on the western coast of Norway, as an inquisitive child, interested in chess, writing poetry, and spending time in the outdoors. His budding interest in Polar adventure was evident when, at the age of thirteen, he convinced his father to let him spend a cold winter's night alone on the top of a local mountain.[10] Ingstad was interested in this type of extreme *friluftsliv*[11] before it became fashionable.[12] While establishing a thriving law practice in Levanger, he continued to hunt and fish in the mountains at every opportunity, and he questioned whether he wanted to spend the rest of his life working in an office. In 1925, he made the bold decision to sell his practice in order to spend time as a trapper in the Northwest Territories in Canada, lured by its large stretches of unmapped wilderness. Ingstad recognized this would be a dangerous life, but he longed for the freedom he thought such a life would bring.[13] Seventy years later, when asked by his grandson, Eirik Ingstad Sandberg, why he had made this decision, Ingstad replied, "It was an inner urge. Besides, as a young man, I felt that I only had this one life. I wanted to make my own decisions."[14]

This typical trapper's tent, combining canvas and caribou hides draped over a wooden frame, belonged to Jack Stark. Stark is thought to have been the first white trapper in the region.

When Ingstad and his new Norwegian acquaintance Hjalmar Dale — an experienced trapper from Hordaland who had already spent several years on the Mackenzie River — travelled to the Northwest Territories from Edmonton in 1926 with the Barrenlands as their goal, the journey was long and convoluted.[15] Travelling by train, foot, steamship, and canoe, and working for a time in a sawmill to earn enough money for a trapper's licence, they eventually reached Reliance on the eastern edge of Great Slave Lake. Along the way they met other trappers as well as traders, clergy, and Dene people. Ingstad provides a colourful picture of these groups in his account.

Ingstad and Dale were given two pieces of advice regarding the Barrens: they should be prepared for extreme cold and they should depart as soon as possible if they were to reach their destination before winter set in. While these two Norwegians were aware of Pike's Portage, which Ingstad describes as "the gate to the Barren Lands ... a steep and rugged pass which winds up through the wall to a chain of waterways ... the only known canoe trail east,"[16] they chose an old Native canoe route on the Snowdrift River to reach the Barrens that Black Basile — an Aboriginal man — had brought to their attention. Ingstad acknowledged that Pike's Portage would have been the safe choice, but he wrote that "The 'old canoe route,' which no one ever used any longer, beckoned invitingly to us."[17] Though they had hopes of reaching the Barrens before winter set in to lead a nomadic existence relying on the caribou for meat and clothing, they were unable to make their way using this route. Instead, they built a cabin to use as their winter base on a lake they named Moose Lake.[18] In the 1990s, Eirik Ingstad Sandberg, Ingstad's grandson, enlisted the aid of several Norwegian adventurers to try to locate the site of this cabin. They were successful in their hunt, and footage of their trip can been seen in *Helge Ingstad: The Man That Proved the Vikings Were First* and *I Helge Ingstads Fotspor*.[19]

Ingstad and Dale spent the winter of 1926–27 trapping and hunting at Moose Lake. Feeling "the call of the Barrens," they spent several weeks that winter exploring the treeless tundra beyond Moose Lake. However, they encountered a blizzard, and, unable to locate an Aboriginal camp they had been told about, returned to their cabin after crossing Artillery Lake and merely getting a small taste of the Barrens of their dreams. According to his account, Ingstad spent the following winter with the Dene and tried unsuccessfully for several weeks to navigate the Snowdrift River route again, this time with a Canadian companion whom Ingstad only identifies as Fred. Only then did Ingstad choose to travel to the Barrens alone for the winter via Pike's Portage. The fact that Ingstad chose to try the Snowdrift River route twice provides evidence of his love of exploration and his persistence, traits that served him well in his successful attempts to locate a North American Viking-Age site more than three decades later. Navigating Pike's Portage and managing for a winter by himself were positive and transformative rites of passage for Ingstad. These events also played a major role in the way in which he marketed and shared his experiences after he returned to Norway.

Ingstad valued the solitude he experienced in the Canadian North, winter and summer, and he spoke and wrote fondly of the times he spent alone with only his dogs as companions:

> One day, along toward the end of June, the fur traders set off south down the lake for Fort Resolution; early next autumn they will return with a fresh supply of merchandise. A short time afterwards the trappers follow

them south. The Indians move out onto the islands, and I am left alone in Snowdrift. Here is my canoe, here my nets, my guns, and my dogs. Forest and lake are at my disposal. I sit in my shirt-sleeves in front of my tent and feel like a millionaire.[20]

Ingstad expressed similar sentiments about his last winter in the Northwest Territories, which he spent alone on the Barrens with his dogs. While he had good and bad days, becoming lost on one occasion without his dogs and barely making it back to camp, he wrote about how his canine companions helped keep his spirits up, and he referred to his tent as his home. He also wrote of the caribou: "I would feel that I was the lord of some vast estate and that these were my herds of kine."[21] Ingstad's comments about ownership, conquering, and disposal not only express a sense of place and belonging, but also reflect his intended European audience and his Western mindset.

While he relished his time alone, Ingstad had considerable contact with others, and his North was populated by Aboriginal men, women, and children, white men, and trappers, as well as by past explorers. Non-Aboriginal women had virtually no presence in his stories, and Ingstad's North was very male-oriented. Though a degree of Eurocentrism is evident in Ingstad's descriptions of the Aboriginals who he encountered as evidenced by stereotypes and caricatures — particularly of women — Ingstad's cultural and gender biases are clear to the contemporary reader. However, it is also evident he had a great deal of respect for Native skills and knowledge and his written account contains valuable ethnographic material. Ingstad eventually distanced himself to some degree from his European cultural context while living with the Dene, and he felt that he became one of them, learning from this group and the other Aboriginal people he encountered. Without this invaluable apprenticeship, Ingstad's solo time on the Barrens might have turned out very differently. Ingstad spoke often of the uniqueness and breakthrough quality of being a white person who lived with a group of Aboriginals in the North for a year, and this became an intrinsic part of his popular and public image.

The elder Ingstad's perspective appears to have been more egalitarian, shaped by additional life experiences with a variety of Aboriginal groups and more progressive views of the latter part of the twentieth century. This attitude is clear in written and oral comments he made as he grew older. At the end of the twentieth century, Ingstad said, "Most people have an instinct. We have it ourselves. Primitive people have it to a greater degree. They understand that I sympathize with indigenous peoples, that I considered them to be equals. It was important to be equal with everybody no matter whom."[22] Indeed, Ingstad's years in the Northwest Territories shaped his life journey in more ways than one, instilling in him a profound respect for Native ways, which grew during his later encounters with the Apache in New Mexico, the Inuit in Greenland, and the Nunamiut of northern Alaska.

Ingstad's stories of his encounters with Aboriginal peoples are often told with humour and frequently focus on cultural contrasts. Though Ingstad may have exaggerated both the humorous nature of these experiences and the cultural differences they exposed for dramatic effect and narrative purposes, his oral and written accounts are key to telling his story today, since only a few of the people with whom he lived and interacted have left records of their encounters with him during his days on Great Slave Lake. One of Ingstad's most memorable tales is of attending an Aboriginal dance with a number of his acquaintances, including the legendary Klondike Bill.[23] While Ingstad quickly tired of dancing, admitting his clumsy attempts were a sight to behold, Klondike Bill enthusiastically danced with women and girls of all ages, proudly displaying the gifts of tobacco, knives, rat skins, and handkerchiefs he had received from them. His companions repeatedly tried to explain the importance of reciprocating with gifts, but Klondike Bill was oblivious to his social faux pas and his companions dragged him away before their hosts became irate.

Ingstad wasn't immune to failing to communicate with and pick up on the social and cultural cues of his Aboriginal friends and hosts either. Indeed, the reason he left the Dene group he lived and came to identify with, was that a young woman's family had her designs on Ingstad as a husband for their daughter. Once it dawned on him that the attention and gifts being showered on him were linked to a possible arranged marriage, he didn't feel comfortable addressing the situation directly. Rather, he bided his time with a poker face, and made his escape by telling his hosts he was travelling to Great Slave Lake to visit some white people. He never returned to this camp, and he lightheartedly wrote:

> During the four years I spent knocking around in northern Canada, it was many times my fate to look anxiously forward to the arrival of the caribou. But the keenest anxiety of all — and I do not exclude those periods when my larder was utterly exhausted — was that which I experienced during my imprisonment in that Indian village when, with marriage hanging over my head, I waited for the bucks to come trekking north through the forest, thus giving me the opportunity to escape.[24]

Told with a great deal of humour and likely dramatic embellishment, this courtship story provides a tidy explanation for the timing of Ingstad's departure from his Dene hosts. However, even allowing for its jovial tone, Ingstad's description of the young woman, Kachesy, and her mother, Phresi, reveal unprogressive gender views on the young Ingstad's part:

> [A]nd Kachesy herself — yes, she had a bewitching gleam in her eye for one and all and was never wanting when it came to the use of the small devices common to women the world over, regardless of their color. At one moment she was a troll, at the next something quite different, but taken altogether, neither better nor worse than the white members of her sex.[25]

Perhaps the most sombre and moving story that Ingstad relates of his time in the North is one of disease. Ingstad learned from a Dene chief, Marlo, that virulent diseases had arrived along with the white people, and that many people had died as a result. Ingstad experienced this first-hand when, on a solo trip, he came upon a group of sick and dying Natives camped on one of the islands off Snowdrift. He helped the only healthy person in camp, an old woman, bury her husband and the other dead, and move the group in canoes to a neighbouring island. A week later, Ingstad became violently ill as a result of his exposure to this illness, revealing the selfless nature of this act. As a thank-you, the woman gave Ingstad her deceased husband's dog. Ingstad named it Skøieren, which means "the rascal" in Norwegian, due to its mischievous nature. Though Ingstad said he did not want anything for his help, he displayed cultural sensitivity by accepting the dog, knowing he would offend the woman if he refused this gift. This dog became Ingstad's favourite, and when Ingstad left the North, this was the only dog he took with him. He was always quick to acknowledge the role the resilient northern sled dogs played in facilitating his travels and survival, and his account is rife with stories of their personalities, work, and what he perceived as harsh treatment of them by the Aboriginal people he encountered.

Ingstad's account was clearly of value and interest to naturalists of his day. In addition to making numerous comparisons between animals found in the forests and mountains of Canada and Norway, he described both harrowing and humorous encounters with wildlife, including moose, wolves, and beaver. A particularly entertaining encounter was with a supposed moose. One day, while attempting to attract a moose during the fall mating season by calling like a lonely moose through a bark trumpet, Ingstad received a grunting response. Excitedly, he continued to call as the moose approached Ingstad's hiding place. Suddenly, he found himself face to face with an Aboriginal man in a canoe who was calling on his own bark trumpet. This man was armed with a rifle, and he was ready to shoot his prey. Ingstad ran toward the man, trying to convince him not to shoot, and the man paddled away as quickly as he could as "though the devil were after him."[26] Clearly, this was a story and legend in the making from two perspectives.

Ingstad recognized the importance of storytelling in the North, demonstrating that its value reached far beyond entertainment. He told of spending time at the trading post in the spring with other trappers who related stories and worked together by sharing observations, plans, and experiences. One year the talk turned to John Hornby, who had disappeared with two greenhorn companions in the wilderness during Ingstad's time in the North. Hornby had a reputation for rash behaviour, but notably, Ingstad did not directly criticize Hornby's daredevil actions and supposed death wish, though he did record the rather unflattering picture others painted of Hornby. Shortly before Ingstad left the North, he learned of the fate of the Hornby party — death by starvation — from RCMP Corporal Williams. Ingstad wrote, "It was the old story: the caribou had disappeared and the three had died of slow starvation."[27] Ingstad also mentioned the diary that young Edgar Christian left, with its stories of this doomed hunting party. Ingstad recognized the role of luck in survival in the northern wilderness, due partly to the unpredictability of the caribou migration, and more than once he found himself in dire straits — facing starvation like the Hornby party and his Native neighbours.

As an old man reflecting back on his life and choices, it is clear that Ingstad had no regrets about giving up his law career as a young man. "I barely escaped the city's shadow. Only in the wilderness did I feel I was free. There I became myself. Position and money were suddenly of no importance. One's future depends upon oneself."[28] Not only was Ingstad transformed by his northern experience — these years setting the stage for the rest of his life — he also recognized that the North was on the cusp of major change when he left in 1930. He had arrived by train in 1926, but he returned south by plane four years later. As he flew back to Edmonton from Fort Resolution, Ingstad made some perceptive observations about the Canadian North, the accuracy of which he proudly pointed out almost sixty years later. Ingstad wrote:

> The wilderness is in the process of being conquered from the air, this conquest being in the name of the yellow metal and radium. Giant corporations from the south send up whole fleets of aeroplanes carrying geologists to strategic points in the wilds. One region after another is being carefully combed for deposits.… The prospector no longer tramps about with his pan. He goes sailing through the air! The romance of the Klondike belongs to a bygone day.[29]

Forty years after his foray into the Canadian wilderness, Ingstad discovered that a creek had been named after him, located about nine miles south of Artillery Lake.[30] This creek was the site of a remarkable coincidence in the northern Canadian journey of the contemporary Norwegian adventurer Lars Monsen, one of many Norwegians inspired

Courtesy of Nicolay Eckhoff.

Helge Ingstad sitting on Warren's Island, Newfoundland, a few miles from L'Anse aux Meadows.

by Ingstad. Introduced to the classic *Pelsjegerliv* as a teenager by an acquaintance forty years his senior, Monsen started to dream of his own solo adventure in the Canadian North.[31] He realized this dream during a span of 947 days in 2000–02 when he crossed a vast tract of northern Canada from the Polar Sea in northeastern Alaska to the coast of Labrador by dog team, skis, and canoe. An immensely popular television series based on Monsen's adventure was shown on NRK (Norwegian Broadcasting Corporation) in 2005,[32] and in 2002, Monsen dedicated the written account of his journey — *Nådeløs Villmark: Canada på tvers* — to Helge Ingstad. Monsen, like Ingstad, focuses at times on the solitary nature of his expedition, clearly aware of its myth and image-making potential, while also highlighting interactions with Aboriginal and non-Aboriginal inhabitants of the North. Monsen's descriptions and images of encounters with wildlife, often with a jovial and at times irreverent tone, are also reminiscent of Ingstad's account. Monsen was on his expedition when Ingstad died, and when he learned of this event was startled to discover that of the hundreds of campsites he stayed at during his trip across the Canadian North, most of them for only one night, he was camped at Ingstad Creek on March 28, 2001 — the eve of Ingstad's passing.[33] Young Norwegians today are more likely to associate the Canadian North with Monsen rather than Ingstad, but Monsen's popularity and the way in which he has influenced the image of Canada — particularly the Canadian North — in the Norwegian collective imagination is undeniably a part of Ingstad's legacy.

Monsen only encountered one person in Lutsel K'e who could remember meeting Helge Ingstad. Morris Lockhart was ninety years old when Monsen met him, and he spoke with respect of this note-taking Norwegian who managed his own trapline. "Of course, I remember Ingstad! He was tall and powerful, and had his own trapline and dog team. There was no trouble with that fellow; he knew how to manage in the wilderness. I also noticed that he always had a pen and paper with him, and he constantly made short notations."[34] These were likely the notes that Ingstad used to write *Pelsjegerliv* a few years later. Though Monsen tried to get more information about Ingstad from Lockhart on several occasions, he gave up after he realized that this old Chipewyan man wanted to be left in peace.[35]

After Ingstad's death, Benedicte Ingstad, his only child, edited and published a collection of the poetry his father had written throughout his long life. Several of these poems, including "Sommer ved den Store Slavesjø" — "Summer by Great Slave Lake" — were inspired by his years in the Northwest Territories.[36] An Ingstad poem that doesn't appear in the published collection, but which he recites in the documentary about his travels, focuses on the solitude he loved so much. Clearly, he continued to value and promote the benefits of adventures off the beaten path throughout his long life:

Wasn't it lonely being alone?
Where forest and tundra chill you to the bone?
There you're mistaken,
It's between people that loneliness is born.[37]

Klondike Bill agreed with Ingstad on this point. Ingstad gave this legendary figure the last word in *Pelsjegerliv*. After flying back to

Edmonton and spending only four days in the city, Klondike Bill told Ingstad, "Lighting out for the north tomorrow. Got to go home to my tent, it's too lonesome out here."[38] The film *I Helge Ingstads Fotspor* also focuses on the solitary aspects of Ingstad's time in the North, romanticizing it to some extent, and ending with footage of a lone paddler in a canoe in the northern Canadian wilderness. In light of the focus on solitude, by Ingstad himself, and by those who emulate and remember him, it seems fitting that the Ingstad name is now attached to a remote Alaskan mountain, a creek on the rugged Barrens near Artillery Lake in the Northwest Territories, and to a monument at L'Anse aux Meadows, Newfoundland, a northeastern Canadian outpost. These, too, are parts of the Helge Ingstad legacy and lore.

Ingrid Urberg
Camrose, Alberta

Part IV

On the Trail to the Present

By now we had reached the eastern edge of the great lake. Here the flat scenery changed and became more rugged, cliffs falling sheer a hundred feet or more to the water's edge, the sunken islands emerald green just beneath the surface of the black water, the blue mists enfolding the hills in a tattered embrace. Below us lay Fort Reliance (Reliance today), on the very eastern tip of the lake. It might just as easily have been named Fort Isolation. The only reason for its existence is its position as gateway to the Barrens, the funnel through which trapper, hunter, scientist, and explorer must pass on their way to the tundra.[1]

— Pierre Berton, *The Mysterious North*, 1956

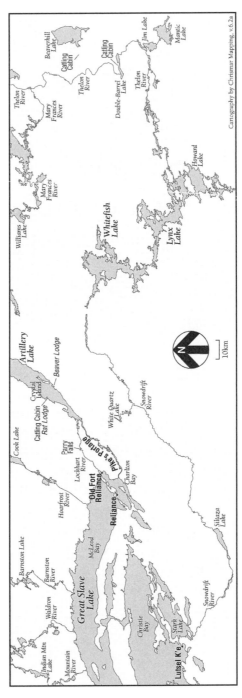

Map 6. Contemporary Travels.

Chapter 14

Gus D'Aoust: Living a Dream on the Barrens

In July 1930, Gus D'Aoust made the long journey from Black Diamond, Alberta, to Fort Reliance, Northwest Territories, in the pursuit of his lifelong dream of trapping in the North. With his brothers Hughie and Phil, he travelled by train to Fort McMurray where they built a thirty-foot barge that was eight feet wide, and loaded on their trapping supplies. They headed down the Athabasca River into Lake Athabasca before joining the current of the Slave River that took them to Great Slave Lake where they navigated the rocky shores to Fort Reliance located at the far east end of the lake. From Fort Reliance, all that lay between Gus and his quest to trap on the Barrens was Pike's Portage — a rite of passage that all early trappers struggled over before reaching the rich trapping grounds beyond. Gus describes it as "the worst one on Great Slave Lake. The first three and a quarter miles were the worst because there is a 350 [foot] rise above the lake level, in a quarter mile distance, we were going uphill all the time."[1] Gus made countless trips over Pike's Portage during the next thirty-six years, before retiring to Fort Reliance in 1966 at the age of seventy. He was a courageous, independent, and tenacious man who let little stand between him and the realization of his boyhood dreams.

Gus D'Aoust displays his furs outside a cabin in Snowdrift (Lutsel K'e).

His life was full of stories that go beyond the imaginations of most people of his time and certainly beyond the imaginations of most people today.

Gus D'Aoust was born near the Riding Mountains of Manitoba in 1896 and was the third oldest of eleven children. His grandfather had been a trapper and fur trader in Quebec and was away from his family for long periods. Gus's father didn't want this life for his family, so he had moved to a farm near Riding Mountain where he could provide a more stable home for his children. In spite of his father's hopes that his boys wouldn't become trappers, the Riding Mountains became Gus's training ground and the source of his hunting and trapping dreams. Years later, when Gus was attempting to persuade his brothers Hughie and Phil to join him in his trapping ventures, his father said to them, "You two had better forget the idea of going trapping. There are enough crackpots in the family already."[2] While Gus's father viewed him as a "crackpot," his mother was his constant supporter and a continuous source of courage and understanding.

On the farm in Manitoba, Gus would snare rabbits with his brothers. The local boys had their own way of setting snares and tried to impress upon Gus that their way was the best. However, Gus would have nothing of it. As would become his modus operandi for most of his life, he developed his own techniques that worked. After Gus skinned the rabbits, his mother made rabbit pies that were a staple in the D'Aoust household and a favourite of Gus's. Years later, while alone on the Barrens, Gus would trap rabbits and "make pies just like mother used to make" and think, "Gee, that was good."[3]

In the summer of 1917, Gus turned twenty-one[4] and his dreams of northern trapping began to come to life. He was working for the Hudson's Bay Railway Line earning thirty-five cents an hour when he learned of an old abandoned cabin north of La Pas, Manitoba. In the fall he used his summer earnings to buy a meagre trapping outfit and boarded the train after arranging with the conductor that he would stop at Mile 156. On a dark November night, the train slowed to a stop as arranged; it was eleven o'clock when Gus stepped off, unloaded his outfit — a bedroll made by his mother, his rifle, snowshoes, a bundle of traps, and a packsack — and stood alone in the snow as the train rumbled into the northern darkness. After putting on his snowshoes, he made his way to the cabin about six hundred feet from the tracks. The cabin was more than he had hoped for. Until the first week in March he lived alone in his little wilderness abode, during which time he trapped marten, fisher, lynx, and rabbit, and lived on moose meat. As he was without a dog team, his daily rounds of setting and checking traps were made on snowshoes: "I had a good winter and by spring I had lots of furs. I was happy in the North but I packed everything and left for Winnipeg and joined the army."[5]

Gus's tenure in the army was short-lived — his independence didn't mesh well with the regimented nature of the army. In hindsight, he claimed that he treated his dogs better than he was treated in the army. Gus was stationed in Wales, where he endured daily drills in grey, rainy weather. He returned to Canada in the spring of 1920 without ever seeing action. After a short period of working on the farm, followed by a winter of trapping in the Riding Mountains, Gus made his way to La Pas to see a dog-team race and saw his first white fox pelts. He was "fascinated by them and at the time thought they were the most beautiful furs"[6] he had ever seen. His dream of trapping in the North was fuelled once more.

After returning from La Pas, Gus left his home in Manitoba, sold his furs in Winnipeg, and boarded a train for Edmonton. He worked for a brief period in the Peace River country before buying a trapping outfit in Fort McMurray and heading north to trap for the winter on the Slave River. Gus trapped there until Wood Buffalo Park was created in 1922, ending his trapping privileges.[7]

In March 1923, Gus learned that his father had died and he returned to Manitoba to be with his mother and family. While in Manitoba, he went to see Nella, a woman he had been introduced to by his cousin and with whom he had corresponded for the past two years. He asked her to come north to trap with him: she agreed on the condition that they get married. Not having enough money to do so, Gus once again boarded a train for Edmonton, but this time with his brother Hughie. To Gus's surprise, Nella met him in Edmonton and they were married and went as far north as Fort McMurray — as far as their money would take them — and trapped for two winters.

Nella soon discovered that she didn't care for the northern trapping life. Every summer she boarded the train for Edmonton, and in the fall, reluctantly made the return journey north to spend the winter with Gus. She soon convinced Gus to take a job as a ranger in Wood Buffalo Park, which he did. However, as a ranger, he continued to spend most of his spare time hunting and trapping. Nella gave birth to two daughters, Rita and Olive, in 1927 and 1929 respectively. As always, once summer came, Nella headed south to Edmonton, now with Rita and Olive in tow. During this time, Hughie had been trapping nearby, and in 1928 he decided to make the move to the fur-rich Barrens. Gus resisted the urge to follow his brother and his lifelong dream, and continued his work with the park.

Although Gus enjoyed elements of his work with the park, he longed for independence and the pursuit of his trapping dreams. However, in the spring of 1929, he quit his job with the park and followed his family south. As Gus said, "After ten years in the North, I came out for the sake of my family."[8] However, after a year with his family in Black Diamond, Alberta, Gus could no longer resist the lure of trapping white fox on the Barrens and once more headed north with his brothers Hughie and Phil in July 1930. For the next ten years, each spring Gus would make a trip by dog team, sternwheeler, and train to Edmonton to be with Nella and their girls for the summer. Then, without warning, he arrived in Edmonton as he had done each spring to find that Nella and the girls had moved east — they had vanished. Gus returned to the Barrens to trap, and each spring he turned his dogs toward Reliance, hoping the mailbag would hold a letter with news from his daughters. It was seventeen years before he heard from them. By this time, they were grown women.

Gus's journey over Pike's Portage in 1930 was an arduous one even though he and his two brothers had their dogs carry much of the load. Phil had a sewing machine and constructed canvas bags that were draped over the dogs' backs — much like saddlebags on a horse — and tied into place, while Gus, Hughie, and Phil carried the bulky things and, of course, the canoes. There were fifty-one portages on their six-week journey from Reliance to their trapping grounds on the upper Thelon River. By the mid-1930s, the float plane arrived in the North and each fall trappers would wait their turn to be flown into their camps with canoes, dogs, and supplies. The trip took one and a half hours, "a hell of a big difference" and "worth every penny,"[9] Gus claimed.

With Pike's Portage behind them, the three brothers continued toward the Thelon. Phil settled in at Tent Lake for the winter while Gus and Hughie headed for the Thelon where they established themselves near Granite Falls — an impressive cascade where the water of the Thelon has carved and smoothed the granite riverbed for centuries. Here they set to work preparing for winter, as Gus would do for the next thirty-six years. First they set up their tent by building a wooden tent frame, covering it with about thirty caribou hides sewn together and laying the hides over the frame with the fur side out. On top of the caribou hides, they draped the canvas tent and secured it to the ground so that it could outlast the frequent tundra blizzards. With a wood stove inside, it made a warm winter home. Once the tent was up, they would put up wood from small clusters of trees found along the river, kill close to sixty caribou to keep themselves and their dogs warm and fed through the long winter, as well as prepare their traps for the trapping season. Once this work was completed, they would have until mid-November to start trapping — when the furs were prime. Their normal seasonal pattern was to trap until Christmas, travel six days by dog team to Reliance around Christmas for supplies and to deliver furs, return to the Barrens to trap until late April, and then go back to Reliance and south to Edmonton for a brief summer retreat. After selling their furs and living the easy life *outside* for a few

Courtesy of Knox/NWT Archives/N-1985-009-0043.

Gus D'Aoust in fur clothing rests with his dog team.

months, they would be back on the trail headed for the Barrens in July. Later in Gus's life he would spend summers in Reliance looking after the other trappers' dogs for a fee of five dollars per month for each dog. He frequently cared for fifty dogs.

The trip to Reliance around Christmas and in the spring was considerably easier than the outbound journey in the fall, as the snow-covered landscape allowed for a more direct route over rocky ground and frozen lakes. Gus's six dogs were hitched one behind the other. At times he would ride on the sled and at others he would run alongside. However, the trip was not without its challenges and unforeseen adventures.

As one descends Pike's Portage, the trail snakes downhill from Artillery Lake through a series of lakes before making the last steep plunge to the shores of Great Slave Lake. From Harry Lake, the last of these lakes, Gus and his dogs raced down the steepest and fastest section of the portage, the same 350-foot rise they had struggled up in the fall. Gus would stop at a height of land where the forest briefly opens up, providing a sweeping vista over Charlton and McLeod bays and marking the beginning of the final descent, to cut down a spruce tree with many broad branches. This he would drag behind the toboggan, heavily laden with furs, to keep it from running over the dogs on the wild downhill ride.

While the trip to and from Reliance by dog team in winter was considerable quicker than by foot and canoe in the fall, it did not always unfold as planned. Three times Gus was lost: once for nine days, once for twenty days, and once for a month. In 1938,[10] Gus was lost for the first time after leaving his camp on the Barrens in early March to check his traps, expecting to be back by dark. He left with little food, his rifle, a few shells and matches, his snow shovel, and an old dull axe. He had no bedroll or tent. After a few hours, the weather "really got dirty,"[11] transforming the land and sky into a world of solid white. Thinking he knew the way to camp, Gus incessantly commanded his lead dog to turn left rather than letting it find its own way as it had done so many times before. This was his first mistake. Gus describes his first night out:

> [T]he dogs buried themselves in a snowdrift and I put the sleigh on its side and used it as a wind break. I slept in the open … since there was nothing there. I was right on the lake. I just flopped down. I spent the [night] covered with the tarp of my cariole beside the dogs. I managed to sleep a little, about an hour, but it got too cold to sleep and I was afraid to fall asleep again. By then it had stopped blowing. At daybreak we struck out.[12]

For nine days Gus roamed the Barrens hoping to find a landmark that would lead him home. He and his dogs ate two caribou that he shot and meat scavenged from wolf kills. He slept little and rarely had a fire. At one point, when he was in an area he was sure he knew, he once again neglected to trust his dogs and walked ahead of them on snowshoes, demanding they follow. When he finally wandered into Reliance, far from the camp he had left, he felt more dead than alive and was in bed for two days. Five days later, Gus and his dogs began making their way back to his trapline, only to be lost again for twenty days before once more returning to Reliance half-dead.

Gus left Reliance with confidence, and was well supplied with a tent, bedroll, down-filled parka, frying pan, matches, stove, and a "damn sharp axe."[13] He had food for ten days, expecting to be on the trail for six — a reasonable emergency ration, he thought. After five

Photo by Morten Asfeldt.

A whiteout on the Barrens makes finding one's way very difficult. It is easy to see how Gus D'Aoust and others got lost, as they often travelled without maps or compasses.

days of good travelling and fine weather, a fierce blizzard engulfed the Barrens; Gus could see nothing. Complicating the poor visibility was the state of Gus's eyes. He was becoming snow-blind. He could see very little, not enough to even shoot a caribou. Again, for some unknown reason, Gus walked in front of his dogs rather than letting them find the way. Later, Hughie would report that he and George Magrum[14] had found Gus's tracks and followed them for some time but were forced to retreat to their camp due to a blizzard and poor visibility. After twenty days of cold, hunger, snow blindness, and having to kill three of his dogs to keep himself and the other dogs alive, Gus once again wandered into Reliance nearly dead. A few days later, near the end of April, Hughie arrived in Reliance to report Gus missing, only to find his brother exhausted, eyes swollen, and lips frostbitten, but alive. Hughie had no idea that Gus had been twice lost in the last two months. Gus was flown to Edmonton where his right eye was removed and he was fitted with a glass eye. He returned to the Barrens in the fall and had to learn to shoot with his left eye, which he did. Gus was lost again a number of years later, en route from Beaverhill Lake to Reliance, when he again made the mistake of not trusting his lead dog and spent a month roaming the tundra aimlessly before stumbling into Reliance, half-dead, for the third time.

It is difficult to understand why Gus refused to trust his lead dogs, given that for thirty-six years they had led him directly to every trap on his line, even though the traps were often cover by hard windswept snow. Countless times his dogs successfully led him through blinding storms back to camp; the dogs' ability to sniff out old trails, traps, and campsites was remarkable. Gus describes his dogs finding an old campsite while travelling with Phil:

> When we picked up the traps in the spring, usually we would stick the toggle[15] alongside a rock so we could find it the following year if we happened to be trapping there. We were both thinking the same thing, that old campsite wouldn't be very far away. Pretty soon the dogs stopped. We looked around but we couldn't see anything. Then we spotted a stick about a foot high. There was a big snowdrift and the dogs stopped right there and lay down. We started kicking the snow around and sure enough, there was the split wood and a few tent poles. Imagine finding a few armfuls of wood on the tundra.[16]

On another occasion when Gus and Phil were travelling together, their dogs lead them directly to an old trapline that they hadn't used for two years. The dogs stopped on the top of a hill and Phil walked several feet from the sled and found an old toggle. Without their dogs, finding their snow-covered traps on the wind-scoured Barrens would have been impossible.

Trapping was an art, and each trapper had his own quiver of tricks they felt held the secret to success. Gus was no exception. To set a trap, Gus would dig a tunnel in the snow four inches below the surface, insert the toggle, and attach the trap. The trap would be set right on top of the bait and covered with soft snow — this was Gus's trick — and then covered with a two-foot mound of snow. A fox would climb up on the mound and start digging for the bait and "[w]hen they hit that pocket of soft snow, the trap goes off and you've got your fox."[17] In contrast, Phil and Hughie covered their traps with a thick, hard crust of snow. After much cajoling, Gus convinced Phil to try his method. After trying it, Phil exclaimed, "I caught a fox in every trap! The hell with that crust from now on."[18] Once again, Gus had developed his own technique that worked.

Gus and his brothers were among a small handful of white trappers on the Barrens. The first white trapper is said to have been Jack Stark, who trapped around Artillery Lake in 1914. In 1926, it was believed that there were only ten or twelve white trappers in the area.[19] Many of these trappers spent from mid-September to April alone, some trapped with a partner, while George Magrum, a friend of Gus's, trapped with his two sons. For all, the winters were long and isolated. Communication with the "outside" was nearly impossible and they received their last mail in Reliance before heading out in the fall and then not again until Christmas or spring when, with weathered faces and bundles of furs, they returned to Reliance. During the winter they would do their best to be sitting warm and cozy in their camps every Friday night with the radio dialed to CBC, listening to the *Northern Messenger*. Pierre Berton describes the program well:

> Over the ether from Winnipeg, a thousand miles to the south, crackle the brief messages sent out by relatives to men and women in the north, read in flat, unemotional voices by two alternating announcers. The program is heard every Friday night as well as on Christmas Day. The entire north listens in, for it is one of the great bonds that unite the country, a giant party line with ten thousand eavesdroppers.[20]

Gus walked many hurried miles and travelled through blinding storms to be home on Fridays to hear the *Northern Messenger*; sometimes he didn't make it. His mother, his constant supporter, and his sister Toni, had a message for him every Friday and Christmas Day all the years he was on the Barrens. While listening to the program in January 1955, Gus learned that his dear mother had died in October. His sister Toni

Photo by Morten Asfeldt.

Gus D'Aoust's cabin, "Chateau Wolverine," (on the right) and trading post at Reliance.

had dutifully sent a message to be read over the *Northern Messenger*'s airways shortly after her death, but Gus didn't get it; he must have been on the trail.

In 1960, Gus received word from his daughter Rita that Nella had passed away. Two years later Gus married Delphine Lockhart of Fort Franklin, Northwest Territories, who had been raised and educated by nuns in Fort Franklin on Great Bear Lake. She was an expert trapper and could speak five languages. By this time, Phil and Hughie had both moved on from their trapping lives. Gus and Delphine would trap together for three years on the Barrens before retiring to Reliance. Here they lived in Gus's cabin that he had dubbed "Chateau Wolverine," operated a trading post, and did some trapping nearby. Later, they built a number of small cabins and earned a living by taking in tourists, providing them meals, and guiding them on fishing and hunting trips.

One cold November evening in 1973, Gus was making supper when he heard their two dogs whining at the door. Delphine had gone out earlier to check the trapline. When Gus opened the door to investigate, the dogs barked and ran toward the trail leading to the trapline. Gus dressed quickly before commanding the dogs to "Get going! Go find Delphine."[21] Not far from the cabin they found her lying in the snow, paralyzed and disoriented. A plane was summoned from Yellowknife. It landed in the dark in front of their cabin on a makeshift runway of snow and ice lit by toilet paper set ablaze in tin cans. Delphine was flown to Yellowknife where she remained in hospital for nineteen months before dying in 1975.

Gus continued his life in Reliance, taking in tourists in the summer and trapping nearby in the winter. In the fall of 1973, Gus took Roger Catling[22] under his wing and mentored him in the hunting and trapping life. Roger, who now refers to Gus as "old Gus,"[23] remains in Reliance today as the only year-round resident, and has become a renowned wolf hunter. Roger enjoyed his winter with Gus and describes a few fond memories of his mentor:

> He was a character. He was one of these people that just slept when he wanted to. He'd sleep for three hours then get up for an hour or two or three, so the winter I spent with him it was really hard to get any sleep because you couldn't just go to bed and sleep all night. He'd be up at twelve o'clock and he'd make coffee and be up at three o'clock making coffee, and he just loved to tell stories and he always wanted somebody to listen to them so he'd get you up at all hours of the night when you're asleep.[24]

Roger laughs when he recounts how Gus would dream of lions and tigers trying to get him. Roger would wake up and Gus's "feet would just be goin' on the bed, he'd be just runnin'"[25] and Roger would tell him to wake up and Gus would respond, "Oh, this lion was comin' through the window — it just about had me."[26] Roger tells of his time with Gus with great enthusiasm and delight, clearly indicating the profound influence Gus had on his life.

Gus died in January 1990 at the age of ninety-three. In the years before his death he had a number of experiences that made him particularly proud. In 1970, he and Delphine were presented to Queen Elizabeth in Fort Smith as representatives of all northern trappers. Gus recalls thinking that his mother "would have been [the] proudest of them all. Imagine, her little Gus shaking hands with the Queen of England."[27] In 1977, Gus again represented northern trappers by posing to have a bronze bust made of him. The bust now finds its home in the Prince of Wales Northern Heritage Centre in Yellowknife. Finally, Gus was proud to learn that there had been a lake, about seventy-two miles southeast of Reliance, named D'Aoust Lake — an honour bestowed on many trappers from his era.

When Gus first reached Reliance in July 1930 he was "taken by the beauty and splendor of the country."[28] At the time, he didn't realize that Reliance and the Barrens to the east, known by the trappers as "the country,"[29] would become his home until 1974 when "if it weren't for [his] knees, [he] would still be on the trapline."[30] After a lifetime in "the country," he moved to Yellowknife. However, he lived out his last years in Manitoba with his sister Toni. Reflecting on his life, he said,

> "You can't buy happiness and the thrill and experience of hunting and trapping. It's the excitement of it all and the love of a clean life, the peace, the freedom, and the tranquility of the North that attracted me. It's the love I had for the Barren Land, my home. It was like magic, the country became part of me, and I part of the country."[31]

It was Gus's last wish that he join his brother Phil by having his ashes scattered on Whitefish Lake as Phil's had been, in the heart of the Barrenlands, the land they both loved so much and where he realized his trapping dream.

Morten Asfeldt
Camrose, Alberta

Chapter 15

Roger Catling: The Last Wolf Hunter in Reliance

I first met Roger Catling on March 3, 2005. I had heard of him for many years from people who had visited Reliance or paddled the upper Thelon River where he trapped in the 1970s and 1980s. I don't remember what preconceived image I held, but it didn't match with my experience when we met that cold and sunny day on the ice of McLeod Bay.

Kristen Olesen, who lives twelve miles away at the mouth of the Hoarfrost River,[1] and I had come by skidoo to visit Roger after confirming by HF radio that he was home. The skidoo we were using was past its prime, and we wanted to be sure he would come looking for us if we hadn't arrived by early afternoon as planned. As we neared Reliance, I was surprised by another skidoo coming toward us — it was Roger. He met us half a mile or so from his home, and I was immediately struck by how big a man he was. Roger was fully dressed for winter, with thick snow pants, a big down parka with a fur ruff around the hood, and wore huge boots that made him five or six inches taller. A rifle was slung across his back in a well-travelled canvas case. He towered above my five-foot-eight-inch frame as I extended my hand to greet him. Roger had come to meet us to be sure that we avoided the thin ice in the narrows that separate McLeod and Charlton bays.

Reliance was once an active community and gathering place. Built on the west end of Fairchild Point, it is at the extreme eastern reach of Great Slave Lake and was the last settlement for trappers striking out over Pike's Portage and onto the Barrens in the first half of the twentieth century. When trappers returned from the Barrens, it was their first opportunity to trade furs, to resupply their grubstake, and to engage in conversation after months of solitude. As the crow flies, it is approximately 170 miles west to Yellowknife, close to fifty miles west and a bit south of Lutsel K'e, nine miles east to Old Fort Reliance[2] at the mouth of the Lockhart River, and six miles southeast to the foot of Pike's Portage.

Today, Reliance is a ghost town most of the year. The weather station built by the military in 1946 is now automated, leaving an empty two-storey wooden house that resembles a typical early Canadian prairie home with its box-like appearance and small enclosed porch on one side. A larger industrial metal warehouse is rusting with age and scheduled for demolition, and the weather information is now transmitted to far-off places from a modest metal tower reaching from the height of land. Further along the shore and slightly set back from the beach is a modern fishing lodge built of logs with large, peaked windows facing west. Surrounding the lodge is a collection of red and white buildings that were once an RCMP post, built in the 1920s. Today, the former jail is a convenience store selling chips, chocolate bars, pop, a variety of fishing tackle, and a sparse selection of non-perishable food during the short summer fishing season. Other buildings serve as sleeping quarters for guests and lodge staff, while one inconspicuous old log cabin farther back from the beach houses a collection of old dog harnesses, skis, snowshoes, dog bowls with names on them, fishing nets, and other items from Reliance's storied past.

Reliance is divided by Police Bay, with the weather station, the old RCMP post, and the fishing lodge set on the south side of the bay. On the north side of the bay, Gus D'Aoust[3] — one of the last professional trappers in the region — built his cabin and later a trading post. These two buildings remain today with sagging roofs, loose floorboards, and timbers grey from sun, wind, and snow, which the storm-driven winds now easily blow through. Also on the north side is Roger's home, the

Photo by Morten Asfeldt.

Roger Catling's house in Reliance is perched on the western tip of the Fairchild Peninsula.

only dwelling where smoke rises from the chimney between September and June.

After our tour of Reliance, my first visit with Roger began with tea at his kitchen table beside a big south-facing window that overlooks Charlton Bay. Roger sat closest to the window on a bit of an angle, allowing him to see out over Charlton Bay and west through the living room window toward the stately cliffs of the Kahochella Peninsula. We entered the house through an unusually large door opposite the south-facing kitchen window. Inside, on the left, there was a large workbench covered with a variety of engine parts, and straight ahead were a large water tank and washing machine. To the right was a long wall broken up by several bedroom doorways and a few wolf hides that stretched from ceiling to floor. As well, there were strange wooden slates on the floor that resembled miniature railway ties extending in from the door. I had to ask: Why the slates on the floor? Roger explained that he keeps his skidoo inside to allow for the quick pursuit of nearby wolves. The slates provide traction for the skidoo to ensure a speedy exit. The big door now made sense. Roger and I visited for several hours that day and he enthusiastically talked about his life and wolf hunting. This was the first of many visits.

As with many people who live in the North, there was an element of chance and circumstance that brought Roger to Reliance. As a child he had lived in Vancouver and Winnipeg before his father, a meteorologist, joined the Canadian Forces so that he and his family could live in Europe. They spent four years in Belgium and Germany before returning to Canada where they spend three years in Toronto before moving to Whitehorse and then on to Yellowknife. While in Yellowknife, his father was responsible for the weather station in Reliance, providing improved weather information and forecasting for the growing northern air industry.

In the early 1970s, Roger was studying biology at the University of Alaska in Fairbanks. In the summer of 1973, he came to Reliance at the request of the weather station's cook who wanted Roger to replace the engine in his cabin cruiser. As Roger talked about that first summer, he commented, "I was looking for a place like this. It was the perfect place. I just never left."[4] That was thirty-six years ago — the good part of a lifetime.

Roger has an astonishing knowledge of the geography and history of the area, including the East Arm of Great Slave Lake, the Barrens to the north and east, and the upper reaches of the Thelon River. The ease at which he describes specific valleys, rivers, eskers, old cabin sites, and hunting grounds reflects the intimate knowledge and personal relationship he has developed with this vast wilderness that has been his home range. Roger is among a very small, and decreasing, number of people with such profound knowledge of this remote landscape.

Back in 1973, once the cabin cruiser's engine was repaired and fall started to grip the land, Roger had decided to stay for the winter. He never did go back to complete his university education. At that time, Gus D'Aoust was still living in Reliance, and Roger received an invaluable mentorship while he lived and trapped with Gus that winter. Gus had been trapping in the region since 1930 and was by then in his late seventies. It would be Gus's last winter of trapping.

Roger's account of his time with Gus makes it clear that he holds his mentor in high esteem. In fact, Roger's son is named after him. That winter, the winter of 1973–74, Roger and Gus trapped around Reliance, travelling by dog team as they set and checked their traps. Gus had always used dogs to get around, but at that time skidoos were becoming popular, though, as Roger says, "they didn't amount to much." Roger brought a skidoo out with him in 1973 but later traded it with a fellow from Lutsel K'e for a dog team. He used dogs for his hunting and trapping until the winter of 1977–78 when he rented his team to a group of young men who spent the winter at Warden's Grove in the Thelon Wildlife Sanctuary.[5] By this time skidoos had improved considerably, and Roger never had a working dog team again.

During his first winter in Reliance, Roger met and married Theresa, daughter of Noel Drybones, a Dene man who had lived and trapped in the region for many years.[6] In the fall of 1974, Roger and Theresa made their way over Pike's Portage to Acres Lake and onto Barrenslands Lake en route to Beaverhill Lake[7] where they refurbished one of Gus's old cabins and trapped for the winter. During that winter they found a location for a home with a bountiful wood supply. They built a cabin and lived there for twelve years, at a widening of the Thelon River southwest of Beaverhill Lake, which they named Double Barrel Lakes. I visited this cabin in the summer of 1995.

The cabin sits back from a long, sandy beach facing east, overlooking Double Barrel Lakes. Along the beach and around the cabin, caribou antlers were scattered about. Peering in through a window, I could see that it had been home for Roger and his family for many years. However, it was also clear that nobody was home. Wide strips of plywood surrounded the cabin with nails driven up through them at close intervals. Likewise, the door was covered by plywood with the nails pointing directly at any would-be intruder. This moat of rusty nails and grey weathered plywood was Roger's defence against bears in his absence. As I walked around the cabin and wandered briefly through the surrounding forest I tried to envision Roger's life out here on the edge of the Barrens, especially in winter. It was a life so far removed from my own that I lacked the ability to gain any sort of vision. The life seemed unimaginable. It was in this cabin that Roger and Theresa raised and home-schooled their two daughters, Jessica and Susan.[8]

For the first few years that Roger and Theresa trapped on the Thelon River, they trapped primarily white fox. This is what Gus had trapped most of his life and what Roger knew best. However, after the first few

Photo by Morten Asfeldt.

Roger Catling's cabin on the Thelon River, where he and Theresa lived for many years, displays the nail-studded plywood used to prevent bears from damaging their cabin.

years, the price of white fox pelts plummeted and they had to focus on other furbearers to provide a sustainable living. It was then that Roger began hunting wolves.

In the mid to late 1970s, a wolf pelt sold for a handsome price of about four hundred Canadian dollars, the equivalent to $1,645 in 2008.[9] Roger and Theresa made a good living and could afford to live on the Thelon, chartering planes to bring in supplies, regularly replacing skidoos, and enjoying a few luxuries of life. In fact, in 1978, Roger bought a Super Cub — a small two-seater airplane — that made getting to and from their remote home much easier. In the late 1980s, Roger upgraded to a bigger Cessna 180, but because of falling fur prices, owned it for only a short time.

Today, a wolf pelt brings Roger between two hundred and 250 Canadian dollars. A large white wolf in prime condition may sell for up to four hundred dollars, but those are rare. To put this in context, in the 1970s, a Twin Otter aircraft (which can carry about three thousand pounds of cargo) could be chartered from Yellowknife to Reliance for about six hundred dollars — the revenue from less than two wolf pelts. Today, that same charter costs close to five thousand dollars — the revenue from more than twenty wolf pelts. As Roger says, "in the early days we didn't think twice about calling for a plane to bring skidoo parts, gas, food, or other supplies from town." Today, it is rare that a chartered plane lands on Charlton Bay in front of Roger's home. I have heard Roger talk for several years about how precarious his life in Reliance is; he seems to be approaching a crossroads with no clear direction for the future.

Most years, Roger and Theresa would make their annual move from Reliance to Double Barrel Lakes in September, flying dogs, skidoos, fuel, food, and other sundry supplies by charter plane and later by Roger's own plane. In September, the dwarf birch, bearberry, and cranberry turned the landscape into a rich pre-winter flood of colour — deep reds and yellows mixed with the last hints of summer green — a final celebration of sorts before the monotonous grey and white and darkness of winter. During this time, Roger and Theresa would prepare for winter: putting up wood, hunting moose and caribou for meat, and repairing equipment. The hunting and trapping started in November, when the furs became prime, and continued until April. For a brief period at Christmas, they would generally return to Reliance to be with family and friends. They also spent the summers in Reliance, preparing furs and enjoying a more relaxed life.

In the late 1980s, when the expenses of hunting and trapping from the remote Thelon River became more than their trapping income could bear, they moved to Reliance. Once settled, they built a cabin at Rat Lodge on Artillery Lake, about fifty miles northwest over Pike's Portage, which they would use for short periods throughout the winter, giving them access to the Barrens and increasing their hunting and trapping range.

I have heard that no one knows wolves as Roger does. He is among a small handful of people whose livelihood is largely dependent on the sale of wolf pelts. To be successful as a wolf hunter requires a great deal of knowledge, skill, and commitment; it is not an easy life. Each morning from November to April, Roger wanders a half mile or so from his house to a lookout point where he can see the great expanse of McLeod Bay. From here, he scans the lake for wolves. When he sees a wolf, or a pack

Photo by Morten Asfeldt.

Roger Catling's cabin on Artillery Lake is found on a spit of sand that connects the shore to the fabled Rat Lodge.

of wolves, he first tries to determine what they are doing — feeding on a carcass, pursuing caribou, or simply travelling about. He then jumps on his skidoo, sled in tow and rifle slung across his back, knowing he has limited time to get within firing range before the wolves reach the safety of the forested shore. The skidoo often bounces over the windswept ice where the snow has been transformed into an endless sea of rock-hard snowdrifts, a pursuit that can loosen every joint in his body. Once close to the wolf, he gets off his skidoo, slides his rifle off his back and pulls it from its sheath. He then takes quick but careful aim in order to hit the wolf that is now running full-tilt away from him and closing in on the shore with every passing second. Once the wolf is dead, the real work begins. If time allows, Roger will skin the wolf on the spot and finish preparing the hide once back home. If he has killed several wolves, he may have time to skin one, two at most, before the rest are too frozen to skin effectively. In this case, the frozen wolves are bought home and stored frozen until he has time to bring them into the house, thaw them out, and skin them. This all happens just inside the big door next to the workbench and water tank. Once skinned, the hide is rinsed in the washing machine to remove the blood, urine, and excrement that commonly foul it. Next, the hide must be fleshed to remove any remaining flesh and fat. This requires a combination of cutting and pounding. Roger's favoured tool for this work is the femur bone from a moose[10] cut at a forty-five-degree angle — the same tool Native people used for centuries. The paws are not skinned in the field so this must be done at home — this is delicate work that takes time. At one time, Miranda Casaway, Roger's second wife, would skin the paws because she could complete the task much faster than Roger and with better results; Roger loathes this fine work.

Once the wolf is fleshed and paws skinned, the hide goes back into the washing machine and is washed with detergent and rinsed with a fabric softener to give it a pleasant smell and make it easier to brush. Once out of the washing machine, the hide is immediately brushed, bullet and knife holes sewn up, and then stretched. The hide remains on the stretcher for twenty-four hours and is then removed, brushed again, then stretched for another twenty-four to forty-eight hours before being ready for auction. It is critical that the hides are absolutely dry so that they don't rot before shipping. Drying requires that extra care be taken to turn the ears inside out — the most common place for rot.

Many fur auction houses recognize Roger for his excellence in pelt preparation and consistent supply of high-quality wolf pelts. In fact, at the Fur Harvesters Auction in Winnipeg, Roger's pelts are put up for auction as a separate collection referred to as the Catling Collection.[11] In addition, Roger has often been called upon throughout the Northwest Territories to host workshops where he shares his pelt preparation knowledge and techniques.[12] He also collaborates with the Northwest Territories Department of Renewable Resources biologists, who fly to Reliance each spring and fill a Twin Otter with skinned and frozen wolf carcasses that they take back to their labs in Yellowknife where they are used in a variety of research projects.

Since 2005, I have been taking students to the East Arm of Great Slave Lake in February as a part of a university course. On a number of occasions we have had the opportunity to witness Roger skinning a wolf; a process that students curiously gather around to watch.

Roger first pulls the wolf from his sled. Even as a big man, grabbing the limp wolf by all four legs and lifting it onto the snow takes considerable

Photo by Morten Asfeldt.

Roger Catling skins a wolf for Augustana students.

effort. While in the sled, Roger wraps the wolf in an old quilted blanket, bloodstained from many years of use, to keep the wolf from freezing before skinning. With the wolf on its back and Roger straddling it, he first makes a cut in the underside of the jaw and splits the lower lip, allowing him to peel back the hide, exposing the bone and muscle of the lower jaw and neck. Roger then turns around, now straddling the wolf facing the tail, and extends the cut back the length of wolf. Stepping to one side, he gets down on his knees while holding a front leg in his left hand. He splits open the hide along the back side of the leg from the wrist all the way to his first cut along the midsection of the wolf. With a combination of pulling with his left hand and smooth, effortless knife-strokes with his right, the hide is removed. However, in order to leave the paws intact for skinning at home, he quickly and with great precision, cuts the tendons and ligaments that hold the wrist joint together. Once they are cut, he grabs either side of the joint and breaks it in one quick and routine motion that is accompanied by a distinct and surprising sound of ripping and cracking as the joint comes apart. The students' response is immediate and vocal. The skinless broken leg of the wolf is now fully exposed. After all four legs are skinned, Roger removes the hide from one complete side before rolling the wolf over and removing it from the opposite side. In the process, he removes the hide from the head. Once again, with a series of smooth and effortless knife-strokes the large powerful cheek muscles are exposed. They are deep red and were once a source of great force. A moment later, a few slow and carefully placed knife cuts reveal an eye that now holds a blank and empty stare. Until now, it has been just a carcass, but looking into the eye surrounded only by steaming red flesh, I found myself feeling uncomfortable and looking away. With what I knew from reading and local biologists, I was aware that Roger's wolf hunting is not threatening the local wolf population. And, while I had hunted and killed moose and caribou as a teenager, I nevertheless began to rethink the practice of killing for fur.

Even so, to watch Roger skin a wolf is to watch a master craftsman at work; in some ways, it is like watching a superb athletic performance or listening to an inspired musical recital. At times a shy and reserved man, there is new life in his eyes and confidence in his voice as he demonstrates his trade and talks about his life. It is clear that he takes great pride in his life as a wolf hunter. Although we experience emotionally difficult moments as we watch this skinning process, and while there are few clear answers to some of the questions that arise from it, the experience spurs an engaged and thoughtful discussion among the students. Time and again, it causes them to revisit and rethink a number of fundamental assumptions and attitudes about hunting and trapping, as well as more global aspects of human–nature relationships. Without careful and respectful consideration of Roger and of wolves, it is as easy to be highly critical as it is to be naively romantic.

In spite of the questions that watching Roger skin a wolf raises, he is a likeable man and his life is an uncommon one that is difficult to fully imagine. Combine this with the iconic and mystical nature of wolves, portrayed over centuries as creators and helpers, as symbols of evil, and now as icons of all things wild,[13] and Roger emerges as an intriguing man who leads a life that presents a confusing mass of contradictions.

One the one hand, Roger has a great respect for wolves and on the other hand, he kills them. However, as he says himself, "I just hunt wolves. I've never had anything against wolves. I like them. It wouldn't be

Roger Catling with his son, Gus, and daughter, Winnie, at the back door of their Reliance home in April 2009.

much of a country out here without the wolf. We can hear them howling all the time. It's pretty spectacular." It is a difficult tension to reconcile. Nevertheless, this tension may not be unique to Roger's life. Perhaps it is a tension in all our lives, though hidden under many layers of modern technology and decades of living far-removed from the natural world for most of us. Perhaps Roger's life, with the realities and tensions facing him daily, is the honest life. To make his living he does the killing, the skinning, the fleshing, and the sewing of holes made by his modern rifle, while we urban dwellers have nameless living beings anonymously killed for us while never having to look into a dying eye or see the last steam rise from a cooling carcass. While this realization doesn't remove the tension in Roger's life, it provides an appreciation for the honesty and authenticity of the hunter and trapper's life.

There are other tensions in Roger's life, too. Aside from losing his first wife to cancer in 1995, Roger recently lost his second wife in an unexpected tragedy. Roger is now alone with his two young children, Winnie and Gus, while trying to make a living as a wolf hunter in a poor fur market. This is complicated by the need for home-schooling, the long days needed for hunting and preparing hides — a task that often drags into July — coupled with an array of factors associated with living in the remoteness of the far east end of Great Slave Lake. For most of the year, their closest neighbours are twelve miles across McLeod Bay. In a recent conversation, Roger expressed his fear that "his days in Reliance are numbered."[14] I cannot imagine the loss that Roger must feel when he contemplates "moving to town" and leaving behind the lifestyle and place that has been his home for most of his life. As I try to imagine what Roger might be feeling, images of prairie farmers being forced from their family farms and pushed to find work "in town" and Newfoundland fisherman having to hang up their nets, beach their boats, and make a life for themselves "on shore" come to mind. Roger and his children face a difficult crossroads that may mark the end of a hunting and trapping era that extends back to the early twentieth century and beyond.

Morten Asfeldt
Camrose, Alberta

Chapter 16

North of Reliance[1]

In 1987, when I was thirty years old, I moved to the silence and severity of this place. I was looking for a new standpoint, a life more difficult and more direct. Amidst this dramatic beauty and pristine integrity, this opposition of power and fragility, I have not found precisely what I came seeking, but neither am I now the same person who first moved north to search. The place has changed me, as I suspected it would, and is changing me still.

My track was not direct from the pastures and moraines of Illinois to the cliffs around McLeod Bay. I came north and west in stages, by way of a two-year stay in Montana and a ten-year stopover in Minnesota and Wisconsin. Even in those waypoints my bent was obvious — the border lakes of Minnesota and the high country of Montana are provinces of the North. Duluth and Missoula are border towns. Upward from them, whether in altitude or latitude, one enters another country: spruce trees, trout lakes, mosquitoes, forty-below nights, bare granite, sled dogs. The northern fringe of the Midwest States straddles the great Canadian Shield. In fact, more than half of all Canadians live in cities farther south than Ashland, Wisconsin.

Dave Olesen resting while out on the trail in April 2009.

In the summer of 1980 I was twenty-two years old. With my friend and mentor Duncan Storlie, I arrived on a little lake outside of Ely, Minnesota. We pitched a tipi on a high bare ridge and began to build a log cabin on a forty-acre parcel of second-growth poplar. On a spur of smooth bedrock out in front of the tipi we passed long summer evenings around a small fire. Our muscles ached from the day's lessons with chainsaw, drawknife, and green logs. We laughed often, and that summer I fell in love for the first time — with a woman, briefly, and with a way of life, forever. As freeze-up came on and the snow fell, I moved from the tipi indoors to the snug cabin we had built. Duncan left for the Twin Cities, and with a handful of sled dogs for companions I began to live full-time in the north woods.

For the next three years Stump Lake was my home. I see now that those years were my apprenticeship. I learned to net fish and hunt animals, learned about sled dogs and wood stoves and root cellars. I learned, too, about isolation, solitude, and loneliness. The cabin was only a mile or so from the nearest road, and on summer evenings I could hear traffic in the distance, but being at the far end of a rough, indistinct trail introduced me to a frame of mind that has since become all too familiar. I passed my days alone at Stump in a mood of constant anticipation, craving visitors and conversation as fiercely as I craved solitude and silence.

Chapter 16

Photo by Morten Asfeldt.

The Olesen's Hoarfrost River homestead as it looked in February 2006.

From Stump Lake I could envision a life farther north. I could make a leap of imagination and trust that it was at least partly accurate. On annual trips to the Subarctic I fleshed out my visions of the Far North, always returning to the little cabin and to the various jobs I held during those years — guiding, woodcutting, and pumping fuel at the local airport. Year by year my starry-eyed infatuation with log-cabin life was tempered by its realities, yet I remained in love with it as the lessons built upon each other.

Having served my apprenticeship in the north woods of Minnesota, in July of 1987 I arrived on the east end of McLeod Bay again, but this time I arrived to stay. My father had accompanied me on an unforgettable father-son odyssey in two dilapidated pickup trucks, with all of my worldly possessions, including nineteen sled dogs. In quiet amazement he set about helping me move my things and animals ashore from the freighting boat we had chartered, and then he helped clean out the interior of the cabin that would be my first home at the Hoarfrost. We spent a long second morning in the heat of summer, carrying piles of broken glass, cardboard boxes, dirty diapers, and spent 30/30 cartridges from the interior of my dream home. The cabin had been used only in passing by a few hunters and trappers. Another father-son pair, eastbound by canoe, stayed with us for a few days and helped fashion some small windows to light the dark room. We cut trees and built crude shore ramps for boats and planes, chinked the cabin's walls with homemade mortar, staked out my dogs, and strung a radio antenna. Everything we did felt immediate and necessary; there weren't enough hours in the day. We worked from dawn to dusk, which even in early August here yields a solid sixteen hours or more.

After two weeks, my father left — he was a high-school teacher and classes were soon to start. I awoke in a sleeping bag on the floor of the cabin the next morning, alone at the place I had held in my mind for so long. This was not Stump Lake. I could not hear any cars in the distance.

That initial flurry of frantic activity took years to wind down. It still returns at certain seasons, and I dash around the place repairing, refining, gathering, building, and provisioning. During those times there is little contemplation of motives. The demands and preparations and improvements fill entire days.

I had learned years ago, though, at the little cabin on Stump, that at least one popular notion of rustic log-cabin life is mistaken. As seasons pass, one's days are less filled with mundane, repetitive tasks. The daily chores, which dilettantes and visitors imagine to be so all-consuming — splitting wood, hauling water, feeding dogs — are nothing. I am certain that I spend no more time working to heat my home, for instance, than does anyone who lives in a bungalow in Yellowknife or Duluth. My work is direct, with saw and sled and axe; that other person's work is at a job, where hour by hour they earn the cash that buys their heat. It all works out at least even, and I enjoy the afternoons I spend up the hill north of the homestead, cutting and stacking wood alongside the trails so we can stop the dogs near the end of a training run and load the sled. I would not happily sell those hours in order to purchase my warmth.

My apprenticeship is done, but I am still a journeyman here. Mastery lies somewhere ahead, or so I hope. Mastery will be making a living here, and making a good life of it. As Annie Dillard wrote in *The Writing Life*,

"There is no shortage of good days. It is good lives that are hard to come by."[2] I am unsure of the specifics of the living that can be made here. There is a new course to be charted.

I generate more questions than answers. I came here with no burning desire to escape, to shut myself away and turn my back on civilization. Such notions creep into my thoughts more frequently now, seven years into this, than they ever did at the outset. At times I see there is no choice. Even in the age of two-way radio and Twin Otter turboprops, sheer distance and contrast and day-to-day concerns cut us off completely from society at large. But when I feel myself leaning too far toward the outlook of the hermit, toward notions of "just me and the missus and my AK-47," as Bill McKibben once described the credo of survivalists, I draw back in suspicion. That is the deadest of dead ends.

We do our share of old-fashioned, outmoded pioneering as we attempt to make a home in this wilderness. With axe and chainsaw and shovel, wheelbarrow and dynamite, gillnet and rifle, we have established our place here. We have changed the character of this beach and these woods, cut new trails through these hills, fed and housed and clothed ourselves. We cut, kill, burn, and harvest our way through the years, just like the rest of humanity.

Life here now is a parade of paradox. Timeless arctic tools and scenes are daily juxtaposed with the latest gadgets: a team of huskies pulls up alongside a sleek snowmobile; the shimmering diaphanous veil of the aurora borealis is bisected by the strobe lights of a Boeing 747. Sand and Styrofoam, birch and polyethylene.

There are signs, there are stories, and there is imagination. When I spent the summer of 1983 camped down the bay, alone much of the time with my ten dogs, I repeatedly conjured up an illusion. It was quite real, and I let myself indulge in it. I would see, usually in the obliquely angled light of late evening, a small bent figure watching me from the crest of a rock island, or peering out through the stunted spruce on the shoreline. Imagination filled in details: his face was wrinkled, darkened and pinched by years of frost, smoke, sun, and hunger: his clothes were skins, dirty cotton, and ragged wool; puckered moosehide moccasins were on his feet; his hair was thin and white. Old timer, boy.

He is the old one, the one I've not known here. Alaska poet John Haines had old Fred Campbell and others, his neighbours in Alaska when he first arrived to homestead along the Tanana.[3] Back in northern Minnesota I knew several old-timers, among them Bill Magie, who'd been around "since Christ was a cowboy," guiding, surveying, flying, and mining. Bill's stories and his detailed memory of that land and its lakes filled in blanks in my own geography; knowing him helped me to better and more quickly come to know the country.[4]

Here it has been different. In the late seventies the grand old man of Reliance, Gus D'Aoust, went away for good, his eyesight failing and his knee joints giving out after more than fifty years of trapping, trading, and hunting. He was gone before I arrived.

Louison Drybones was the last of the Chipewyan Barrenland trappers to depend on a dog team. Late in that summer of 1983 I had a fleeting opportunity to join him, to go out to his trapping grounds as his green sidekick and spend the autumn with him at Williams Lake. He wanted a partner, being in his seventies then and having had a colostomy, and none of the Native fellows from Snowdrift were inclined to join him. But I called Minnesota from the radiotelephone station in Reliance and was told that I still had a job waiting for me. I went dutifully south at the start of September and I never met Louison, who, like Gus, had died by the time I moved to the Territories. I will always muse over that lost opportunity, and wonder what insights and lessons I might have gleaned in that remote autumn.

The peers of Louison and Gus are gone, as well. The younger Natives that pass this way now come roaring through, always bound somewhere in a rush, astride gleaming skidoos or hurtling down the lake, pushed by the latest outboards. A bit baffled by our ongoing efforts here, they stop by to borrow something or to spend the night. Their elders have all moved to town, taking their memories and knowledge with them.

I talk with my handful of non-Native cohorts, but not one of us living out here is over fifty years old (alas, not true as I revise these excerpts!), and we are all from somewhere else. All that we have seen for ourselves is the latest drawn-out decline of what has gone on here. This has been a land of transient lives, of boom and bust, of forays and temporary establishments. I sometimes find myself adopting the local parlance and referring to our home here as our "camp," as if tomorrow or the day after we might pull it all down, pack it up, and head off. The canoe that hangs on the back wall of the little cabin seems to announce that possibility.

I crave a history. I want to weave myself and my own story into the ongoing terse narrative of this place, a narrative I can only dimly discern. I hungrily gather whatever fragments, glimpses, and signs I can find, in order to patch together a backdrop for my own years here.

The country is full of vague leavings. Old camps in ruins, traps hung in trees, rock cairns on tundra hilltops, the ancient remains of a bark canoe in the moss alongside a secluded cove. Old axe-cuts or blazes on spruce trunks lead up small drainages and outline the perimeters of some forgotten prospector's claims. Crystalline sap, brittle and bitter, is congealed over the old wounds in the bark. I wander the hills and try to flesh out old splinters of bone, metal, and wood. I circle my plane over the twisted wreckage of a by-gone crash. I rummage through the archives and read the words of Hearne, Seton, Pike, Anderson, and Ingstad.

Things surface. Out feeding the dogs one summer night, I found a trade-axe head, crudely cast and crimped in an archaic style at least 150 years old. Esker, a wolf I once raised from a pup, had uncovered it as she dug a cool place to lie in the moist sand. Her burrow was almost two feet deep, and the small axe-handle lay on top of her pile of diggings. On the wall in the kitchen hangs a weathered paddle blade, cedar and narrow in the style of the fur-trade voyageurs. It, too, I found in the sand on the beach here. Up the hill beyond our cabin is an old grave, a small rectangle sunk into the ground, with shards of carefully carved spruce along its outline. A Native child must be buried there.

To move through a wild land and know nothing of its human history would be an impoverishment. An understanding of the past enables a clearer appreciation of the present. In a time of rapid change, historical perspective can help to place that change in context. I gain a fresh outlook on the present whenever I deliberately set out to do something the old, outmoded way: to sail a canoe; to steam and bend a wooden dogsled runner; to read a sextant; to make a basket from birchbark or a fire without matches.

In learning archaic skills, in looking back, one must be careful. That historical perspective, especially in the wilderness and along a frontier, can all too easily become a fuzzy and simplistic nostalgia. Like any rigid doctrine, a blind belief that the old ways were better, that other times and people were better, is shallow. To think that one was "born too late," that one's own culture is completely trivialized, polluted, and destructive, provides no clear vision and slim hope of happiness. Tempting as that line of thinking may be, it does not lead to the lesson I am trying to learn from old blazes, from history. I want to move forward down the trail, even blaze new trails, but I want to keep clear the view back over my shoulder, to remember where I came from, and to learn what journeys through this place have been like for others.

As seasons pass, the history of this place includes us, whether or not we take notice of or strive for that inclusion. The blazes we see up in the countless small drainages north and east of here are now more likely to be our own than anyone else's. We skim our own history as the dogs tow us along a familiar trail; there's where I got that damned skidoo bogged down in slush and nearly froze my toes; there's where we camped and saw the muskox tracks; that flat is where the cabin logs came from. I have a rare chance to date precisely the signs of a people's activities on the land: here's what a blaze on a spruce trunk looks like after a year, after three, after seven (and now, after twenty-two) … I know exactly how old most of those blazes immediately northeast of here are, because I cut nearly all of them.

I have not seen the old one lately. My first years here have been a flurry of work and activity, with most of my days dominated by immediate concerns and preoccupations. I have drifted, I think inevitably, from the contemplative and receptive frame of mind which, in that initial summer of exploration, helped me to conjure the old timer's image.

Perhaps — and this is my hope these years — I can over time circle back to that more receptive and visionary stance. If I do, I trust that my glimpses of the old one will revive. The sight of him will then be more empathetic, more understanding and appreciative, than those first encounters. I will have tasted by then some parallels of his own seasons in the North; hard and easy years, weeks and months both lean and plentiful. I might even by then have gained some measure of respect in his wizened gaze.

Given even more time — decades, or a lifetime — my own doings here, my flesh and bone, kin and offspring may meld with the land. In some distant year I may peer out from the shadows myself. Some lingering part of me may watch, bemused and a bit skeptical, as some starry-eyed new arrival cuts a first tentative blaze into the bark of a spruce tree.

As I read these passages from *North of Reliance* today, I find, surprisingly enough, that for the most part they still ring true for me. Today, writing this and looking at these passages, I am windbound on a caribou-research flying job based in Gameti, a small Native settlement about halfway between Yellowknife and Great Bear Lake. The Hoarfrost River is still home, and has been for nearly twenty-one years since that July described above. I have lived there longer than I have lived in any other place in my life. I call there each morning when I am away, and talk on the internet-linked radiotelephone phone with Kristen — my wife of twenty years now — or to one of our two daughters, now thirteen and ten years old.

My father is gone, my kid sister also — there are places around the homestead that call each of them so clearly to mind. Lawrence, one of our closest Native friends, died suddenly in a tragic accident just a few weeks ago. His brother Joseph is at our place now, gathering his strength and biding his time after the loss of his brother. Even the old Grampa tree that I long admired at the top of the sand flat a mile north of our home is dead, as of just this past summer. It has long been the patriarch of that piece of woods, its top broken off years ago by lightning or wind, a few green tendrils still showing that it was somehow clinging to life, year after year. I joked for more than ten years with my daughters and my wife that the old Grampa tree and I were having a race — "first one to die, loses." Now we talk of cutting it this coming spring, to make some appropriate use of its magnificent girth. Perhaps it will turn out to be all rotted inside — we won't know until we do it. Like many other big white

Photo by Kristen Olesen.

(Above) The Olesen daughters, Annika (age thirteen) and Liv (age ten), pose with their dogs, Shade and Bone, in 2009.

(Left) Kristen Olesen in 2006 wearing an anorak that she made herself, trimmed with local fur.

spruce on south-facing sandy slopes around here, Gramps was almost certainly more than a hundred years old when George Back wintered at the mouth of the Lockhart. Life goes on.

The human history of the North's wild backcountry continues its odd evolution. It is home to fewer humans now than at any time since the last ice age. The weather station at Reliance is boarded up and automated and the younger generation of Natives at Lutsel K'e seems more and more focused on parts of the world other than their ancestral homeland. There is sporadic talk of a national park for the area, with some momentous consequences for those of us who have chosen to live here.

Life in a place like the east end of McLeod Bay can seem timeless, because at first glance so few things visibly change. But change does come. I think this is the biggest lesson I take from my two-decade stint at the Hoarfrost: Change. We now see muskox in large herds right at the beach between our buildings and the mouth of the river. If, in 1989, you had told any of us out here that in 2009 there would be a herd of forty muskox grazing the shore of McLeod Bay a stone's throw from the mouth of the Hoarfrost River, none of us would have believed it.

The country changes. It is always changing. This is one of the lessons I never saw coming. The politicians who talk of "stopping climate change" may as well talk of stopping the sunrise, for the one thing that is constant in the universe is change. We cannot afford to forget that, willy-nilly, the climate will change.

But I digress. Suffice it to say that we are still out here. We are still happy and our eyes are still wide open most days, though on some days we seem to be afflicted by a tunnel vision brought on by our own choices: home-school French lessons, Transport Canada regulations for our little air service, Revenue Canada tax returns … the computer spouting the latest inbox full of email or perhaps the nearly instant replay of the Kentucky Derby on YouTube … (And who could possibly turn away from the image of Calvin Borel on Street Sense, coming up the rail like a locomotive to take the roses in 2007? Certainly not I.) And we watched it — my girls and my wife and I, shrieking and moved to tears, right there in our log house at the mouth of the Hoarfrost River! "Whodathunkit?" as a musher friend of mine likes to say. John Hornby would be dumbfounded, along with old Gus, and George, and Helge, and Noel, Warburton and Louison, and all the rest.

Meanwhile, back at the Gameti Motel.... The wind will ease up and tomorrow, or the next day, we will finish our work and I will fly back home. We are short of firewood at this point in the winter — that, at least, never does seem to change. So, I will hitch up the dogs and go cut some — that free and easy privilege in this day and age is a rare and wonderful gift. The other day I was cutting standing dead spruce with the bow saw, and I suddenly realized I was cutting in a little group of trees where I had cut twenty-one years earlier, in the spring of 1988. I remembered the day, and thus I knew that the trees I was cutting had died in the interim, or I would have taken them back then. Nature provides and provides. (And with that he climbed down from the soapbox.)

Dave Olesen
Hoarfrost River, Northwest Territories

Part V

Epilogue

We are attached to place and long for freedom. What begins as undifferentiated space becomes place as we get to know it and endow it with value.[1]

— Yi-Fu Tuan, *Space and Place: The Perspective of Experience*, 1977

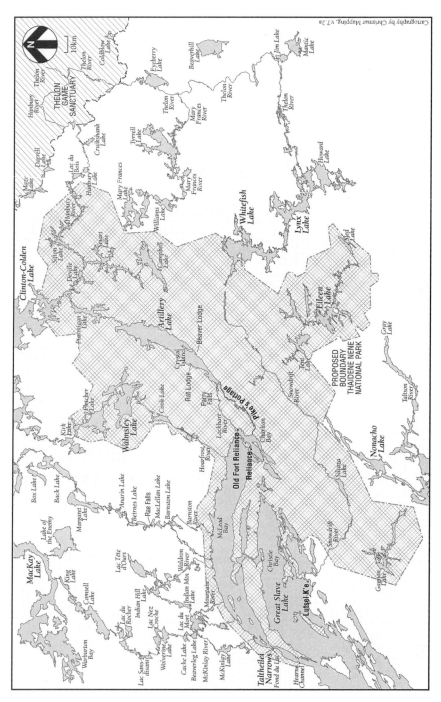

Map 7. Proposed New National Park Boundary.

Chapter 17

Thaidene Nene: The Land of the Ancestors

Portages are more than trails. They connect otherwise inaccessible points and sustain vital connections between them. As the experienced northern traveller knows, the portage is also a place where one's burdens must be shouldered, if the journey is to continue.

Canada's boreal region has been traversed in this manner for thousands of years, and the land is little changed for it. The signs of our passing — lob sticks, blazes on trees, campfire pits, and tent rings, and the narrow track worn through the carpets of caribou moss and Labrador tea — endure, renewed through the countless generations by each traveller in their turn. But in much of the rest of the world, footsteps have not been so light. In the time since the glaciers receded from Great Slave Lake to the present — a mere instant in geological terms — our planet has been radically transformed by human activity. There are few places left where the relationships between people and environment continue intact and unimpaired.

Canada's boreal is one of those places. Representing more than a third of the remaining originally forested landscapes left on Earth, and nearly all of North America's remaining original forest,[1] it has rightly become a

Photo by Morten Asfeldt.

These are life-sustaining caribou of the Bathurst herd migrating on the Barrens.

global focus for conservation as a new wave of development is pushing north, driven by prospects of diamonds and uranium, petroleum, and abundant and untapped hydroelectric potential.

It is in this context that the people of Lutsel K'e have determined to move ahead with a proposal for a new national park within the area they call Thaidene Nene, "the Land of the Ancestors," extending from the East Arm of Great Slave Lake to the Barrenlands of the upper Thelon River Basin. What is truly remarkable, however, is not simply the size, scope, or significance of the area proposed for protection — although it is hard to find the right superlatives to describe 12,700 square miles of spectacular glacier-wrought landscape, rich with lakes, forests, wetlands, culture, and wildlife. It is the deep resolve on the part of the community to transcend past experiences, to shoulder the burdens of history and their responsibilities to future generations, and to set forward once again on an arduous journey to define a new relationship with the Government of Canada.

Conservation and Colonialism in the Twentieth Century

As in many other parts of North America, parks have a checkered history in the Northwest Territories. Historically, North American conservation efforts have been centred on charismatic wildlife and scenic places, resulting in a system of parks and protected areas that are often only fragments of the underlying landscape, and are accordingly unable to protect the full ranges of wide-ranging species such as grizzly bear, caribou, or wolves, resulting in a gradual impoverishment of the very ecological values they sought to protect.[2]

Compounding this problem, the process of establishing new protected areas in the nineteenth and twentieth centuries involved the dispossession and displacement of local communities on the premise that their activities were "management problems" that only served to undermine or complicate conservation efforts. Aboriginal communities in particular have been disproportionately impacted, resulting in a legacy of dispossession and distrust that continues to colour conservation efforts today.[3]

Conservation, of course, is not only a Western concept, nor is it solely a scientific endeavour. Under Dene law and tradition, each generation has the responsibility to ensure that their lands remain capable of sustaining the Dene way of life for generations to come, and maintaining proper relationships with the animals on which the people depend. This requires active engagement in hunting and other traditional activities. These two views of conservation — one rooted in a rational paradigm of resource management and central planning, the other in communal values and individual responsibilities — could not have been more distant, but collided with dramatic effect in the Northwest Territories in the early part of the twentieth century.

Alarmed by precipitous declines in the range and populations of formerly plentiful bison and other game species as settlers expanded westward and into the Mackenzie Region, the Government of Canada took bold, unprecedented steps to establish the Wood Buffalo National Park and the Thelon Game Sanctuary to secure a future for threatened wood bison, muskox, and caribou populations. However, the closure of these sanctuaries to Aboriginal subsistence, together with the introduction and enforcement of game ordinances that restricted Aboriginal hunting and trapping activities, created significant hardships for Aboriginal communities, as these were the only viable forms of economy available to the Dene.

These actions gave rise to bitter disputes between the Dene chiefs and government officials. The Dene maintained that these closures and new laws violated the letter and spirit of Treaty 8, which promised that traditional activities would continue. These disputes gathered strength with each new incident or settler incursion, and by 1937, Dene leaders throughout the Territory — including Lutsel K'e — were actively boycotting the treaty.[4]

The political consequences of these early efforts to impose central authority and "scientific" resource management on a territory and a people accustomed to autonomy and traditional ways of life was profound. As John Sandlos, an environmental historian, notes in his study of this period, resistance to government conservation initiatives transformed whole communities, and shaped the substance of Aboriginal politics in the North: "The assertion of state authority over wildlife ... was not limited to restrictions on Native hunting and trapping activities, but also caused dramatic changes to community, kinship, and cultural relationships among the Cree and Chipewyan communities in the region.... To ignore the game regulations was, in a sense, an act of political restoration.[5]

It is in this context that efforts by Parks Canada in the late 1960s to establish the East Arm of Great Slave Lake National Park were rebuffed by the people of Lutsel K'e. The headline of the July 31, 1969, edition of Yellowknife's *News of the North* says it succinctly: GOVERNMENT STUPIDITY UNITES INDIANS — but the story bears repeating. Early that year, Chief Pierre Catholique was invited to a meeting in Yellowknife by government officials. He was sent home partway through, after being advised "what we have to discuss tomorrow doesn't concern you." What "didn't concern" him turned out to be a proposal to establish a new national park, which he discovered accidentally, after the minutes of the entire meeting were forwarded to the Band office in Lutsel K'e. Caught out, the government sent a twenty-one person delegation to meet with the chief and his council to try to convince them that the park was in their interest. Incensed, the community steadfastly refused to endorse it, and the proposal stalled, but not before a land withdrawal for a future park was advanced by Order-in-Council, protecting a small corridor along the East Arm from mining and other forms of development.

Chief Catholique told the press, "Never again will one Chief sit down with twenty-one government people. From now on, if twenty-one government people come to meeting, twenty-one Indian leaders must come and sit across the table from them."[6] The chief's words quickly spread throughout the region, and the "East Arm Incident" is widely credited for galvanizing the nascent political movement among the Dene that emerged a few years later as the Dene Nation, an organization that gained national attention and credibility during the Berger Inquiry into the Mackenzie Gas Project in the mid-1970s, and has continued to significantly influence regional and Aboriginal politics across the country.[7]

Diamonds and Uranium

The Northwest Territories has always been known for mineral riches. Yellowknife was a gold-rush town long before it became the territorial capital, and several small gold and uranium mines operated throughout the territory during the 1950s and 1960s. Every summer, dozens of prospecting companies would set out to find their fortunes in the vast and still largely unexplored reaches of the region. The vast majority of these activities would return having done nothing of economic significance, but an unlikely discovery of diamonds near Lac de Gras, some 190 miles north of Yellowknife, in 1991, resulted in a renewed rush to stake and explore land for all forms of minerals throughout the Northwest Territories.

For much of the 1990s, "diamond fever" gripped the North, as mining majors BHP Billiton and Rio Tinto sought to bring the first Canadian diamond mines — Ekati and Diavik — into production. During this period, an area the size of France was staked for mineral exploration, and hundreds of exploration camps were established.

The Lutsel K'e Dene First Nation recognized early on that the dramatic expansion of exploration and mining activities was likely to have significant and irreversible effects on their lands, on wildlife, and on the community. As mining developments advanced, the community responded by initiating monitoring programs to help identify impacts,

Photo by Morten Asfeldt.

Ekati Diamond Mine on Lac de Gras was the first diamond mine to open in Canada.

and to actively negotiate the implementation of measures to address their findings and concerns.[8] However, the community was also well aware that monitoring and mitigation strategies were not sufficient to address the full range of impacts from mining, and that other means needed to be found to protect land from development at the outset.

Thaidene Nene

In 2000, the community leadership approached Canada with an invitation to resume discussions over the East Arm National Park. The people of Lutsel K'e had learned from other First Nations that the policies, which used to exclude people from national parks, were changing, and that new legislation was in place that would ensure that Aboriginal and treaty rights would be respected, and that harvesting and access by Aboriginal people would no longer be restricted.

256

Photo by Larry Innes.

Minister of the Environment Rona Ambrose and Chief Adeline Jonasson sit together at the park signing ceremony in Lutsel K'e in October 2006.

One model frequently cited with approval by the community was the establishment in 1993 by the Haida Nation and Parks Canada of the Gwaii Haanas National Parks Reserve on Haida Gwaii (formerly the Queen Charlotte Islands) off the northwest British Columbia coast. This was accomplished through an innovative agreement that recognized the rights and interests of both the Haida and the Government of Canada, and established a process of joint management and consensus decision-making over the operation of the national park reserve.[9]

Beyond the fundamental issues of Aboriginal rights and decision-making, the community was also careful to consider the impacts and the benefits of a national park, and took great care to inform themselves about the possibilities and precedents for direct employment, tourism businesses, contracting for goods and services, community infrastructure, and other issues related to the operations of a national park. Having satisfied themselves that such a park could be implemented in such a way that it would respect Dene rights, ensure protection of priority lands, and provide opportunities to secure economic development and cultural benefits, the community entered into negotiations in 2005 with Parks Canada toward establishing a partnership to examine the feasibility of a new national park. These discussions occurred within the broader context of negotiations between Canada and the three Akaitcho Dene First Nations communities toward recognizing and implementing Dene rights under Treaty 8 through the formal Akaitcho treaty implementation process.

In 2006, the community welcomed the minister responsible for Parks Canada, Rona Ambrose, to Lutsel K'e to enter into a formal agreement to advance a feasibility study for a new national park. In March 2007, a delegation from the community travelled to Ottawa for the announcement of the largest land withdrawal in Canadian history, of an area totalling 37,000 square miles: 13,000 square miles for inclusion as a future national park and the remainder to be formally designated as Akaitcho lands through the treaty implementation process.

Although further studies, detailed discussions, and written agreements to guide the management of the future park must still be completed before official lines can be drawn, it is notable that the proposal now on the table is more than four times the area that was originally proposed by Parks Canada in their ill-fated attempt to establish a park in the 1970s.

Pressing On

As Elder Madeline Drybones of the Lutsel K'e Dene First Nation said, "We can't let go of the land. We have to hang on to the land for our children. They have to follow in our footsteps."[10]

Thaidene Nene is now in view, but many challenges remain. Government interests in conservation are always contingent, and in difficult economic times development interests are often given priority. The community remains committed, but development pressures continue unabated in the region immediately adjacent to the lands withdrawn for the park.

In May 2007, the community won a major victory when the Mackenzie Valley Environmental Impact Review Board, in an unprecedented decision, recommended that a uranium project near the ancient portages between Artillery Lake and the Thelon River not proceed because of the significant impacts that it would have on the cultural and spiritual values of the region.[11] The community is gaining ground, but moving the park forward will require the community to press forward on the portage trail, and to shoulder the difficult burdens of carrying forward thousands of years of history and traditions to a place where they can be safely passed on to a future generation.

Lutsel K'e is not alone on this trail, however. Their path has converged with the ones taken by other Canadians who value wilderness and the spirit of places where our tracks remain traces. As noted northern author David Pelly told the review board:

> [T]he very heart of the largest tract of wilderness left in North America has an importance to Canadians who do not even know exactly where it is. It is part of the Canadian psyche, part of our national identity and culture that we have in this country, a vast untouched wilderness to the north. We erode that wilderness at our peril. Eventually, when the map of northern Canada is dotted with mines and then roads and the infrastructure which would inevitably follow, there would no longer be a distinct Canada. The popular Canadian singer-songwriter Murray McLauchlan sang that the "soul of Canada lies out past the timber line." He is right.[12]

It is here, in the meeting between cultures, too often in conflict over lands too fragile, that we can find a means to conserve places and peoples. Here we find the beginnings of a journey that we can take together, toward "Thaidene Nene — The Land of the Ancestors."

Larry Innes
Goose Bay, Labrador

Notes

1. Warburton Pike, *The Barren Ground of Northern Canada* (London, UK: Macmillan, 1892), 205.

Introduction

1. George Luste, "Lower Lockhart," in *Nastawgan, The Quarterly Journal of the Wilderness Canoe Association* (Summer 1987), 1–5. Also see Bruce W. Hodgins and Gwyneth Hoyle, *Canoeing North into the Unknown: A Record of River Travel: 1874–1974* (Toronto: Natural Heritage Books, 1994) for a chronology of travel over Pike's Portage and the Lockhart River.
2. Lutsel K'e is a community of about four hundred people located on Christie Bay on the south shores of the East Arm of Great Slave Lake. Lutsel K'e means "place of small fish" and was formerly called Snowdrift.
3. The course AUIDS 270: Explorations of the Canadian North is taught at the Augustana Campus of the University of Alberta in Camrose,

Alberta. Course instructors have included Morten Asfeldt, Ingrid Urberg, and Bob Henderson, along with hosts Dave and Kristen Olesen. See Morten Asfeldt, Ingrid Urberg, and Bob Henderson, "Wolves, Ptarmigan, and Lake Trout: Critical Elements of Northern Canadian Place-Based Pedagogy," in *The Canadian Journal of Environmental Education*, Vol. 14 (2009), 31–44, for more about this university course.

4. Helge Ingstad, "Vinland Ruins Prove Vikings Found the New World," in *National Geographic*, Vol. 126, Issue 5 (November 1964), 708–35.

5. A lobstick, or lopstick, is a conifer tree that has had all but its uppermost branches purposely removed, leaving a trunk and crown of branches to create an obvious landmark.

6. This wood stove is in storage at the Prince of Wales Northern Heritage Centre in Yellowknife. Along with eight Augustana students, Morten and I had a tour of various artifacts from the region, including the 1926 Hornby stove, prior to our Hoarfrost visit. It was riveting for Morten and me, both of us knowing the 1926 story of Hornby's final wanderings and the final contents of the wood stove being Edgar Christian's diary. For the students, we believe it was a moment to be in the presence of rich stories to come. We thank Susan Irving for sharing these artifacts with us and for her wealth of knowledge and endless enthusiasm — and for meeting with us on a Saturday, not her normal workday!

7. Throughout this book we use the names Reliance, Fort Reliance, and Old Fort Reliance. To clarify, Fort Reliance was built at the mouth of the Lockhart River by Alexander McLeod in 1833 as winter quarters for the George Back expedition and given the name Fort Reliance. Once Back's Fort Reliance was abandoned it was called Old Fort Reliance. When the present day Reliance was first established in the early 1900s, it was called Fort Reliance and later simply Reliance. Therefore, Old Fort Reliance always refers to Back's Fort Reliance and Reliance always refers to the present day Reliance. And finally then, Fort Reliance is used for both sites based on the time period we are writing about. We hope you as a reader can follow but know of no other way of dealing with this aside from a manuscript cluttered with explanations.

8. George Back, *Narrative of the Arctic Land Expedition to the Mouth of the Great Fish River and Along the Shores of the Arctic Ocean in the Years 1833, 1834, and 1835.* (Boston: Adamant Media Corporation, 2005), 53. Originally published in 1836 by John Murray in London, England.

9. Activeness and activity is a distinction used by Norwegian educator Aage Jensen and others to denote a *friluftsliv* education's attention to a deeper relationally with skills, place, and traditions. See Bob Henderson and Nils Vikander, eds. *Nature First: Outdoor Life the Friluftsliv Way* (Toronto: Natural Heritage Books - Dundurn Press, 2007) and Roger Isberg and Sarah Isberg, *Simple Life: Friluftsliv* (Victoria, BC: Trafford, 2007).

10. This quote has been used before in Bob Henderson, "An Effort to Capture an Elusive Friluftsliv," see Bob Henderson and Nils Vikander, eds., *Nature First: Outdoor Life the Friluftsliv Way* (Toronto: Natural Heritage Books - Dundurn Press, 2007), 143. The quote is from Miyamoto Musashi, *A Book of Five Rings: The Classic Samurai Guide to Strategy* (London: Allison Basby, 1982).

11. Warburton Pike, *The Barren Ground of Northern Canada* (London, UK: Macmillan and Co., 1892), 276.

12. Gwen Hayball, *Warburton Pike: An Unassuming Gentleman* (Poole, Dorset: Gwen Hayball, 1994), 9.

13. George Whalley, *The Legend of John Hornby* (Toronto: Macmillan, 1962).

14. Elizabeth Hay, *Late Nights on Air* (Toronto: McClelland and Stewart, 2007), 230.

Prologue: "Wolf"

1. Reprinted by permission of the author and Novalis Publishing Company.

Part I: A Storied Tale

1. Elliott Merrick, *True North* (New York: Charles Scribner, 1942), 114.

Chapter 1: Pike's Portage: A Story in Deep Time

1. Warburton Pike, *The Barren Ground of Northern Canada*. London: Macmillan, 1892.

2. Alexander Mackenzie, *Exploring the Northwest Territory: Sir Alexander Mackenzie's Journal of a Voyage by Bark Canoe from Lake Athabasca to the Pacific Ocean in the Summer of 1789*, edited by T.H. McDonald. Norman: University of Oklahoma Press, 1966. See also Samuel Hearne, *A Journey to the Northern Ocean: The Adventures of Samuel Hearne*. Surrey, BC: TouchWood Eds., 2007.

3. Diamond Jenness, *Arctic Odyssey: The Diary of Diamond Jenness, Ethnologist with the Canadian Arctic Expedition in Northern Alaska and Canada 1913–1916*, ed. by Stuart Jenness. Hull, QC: Canadian Museum of Civilization, 1991. See also Bryan Gordon, *People of Sunlight, People of Starlight: Barrenland Archaeology in the Northwest Territories of Canada*. Hull, QC: Canadian Museum of Civilization, 1996.

4. Richard S. MacNeish, "An Archaeological Reconnaissance in the Northwest Territories." in National Museum of Canada Bulletin 123 (1951), 24–41.

5. Sam Otto was born in Morris, Manitoba, in 1907, one of a family of seventeen. In 1929, at the age of twenty-two, he came to the Northwest Territories to search for gold as a prospector with Dominion Explorers in the Dubawnt Lake area, near the Thelon Game Sanctuary. He travelled far and wide, ending up paddling to Great Bear Lake, where he stayed without a break for four years. He worked for uranium mines and prospecting outfits in the Great Bear Lake region, sailing with the *Great Bear* and mining for the BEAR mine at Contact Lake. In 1935, he pitched his first tent on Latham Island in Yellowknife, working at Burwash, Ptarmigan, and Con mines, and continued to prospect. In 1937, he raised his first log cabin in the same area where he lived for the next four decades. Also that year, he received his trapper's licence after the requisite four-year waiting period. Otto spent the better part of fourteen winters at his two-hundred-mile trapline, prospecting in the summer to supplement his income. In the fall (August/September) a plane

would fly him out to his trapline near Artillery and Clinton-Colden lakes. The plane returned to pick him up in April. He had a main cabin, ran dogs, and did the rounds of his trapline. Sam Otto also spent one year (1942–43) working on the CANOL project. In 1952, he married Myrtle Ritchie of Edmonton and settled in Yellowknife, though he continued to prospect in the summer. Myrtle had three children from a previous relationship who came with her to Yellowknife: Sharon, Sherman, and Sheldon. In 1953, she gave birth to Lorraine. Myrtle stayed in Yellowknife, running the household, working at Imperial Oil, and expediting for Sam when he was in the bush. Sam died in Yellowknife in 1974. Myrtle remarried, became Myrtle McNeil, and lived in Grand Cache, Alberta. She passed away in Penticton, British Columbia, in 1994. Information from the "Sam Otto Fonds." NWT Archives (database online *pwnhc.learnnet. nt.ca*) at the Prince of Wales Natural Heritage Centre in Yellowknife, accessed on May 27, 2009.

6. William C. Noble, "Archaeological Surveys and Sequences in the Central District of the Mackenzie, N.W.T.," in *Arctic Anthropology*, Vol. 8, No. 1 (1971), 102–35.

7. Willy Laserich was an immigrant from Germany who lived a storied life as a pilot based out of Cambridge Bay, Nunavut. He created a company called Adlair Aviation, and continued to fly throughout the North until he was seventy-five years of age, when he died suddenly of heart failure. In a recent magazine article, Willy is described as "a rule-breaking, seat-of-your-pants bush pilot, a thorn in the side of aviation regulators, and, for half a century, a hero to the residents of the far-flung Northern communities he served." Margo Pfeiff, "Remembering the Flying Bandit," in *UpHere* Vol. 24, No. 2 (March 2008), 22–25. A local Yellowknife band, The Gumboots, have written a song titled "Willy and the Bandits" that is included on their album *Northern Tracks*.

8. See chapter 14 for the Gus D'Aoust story.

9. E.C. Peilou, *After the Ice Age: The Return of Life to Glaciated North America* (Chicago: University of Chicago Press, 1991), 156–60.

Chapter 2: The Denesoline: Where Are All Their Stories?

1. Taken from Hugh Brody's "Inuit Worlds: They Do Not Stay the Same." Keynote Lecture for the University of Alberta Centenary Series / Canadian Circumpolar Institute. University of Alberta Convocation Hall, Edmonton, AB, February 6, 2009.

2. Hugh Brody's experiences in Sanikiluaq, Nunavut, are told in his book *The People's Land: Eskimos and Whites in the Eastern Arctic* (Markham, ON: Penguin Books, 1975).

3. Janet Pivnick, "In Search of an Ecological Approach to Research: A Mediation on Topos," in *Canadian Journal of Environmental Education*, Vol. 8 (2003), 148.

4. Matonabee (1736–82) was a Denesoline-Métis man who was an important diplomat, explorer, and trader and Samuel Hearne's guide to the Coppermine River. Thanadelther was a Denesoline woman who was captured and enslaved by the Cree, and who came to stay with British traders at York Factory on Hudson Bay. She was celebrated by her contemporaries as instrumental in the expansion of the fur trade, and is credited with the peace treaty forged between the Cree and Denesoline.

5. James Raffan is a geographer who worked with the community in the late 1980s and early 1990s. His doctoral work is entitled "Frontier, Homeland, and Sacred Space: A Collaborative Investigation into Cross-Cultural Perceptions of Place in the Thelon Game Sanctuary, NWT." He also the author of "The Experience of Place: Exploring Land as Teacher," in *The Journal of Experiential Education*, Vol. 16, No. 1 (May 1993), 39–45.

6. Ellen Bielawski is an anthropologist, now at the University of Alberta, who worked with Lutsel K'e Dene First Nation in the early 1990s. Her doctoral thesis is entitled "The Desecration of Nanula Tue: The Impacts of the Talston Hydro Electric Project on the Dene Soline." She is also the author of *Rogue Diamonds* (Vancouver: Douglas & McIntyre, 2003).

7. John Sandlos, *Hunters at the Margin: Native People and Wildlife Conservation in the Northwest Territories* (Vancouver: University of British Columbia Press, 2007).

8. P.J. Usher, "Caribou Crisis or Administrative Crisis? Wildlife and Aboriginal Management Policies on the Barren Ground Caribou 1947–60" in David G. Anderson and Mark Nuttall, eds. *Cultivating Arctic Landscapes: Knowing and Managing Animals in the Circumpolar North* (New York: Berghahn Books 2002).

9. Helge Ingstad, Eugene Gay-Tifft, trans. *The Land of Feast and Famine* (Montreal and Kingston: McGill-Queen's University Press, 1992).

10. See Denesoline Fishing Knowledge of the East Arm of Tu Nedhé (Great Slave Lake) Final Report on Thirty Interviews (April 2002), 12. Retrieved from *www.dfo-mpo.gc.ca/Library/265821.pdf*, accessed on September 30, 2009.

11. For more on this legend, see the reference in note 10 above as well as chapter 4 of this book including notes 21 and 23 for that chapter.

Part II: On the Trail

1. George Back, *Narrative of the Arctic Land Expedition to the Mouth of the Great Fish River, and Along the Shores of the Arctic Ocean, in the Years 1833, 1834, and 1835* (Boston, MA: Adamant Media Corporation 1836/2005), 133–34.

Chapter 3: Warburton Pike: No Ordinary Shooting Expedition

1. C.H. French, "Warburton Pike," in *The Beaver*, Vol. 6, No. 1 (December 1925), 25.

2. Graeme Wynn, "The Enigmatic North" in John Sandlos, *Hunters at the Margin* (Vancouver: University of British Columbia Press, 2007), xi.

3. Farley Mowat, *People of the Deer* (Toronto: McClelland and Stewart, 1975), 20–21.

4. Warburton Pike, *The Barren Ground of Northern Canada* (London, UK: Macmillan, 1892), vi.

5. *Ibid.*, 87. It is awkward to think in terms of "first white man." One must consider the possibility of early travellers who did not write

or couldn't. Then there is the issue of the early Métis population. Are they to be considered Euro-Canadians or indigenous to the North after a few generations? Certainly the Yellowknife chief Zinto considered the Beaulieu clan and other Métis families indigenous. See chapter 9 in this book for more on this issue.

6. Pike, *Barren Ground*, v, viii.

7. Gwen Hayball, *Warburton Pike: An Unassuming Gentleman* (Poole, UK: Gwen Hayball, 1994), 2–3.

8. See Warburton Pike, *Through the Subarctic Forest* (New York: Arno Press, 1967). Originally published in 1896 by E. Arnold, London and New York.

9. Hayball, *Warburton Pike*, 33–34.

10. *Ibid.*, 38–39.

11. *Ibid.*, 39.

12. *Ibid.*, 40.

13. See chapter 5 in this book for more information on the James Anderson and James Stewart route.

14. Pike, *Barren Ground*, 249.

15. See chapter 9 in this book for more information on the Beaulieu clan.

16. Pike, *Barren Ground*, 18.

17. Ernest Thompson Seton, *The Arctic Prairies* (New York: Harper Colophon Books, 1981), 172. Originally published in 1911 by C. Scribner's Sons of New York.

18. The exact location of the Beaulieu's East Arm trading post named Fond du Lac is difficult to ascertain. As editors, we have searched high and low in the literature, on archival maps, and spoken to local people in our attempt to pinpoint it. There seems to be consensus that this Fond du Lac was somewhere near Taltheilei Narrows and perhaps where Plummer's Great Slave Lodge sits today. In the process of writing chapter 9, Randy Freeman asked Danny Beaulieu where Fond du Lac was and Danny indicated that it was at different locations at different times. What is clear is that Fond du Lac was a Beaulieu camp.

19. Pike, *Barren Ground*, 33.

20. *Ibid.*, 65.

21. *Ibid.*, 66. Beaulieu is referring to Fort Enterprise, which Franklin established to support his 1819–21 journey to the shores of the Polar

Sea. On this expedition, eleven of the original twenty expedition members died. See C. Stuart Houston, ed. *To the Arctic by Canoe 1819–1821: The Journal and Paintings of Robert Hood, Midshipman with Franklin* (Montreal and London: McGill-Queen's Press, 1974).

22. *Ibid.*, 71.
23. *Ibid.*, 98.
24. *Ibid.*, 107.
25. *Ibid.*, 108.
26. *Ibid.*, 115–16.
27. *Ibid.*, 131.
28. *Ibid.*, 152.
29. *Ibid.*, 160.
30. *Ibid.*, 161. Here Pike also tells the story of how two blind men, Pierre and Antoine Fat, were helped in travel and contributed to the "wandering life" rather than preferring the support they would receive at Fort Resolution.
31. *Ibid.*, 162.
32. *Ibid.*, 164.
33. *Ibid.*, 170.
34. *Ibid.*, 177.
35. *Ibid.*, 180.
36. Hayball, *Warburton Pike*, 9. Florence Catholique, a Lutsel K'e elder, indicates that the Chipewyan, or Denesoline, name for Pike's Portage is Teho a tue xakethe. It is possible that Ka a Ku is a short form of *Teho a tue xakethe.*
37. Pike, *Barren Ground*, 205. This is one of the truly charmed and descriptive passages from the Barrenlands literature. The mention of the ancestral Chipewyan name of the portages in Gwen Hayballs's book is unusual given this is the only reference we have found in the exploration literature. It was Tyrrell, just ten years later, who gives the name Pike's Portage to this main line portage to the Thelon and Back rivers.

James Mackinlay, Pike's travel companion, also describes the portage in his journal:

> Thurs. 14th: Wind southerly. Got away from the Indian camp about 9 o'clock and a paddle of 2 miles or so

brought us to the end of Artillery Lake, the bay being just like a river, long and narrow from which point the route lies through a chain of small lakes. We finished 5 portages and camped on the beginning of the 6th. Some of the lakes through which we passed were mere ponds, others a mile or so in length. The country we are now passing through is high and rocky and very rough and cut up, being the range of hills near the Slave Lake. We probably have got about half of the portages finished between Artillery and Slave. Came about 8 miles from the end of Artillery Lake …

Fri. 15th: Wind northerly. Started packing over the 6th portage by 6 o'clock in the morning into a small lake and before dinner had finished 2 more portages and on the next lake we saw a boy with a shirt too white and clean to have been long in the woods so we reckoned he must have come from the boat…. Our supposition was correct. The boat had arrived on the evening of the 14th and three or four of the crew had been sent to meet us, but finding the caribou had scattered over the country in pursuit leaving us to our fate. The small supply of tobacco etc. sent us they cached in an Indian lodge a little farther on from where we met, which we lost no time in reaching and had a good smoke. A little farther on we came to another small portage into the last lake and then a portage, the last, and fell on the Great Slave Lake. 3 canoes were in sight sailing for our destination, the boat landing. So we fired several shots which were responded to by the boat people and canoes. This route from Artillery Lake is by far the most feasible we have passed through. The country tho' rough and hilly affords a good and serviceable road in the valleys from lake to lake and the surroundings during the whole way are much more interesting than the general aspect of the country which has the general fault of sameness. The hills are high and rocky while here and there you fall on a fine sandy shored

lake and slope of sandy hills. On falling on the Slave Lake
we found what appeared a lake of some 4 miles or so in
length and 2 in breadth, in appearance surrounded by
high rocky hills. Where the boat is hauled up and crew
camped is a sandy bay and a flat, which from the stumps
showing has been evidently well wooded and showing
that this route is much used by the Indians."

— James Mackinlay, "Journal Fish River Exploring Party," in
The Arctic Circular, Vol. X, No. 4 (1958), 67–68.

38. *Ibid.*, 206.
39. *Ibid.*, 98.
40. *Ibid.*, 209.
41. *Ibid.*, 210.
42. Margaret Hobbs, "Purposeful Wanderers: Late Nineteenth Century
    Travellers to the Barrens," in Bruce Hodgins and Margaret Hobbs, ed.,
    Nastawgan: The Canadian North by Canoe and Snowshoe (Toronto:
    Betelgeuse Books, 1987), 57.
43. *Ibid.*, 58.
44. *Ibid.*, 74.
45. Patrick Dunae, *Gentlemen Emigrants: From the British Public Schools
    to the Canadian Frontier* (Vancouver: Douglas and McIntyre, 1981)
    as quoted in Hobbs, "Purposeful Wanderers," 58. See Note 42.

Chapter 4: George Back: An Unsung Arctic Explorer

1. George Back, *Narrative of the Arctic Land Expedition* (Boston, MA:
   Adamant Media Corporation, 2005), 58. Originally published in
   1836 by John Murray, London.
2. Beverly was a friend of Back's who accompanied Sir William E. Parry
   on his attempt to reach the North Pole.
3. Back, *Narrative of the Arctic Land Expedition*, 5.
4. Peter Steele, *The Man Who Mapped the Arctic: The Intrepid Life of George
   Back, Franklin's Lieutenant* (Vancouver: Raincoast Books, 2004), 6.
5. *Ibid.*, 43.

6. *Ibid.*, 150.

7. Back, *Arctic Land Expedition*, 59.

8. *Ibid.*, 59.

9. Alexander McLeod's name is spelled McLeod in George Back's journal and MacLeod in Peter Steele's book *The Man Who Mapped the Arctic*. We have chosen to use Back's spelling.

10. Back, *Arctic Land Expedition*, 60.

11. Since Back's journey up the Hoarfrost River in 1833, we know of only one other attempt to ascend the river by canoe. This was by veteran Arctic paddler Ed Struzik and three others in 1993. After one day, Struzik and crew abandoned their attempt finding "the route was far worse than anything [Back] had hinted at in his journal or drawings" and "no matter how hard we tried, there was no way we could figure out how [Back] and his men managed to haul their canoe and gear up through this tangled mess of spongy muskeg, fallen-down trees and continuous stretch of whitewater. In the end, we were left with no choice but to retreat." And retreat they did, after arranging to have Dave Olesen ferry some gear by plane to Harry Lake — the first lake on Pike's Portage after the toughest climb from Great Slave Lake — Struzik and crew paddled south to the foot of Pike's Portage and began the long portage to Artillery Lake en route to the Back River. In a recent email, Struzik commented: "I don't know of anyone else who is crazy enough to try portaging up the Hoarfrost. I still find it hard to believe that Back and his men did it. It was a nightmare."

12. Back, *Arctic Land Expedition*, 61.

13. Dave Olesen, *North of Reliance: A Personal Story of Living Beyond the Wilderness* (Minocqua, WI: Northward Press, 1994), 37.

14. Back, *Arctic Land Expedition*, 69.

15. *Ibid.*, 75.

16. *Ibid.*, 90.

17. *Ibid.*, 88.

18. *Ibid.*, 89.

19. *Ibid.*

20. *Ibid.*

21. James Raffan, "The Lessons of Old Woman Falls," in *UpHere* (April 2005), 26.

22. Based on archeological evidence presented in William C. Noble, "Archeological Surveys and Sequences in the Central District of Mackenzie, N.W.T." in *Arctic Anthropology*, Vol. 8, No. 1 (1971), 102–34, it appears the Pike's Portage was used as long ago as 3,500 to 4,500 years. (Mr. Peter Carruthers (see chapter 1) assisted Noble with some of the research presented in this article. Also, Noble thanks Delphine and Gus D'Aoust (see chapter 14) as well as Mr. Noel Drybones (see chapter 2) for their assistance during his time in the North. Further evidence presented by Bryan Gordon, *People of Sunlight, People of Starlight: Barrenland Archaeology in the Northwest Territories of Canada:* (Hull, QC: Canadian Museum of Civilization, 1996), 18, suggests that Pike's Portage was in use long before Back descended the Lockhart River in 1833. In fact, when talking about Back, Gordon writes, "[Back] was followed by adventurers and trophy muskox hunters who sought an easier route to Artillery Lake and the Barrenlands. They eventually followed an old Indian portage route that Back had missed, naming it after the adventurer, Warburton Pike."

23. There is some dispute regarding the exact location of Beaver's Lodge and Rat's Lodge. According to Maufelly, Beaver's Lodge is on the east side of Artillery Lake about ten miles northeast of Rat's Lodge, yet on some maps Beaver's Lodge is marked directly across the lake from Rat's Lodge. There is no dispute regarding the location of Rat's Lodge, which is very distinct. Roger Catling has a cabin on the peninsula that is home to Rat's Lodge (locals today refer to them as Rat Lodge and Beaver Lodge) and when Roger was asked about the location of Beaver's Lodge, he replied that is was directly across the lake. Among the locals, there is not doubt that Beaver's Lodge is directly across from Rat's Lodge. However, Richard Galaburri in "The Rat Lodge Revisited," in *Arctic*, Vol. 44, No. 3 (September 1991), 257–58, makes a case for Beaver's Lodge being as Maufelly described it.

24. Back, *Arctic Land Expedition*, 95.

25. This alternate route is not commonly used today although it is known to locals. In addition, it is marked on several maps including J.W. Tyrrell's map number one from his 1900 report titled "Great Slave Lake and Hudson's Bay." See the map on page 94.

26. Back, *Arctic Land Expedition*, 90.

27. We can confirm only one contemporary canoe trip down the Lockhart River. This was made by George Luste and his son along with two other companions in 1986. The story of their trip can be found in George Luste, "Lower Lockhart," in *Nastawgan: The Quarterly Journal of the Wilderness Canoe Association* (Summer 1987), 1–5.

28. Steele, *Mapped the Arctic*, 101.

29. Back, *Arctic Land Expedition*, 89.

30. *Ibid.*, 107.

31. *Ibid.*, 106.

32. *Ibid.*, 114.

33. *Ibid.*, 128.

34. *Ibid.*, 230.

35. *Ibid.*, 235.

36. *Ibid.*

37. *Ibid.*, 245.

38. Steele, *Mapped the Arctic*, 285.

39. L.H. Neatly, "George Back (1796–1878)" in *Arctic*, Vol. 36, No. 1 (March 1983), 104.

40. *Ibid.*

41. Steele, *Mapped the Arctic*, 276.

Chapter 5: Anderson and Stewart: The Byways to the Barrens

1. C.H. Stockwell, "Great Slave Lake: Coppermine River Area, Northwest Territories," in *Summary Report 1932*, Part "C" *Geological Survey of Canada*, 39C. The river they call the Barnston is, in fact, the Waldron River.

2. *Ibid.*, 43C.

3. Caspar Whitney (1861–1929) was an American author, editor, sportsman, and outdoorsman. His name may be most familiar to many canoeists as the editor of *The Outing Magazine* and employer of Leonidas Hubbard (of Labrador fame). He travelled north of Great Slave to hunt muskox in the 1890s as well. See Caspar Whitney, *On Snow-Shoes to the*

Barren Grounds. New York: Harper & Brothers, 1896.

Henry Toke Munn (1864–1952) was another gentleman English immigrant. He farmed and raised horses in Manitoba, then headed north to hunt muskox in 1894, north of Great Slave Lake. After his return, he went to the Yukon Gold Rush, served in the Boer War, and pursued prospecting and trading ventures in the North — with little success, developing a poisonous dislike of the Hudson's Bay Company (who bought him out) in the process. He eventually retired to the Seychelles Islands in the Indian Ocean, where he died. See Henry Toke Munn, *Prairie Trails and Arctic Byways*. London: Hunt and Blackett, 1932.

4. Stockwell, *Great Slave Lake*, 43C.

5. *Ibid.*, 43C.

6. *Ibid.*

7. The Anderson Log: "Chief Factor James Anderson's Back River Journal of 1855," in *The Canadian Field-Naturalist*, Vols. 54–55 (1940–41). This article was published serially in five monthly installments — in Vol. 54 (1940), 63–67; in May, 84–89; in September, 107–09; in October, 125–26; in November in Vol. 55 (1941), 38–40. C.H.D. Clarke, ed. All quotes pertaining to the Anderson and Stewart route are from "The Anderson Log." The editor (Clarke) worked from (as per the introduction in the May 1940 installment) "a bound volume of typewritten sheets in the library of the Lands, Parks, and Forests Branch, Department of Mines and Resources, Ottawa." Clarke noted there was a more "polished version" of the log in the HBC Archives, and felt he was working from a transcription of Anderson's field notes. The Anderson Log was also reprinted by the Hakluyt Society in 1999 as "Searching for Franklin: The Land Arctic Searching Expedition, 1855. James Anderson's and James Stewart's Expedition via the Back River," William Barr, ed.

8. James Green Stewart was born in Quebec City in 1825, and joined the Hudson's Bay Company in 1844. He was soon sent to the northwest and worked as Robert Campbell's assistant in the Yukon trade, which was not terribly successful and ended when the Tlingit ransacked Fort Selkirk in 1852. The fort was subsequently abandoned. Anderson and Stewart did not get along well on their journey: Anderson

criticized Stewart's judgment, and Stewart was later reprimanded by George Simpson for his conduct. Despite that damaging rebuke, he remained with the HBC until 1871. Stewart died in 1881.

9. This is very likely the same creek that McLeod expected George Back to use in 1833 when you descended from Artillery Lake to Fort Reliance via the Lockhart River. This creek can be seen on Map 2 on page 18 and in image on page 94.

10. Anderson, *Back River Journal*, 107.

11. *Ibid.*, 107.

12. *Ibid.*

13. *Ibid.*

14. *Ibid.*

15. *Ibid.*

16. *Ibid.*

17. *Ibid.*

18. *Ibid.*, 89.

19. *Ibid.*

20. *Ibid.*

21. *Ibid.*, 87–89.

22. *Ibid.*, 87.

23. *Ibid.*

24. *Ibid.*, 89.

25. *Ibid.*, 87.

26. *Ibid.*

Chapter 6: Ernest Thompson Seton: On the Portage

1. The reader is directed to any one of a number of biographies, each quite different, for further reflections on this brief introduction: John Wadland, *Ernest Thompson Seton: Man in Nature and the Progressive Era, 1880-1915* (New York: Arno, 1978); Magdalene Redekop, *Ernest Thompson Seton* (Don Mills: Fitzhenry and Whiteside, 1979); Betty Keller, *Black Wolf: The Life of Ernest Thompson Seton* (Vancouver: Douglas and McIntyre, 1984); H. Allen Anderson, *The Chief: Ernest Thompson Seton and the Changing West* (College Station: Texas

A&M University Press, 1986); Brian Morris, *Ernest Thompson Seton, Founder of the Woodcraft Movement 1860–1946: Apostle of Indian Wisdom and Pioneer Ecologist* (Lewiston: The Edwin Mellen Press, 2007). See also, Ernest Thompson Seton, *Trail of an Artist-Naturalist: The Autobiography of Ernest Thompson Seton* (New York: Scribner's, 1940).

2. Ernest Thompson Seton, *The Arctic Prairies: A Canoe Journey of 2,000 Miles in Search of the Caribou; Being an Account of a Voyage to the Region North of Aylmer Lake* (New York: Charles Scribner's Sons, 1911). Like Seton, Edward Preble had no formal scientific background. A strong, vigorous man, Preble was as reticent as Seton was loquacious. "It is characteristic of Mr. Preble that he speaks little at any time. But his very appearance proclaims him a man fitted for the difficult voyages repeatedly allotted to him by his government.... [He was] a man of superb physique ... who looked his reputation of being a dead shot and an expert canoeist." *Edmonton Journal*, December 25, 1907. He had already travelled twice to the Arctic, once wintering over at Fort Simpson. For the results of these two expeditions, see Edward A. Preble, *A Biological Investigation of the Hudson Bay Region* (Washington: United States Department of Agriculture, North American Fauna No. 22, 1902); *A Biological Investigation of the Athabaska-Mackenzie Region* (Washington: United States Department of Agriculture, North American Fauna No. 27, 1908). Seton deferred throughout the expedition to Preble's superior scientific knowledge of the land and of wildlife. All of the appendices in *The Arctic Prairies* that relate to birds, insects, plants, or mammals bear Preble's analytical input. In addition, Preble sterned their canoe for the entire expedition. For a brief biography on this remarkable man, see W.L. McAtee, "Memorial: Edward Alexander Preble," in *The Auk*, Vol. 79, No. 4 (October 1962), 730–42.

3. Billy Loutit was born at Fort Chipewyan and worked for the Hudson's Bay Company as a temporary employee and mail carrier until 1912, including fourteen years in charge of the Poplar Point Outpost during the winter season. After that he served primarily as a pilot on HBC scows and steamers. Winnipeg, Hudson's Bay Company Archives RG3/59/17; RG2/37/115; RG# 59B/17. In the

spring of 1904, Athabasca was severely flooded. The Hudson's Bay Company sent two employees, one on horseback, to secure help in Edmonton. Billy Loutit, the second messenger, ran the nearly one-hundred-mile distance cross-country in sixteen hours on foot and, as legend has it, arrived in Edmonton an hour before the horseman. Other similar feats are recorded for Billy. He is remembered in his community as "a man that discouraged bragging but encouraged honesty, diligence and humility." In his honour, the annual one-hundred-mile Billy Loutit Triathlon was established at Athabasca in 2004. *www.thenewmessenger.ca//=16*, accessed on April 10, 2009.

In an interview with the American author Fullerton Leonard Waldo, Billy reported, "Mr. Seton is a nice man. I read his book. The pictures are not in his book the way they really are. He brings everything — so — close up to his tent. It is not really that way. He make believe it all happen right outside the tent. But I like to see him again. An' the other gentleman that was with him, Mr. Preble, mos' of all." Fullerton Leonard Waldo, *Down the Mackenzie Through the Great Lone Land* (New York: Macmillan, 1923), 47.

[Editors' Note: Shannon Loutitt (she spells her name with two *t*s) first learned of her great-grandfather, Billy Loutit, and the stories of his endurance and strength in February 2004. Later that year she discovered the Billy Loutit Triathlon and offered to enter the race along with a number of other relatives. Shannon had no idea what a triathlon was, and was stunned when she realized she would have to swim, run, and bike. She hadn't done either for some time and had just quit smoking after fifteen years. She finished third in the Athabasca race. The next year (2005) she completed six triathlons, and went on to qualify for the Boston Marathon in 2007. More of her inspiring story can be read at *www.thenewmessenger.ca.php5-8. websitetestlink.com/index.php?id=4*, accessed May 26, 2009.]

4. Seton, *Arctic Prairies*, 41, 42, 53.
5. *Ibid.*, 80.
6. *Ibid.*, 94.
7. *Ibid.*, 117. Italics in the original.
8. "Report of Inspector A.M. Jarvis, C.M.G. on Wood Buffalo in the Mackenzie River District." Canada, Report of the Royal North West

Mounted Police, 1907. Sessional Paper No. 28. (Ottawa, 1908), 122–29.

9. Seton, *Arctic Prairies*, 320. The law he refers to is the Unorganized Territories Game Preservation Act of 1894. H.A. Conroy, Treaty 8 inspector, reported to Frank Pedley, deputy superintendent general of Indian Affairs in 1909, that Pierre Squirrel "told me some years ago that if they did not preserve the buffalo their children would never see that animal, and for that reason it was their duty to see that they were not killed. Two years ago when Seaton-Thompson [sic] was up in the buffalo country he reported that it was the Indians who were killing them off, not the wolves as had been reported.... The Indians told us that they had always protected the buffaloes and would continue to do so. They are a very law-abiding people, and as moral as any in my district." H.A. Conroy, Inspector, Treaty 8, to Frank Pedley, Deputy Superintendent General of Indian Affairs, Ottawa, February 19, 1909, in "Supplementary Report of Inspector for Treaty No. 8." Canada, Annual Report of the Department of Indian Affairs, 1910. Sessional Paper No. 27. (Ottawa, 1910), 201. There is a good deal of confusion about who said what to whom. Seton commented to the press immediately upon his return to New York in November 1907 that "throughout the region the game laws are being well administered and the game being conserved. When a game law is carefully explained to an Indian in his own language he is fully as ready to observe it as a white. "Thompson Seton Describes His Farthest North," *New York Times*, November 24, 1907. However, in a speech to the Canadian Club of Edmonton, earlier in the same month, immediately after coming out of the river, Seton made it clear that he still favoured the creation of a new national park for the protection of the bison. *Edmonton Bulletin*, December 25, 1907. See also, Janet Foster, *Working for Wildlife: The Beginning of Preservation in Canada* (Toronto: University of Toronto Press, 1998), 106–09. 2nd edition. One of the nicest, most succinct analyses of the issue and its confusions is Theresa A. Ferguson, "The 'Jarvis Proof': Management of Bison, Management of Bison Hunters, and the Development of a Literary Tradition," in *Proceedings of the Fort Chipewyan and Fort Vermillion Bicentennial Conference*, edited by Patricia A. McCormack

and R. Geoffrey Ironside (Edmonton: Canadian Circumpolar Institute, University of Alberta, 1990), 299–304.

10. Seton's Peterborough canoe was likely in the eighteen to nineteen-and-a-half-foot Rib and Batten Canvas class — probably a Spruce, Stream, or Pine model. See the historical models and serial numbers for the Peterborough Canoe Company at *dragonflycanoe.com/id/peterborough.html*, accessed on April 15, 2009.

11. Seton, *Arctic Prairies*, 174.

12. *Ibid.*, 145.

13. *Ibid.*, 194–95.

14. Seton had suffered from a hernia in his twenties and was obviously reluctant to revisit the operation that had cured it in 1883.

15. Seton, *Arctic Prairies*, 202.

16. *Ibid.*, 204–05.

17. Glen M. MacDonald et al., "Response of the Central Canadian Treeline to Recent Climatic Changes," in *Annals of the Association of American Geographers*, Vol. 88, No. 22 (1998), 192–96.

18. R.W. Brock to Seton, January 14, 1910. Seton Papers, Trent University, 81-014/2/33.

19. Seton, *Arctic Prairies*, 185.

20. *Ibid.*, 210.

21. *Ibid.*, 220–21.

22. *Ibid.*, 221.

23. *Ibid.*, 223. I assume the map he is referring to is that attached to George Back, "An Account of the Route and Appearances of the Country Through Which the Arctic Land Expedition Passed, from Great Slave Lake to the Polar Sea," in *Journal of the Royal Geographical Society of London*, Vol. 6 (1836), 1–11.

24. *Ibid.*, 223. Gwyneth Hoyle mentions that Guy Blanchet came upon a cairn with this same wording at the portage leading from Aylmer to Sussex Lake. Seton did not reach that portage until August 20, so I am puzzled by this observation. Gwyneth Hoyle, *The Northern Horizons of Guy Blanchet, Intrepid Surveyor, 1884–1966* (Toronto: Natural Heritage Books-Dundurn Press, 2007), 76–77. Following Back's example, Seton spoke to the Royal Geographical Society in London about his expedition shortly after his return. In this lecture he said,

"Several weeks were given to compass surveys of Lakes Aylmer and Clinton-Colden. Two great rivers were here discovered: one running into Aylmer from the north was by permission named after the Governor General of Canada, 'Earl Grey river;' the other running into the east end of Clinton-Colden was by permission named in honour of the premier, 'Laurier river.'" Ernest Thompson Seton, "A Canoe Trip to the Plains of the Caribou," in *The Geographical Journal*, Vol. 32, No. 3 (September 1908), 275–77. Upon reading this, Caspar Whitney wrote to Seton somewhat incredulously, inquiring, "Where do you presume that the 'one running into Aylmer' rises, and where the one 'running into Clinton-Colden' takes its source…? Did you ever hear of Hanbury?" Caspar Whitney to Seton, Seton Papers, Trent University, 81-014/2/33. Whitney is referring to David T. Hanbury, "A Journey from Chesterfield Inlet to Great Slave Lake, 1898–9," in *The Geographical Journal*, Vol. 16, No. 1 (July 1900), 63–77. Seton never mentions Hanbury in *The Arctic Prairies* and may indeed not have read this account — though I doubt it. Whitney may have thought that Seton had simply rediscovered Hanbury's route to Clinton-Colden from the east. The inaccuracy of Hanbury's map would have made it possible to draw this conclusion.

25. Seton, *Arctic Prairies*, 228.

26. *Ibid.*, 230.

27. *Ibid.*, 234–35. Seton dressed, skinned, measured, weighed, photographed, and sketched the carcass. "In the many portages afterwards the skull was part of my burden; its weight was actually forty pounds, its heaviness was far over a hundred." Seton provides the detailed measurements of the animal in Appendix F. Seton, *Arctic Prairies*, 342.

28. G.H. Blanchet, *Great Slave Lake Area Northwest Territories* (Ottawa: King's Printer, 1926). The excellent fold-out map accompanying this very useful monograph is "compiled and drawn by the Topographical Survey of Canada, 1926." Whitney's map is in Caspar Whitney, *On Snow-Shoes to the Barren Grounds* (New York: Harper and Bros., 1896), 185.

29. Seton, *Arctic Prairies*, 237. Hanbury had reached Aylmer Lake but did not get this far north.

30. *Ibid.*, 251.

31. Ernest Thompson Seton, *Lives of Game Animals* (Boston: Charles T. Banford Co., 1953). Four volumes. This is a reprint of the 1925–28 edition, but the only one available to me. The four volumes of the first, limited edition were broken down into eight, each of the original volumes thus having two parts. The Barren Ground Caribou are covered in Volume 3, Part 1, 95–135; the Muskox in Volume 3, Part 2, 595–637; the Wood Buffalo in Volume 3, Part 2, 705–17. In each case, Seton uses drawings in the journals from the 1907 expedition to illustrate his text, large parts of which are also based upon journal entries.

32. Seton, *Arctic Prairies*, 255.

33. Verification of this can be found by a visit to the Special Collections in the Trent University Archives, to which Seton's family donated the main portion of his fully annotated library of northern books in 1981.

34. Seton, *Arctic Prairies*, 220, 259, 261.

35. *Ibid.*, 262.

36. *Ibid.*, 264.

37. *Ibid.*, 268–69.

38. *Ibid.*, 285.

39. Robillard was one of three Métis to replace Weeso at points between Resolution and Athabasca Landing, the other two being George Sanderson and Grégoire Daniel, also known as Bellelisle. Francis Harper reported to W.L. McAtee that "Elzéar Robillard, one of the men on the towline, told him that the upset was altogether Seton's fault." McAtee, "Memorial," 732.

40. Seton, *Arctic Prairies*, 295.

41. *Ibid.*, 308.

42. Seton has come under renewed critical scrutiny from a number of fine young scholars. See, for example, John Sandlos, *Hunters at the Margin: Native People and Wildlife Conservation in the Northwest Territories* (Vancouver: University of British Columbia Press, 2007); Misao Dean, "'The Mania for Killing': Hunting and Collecting in Seton's *The Arctic Prairies*," in *Other Selves: Animals in the Canadian Literary Imagination*, edited by Janice Fiamengo (Ottawa: University of Ottawa Press, 2007), 290–304; Brian Johnson, "National Species: Ecology, Allegory and Indigeneity in the Wolf Stories of Roberts,

Seton, and Mowat," in *Other Selves: Animals in the Canadian Literary Imagination*, edited by Janice Fiamengo (Ottawa: University of Ottawa Press, 2007), 333–52; Manina Jones, "Wildlifewriting? Animal Stories and Indigenous Claims in Ernest Thompson Seton's *Wild Animals I Have Known*," in *Journal of Canadian Studies*, Vol. 42, No. 3 (Fall 2008), 133–49.

43. Carl Berger, *The Sense of Power: Studies in the Ideas of Canadian Imperialism, 1867–1914* (Toronto: University of Toronto Press, 1970). A classic statement is found in appendix A, "The New North-West," where Seton writes, without hesitation, "The highest product of civilization we believe to have been the white man of northern Europe — a product indeed of the snow. This should help us to forecast the future of the North." Seton, *Arctic Prairies*, 316. One has to believe that Seton's sense of irony would have invited a reconsideration of these thoughts could he have been here to witness the effects of the Bennett Dam, or the Athabasca Tar Sands, on the descendants of his friends at Fort Chipewyan.

44. Ernest Thompson Seton, *Life Histories of Northern Animals*. (New York: Charles Scribner's Sons, 1909). Two volumes: *Lives of Game Animals*. (Doubleday, Page, 1925–28). Four volumes. Edward Preble was Seton's chief consultant on both books. See also note 35.

45. Ernest Thompson Seton, *The Book of Woodcraft and Indian Lore* (New York: Doubleday, Page, 1912), 57. In this volume Seton's spirited defence of Native people is quite remarkable, especially given the time at which he was writing. He routinely cites sources like Helen Hunt Jackson's *A Century of Dishonor: A Sketch of the United States Government's Dealings with Some of the Indian Tribes* (New York: Harper, 1881) demonstrating a thorough understanding of the abuse suffered by Native people in North America. He pinpoints and explores in detail specific cases — such as the Battle of Wounded Knee (1890) which occurred when he was thirty years old. He has read and, to support his angry and passionate critique, quotes directly from James Mooney's "The Ghost Dance Religion and the Sioux Outbreak of 1890," *Fourteenth Annual Report of the Bureau of Ethnology to the Secretary of the Smithsonian Institution, 1892–93* (Washington: Government Printing Office, 1894), 641–1,136. He

was a close friend of Charles Eastman (Ohiyesa) a Dakota Sioux medical doctor at the Pine Ridge Reservation in South Dakota who ministered to the victims. In other words, he is not easily dismissed as ignorant of or unsympathetic to Native cultures. *Book of Woodcraft*, 16, 59, 534–37.

Chapter 7: Buffalo Jones: God's Work, But Whose God?

1. Robert Easton and MacKenzie Brown, *Lord of Beasts: The Saga of Buffalo Jones* (Tucson, AZ: University of Arizona Press, 1961), 161.

2. I fully appreciate that the convention of the word *exploration* used here is merely a device Euro-Canadian travellers used, and are still using, to denote their trips on the well-explored, travelled landscape of indigenous populations. Warburton Pike put this well: "In following out this plan I naturally passed through a great deal of new country, and discovered, as we white men say when we are pointed out some geographical feature by an Indian who has been familiar with it since childhood, many lakes and small streams never before visited except by the red man." Graeme Wynn in "The Enigmatic North," the foreword to *Hunters at the Margin* by John Sandlos (Vancouver: University of British Columbia Press, 2007) wisely acknowledges Pike's self-identification as a "translator" more than a creator of information. "Most of those who came from afar to draw the features of the land into European atlases and western worldviews were translators as much as creators of information about these vast spaces. Few were as explicit about their borrowing and dependence as the English adventurer Warburton Pike...."

3. Randy Freeman, a northern historian and author of chapter 9 in this book, tells a story from the local oral tradition, that John Franklin had to be tied up by his Yellowknife helpers to get him finally out of the country.

4. Easton and Brown, *Lord of Beasts*, 235.

5. *Ibid.*, 235.

6. See Grey Owl, *A Book of Grey Owl* (Toronto: Macmillan of Canada, 1964).

7. Easton and Brown, *Lord of Beasts*, 181. Ernest Thompson Seton (see chapter 6) attended the farewell dinner in New York City (1909) to honour Buffalo Jones en route to African adventures. Seton had just returned from his own Arctic adventures. Easton and Brown, *Lord of Beasts*, 162.

8. As for big game hunters before Jones (1897) there was Warburton Pike (1890). After Jones there was David Hanbury (1902) and Ernest Thompson Seton (1907). Of course, local Native tribes from all directions were occasional hunters of muskox.

9. Charles Jesse Jones, with Henry Inman, *Buffalo Jones' Forty Years of Adventure* (London: Sampson Low, Marston and Company, 1899), 307.

10. Jones does not mention Warburton Pike's travels in the region (1889–90, completed six years earlier). However, he regularly mentions George Back. One might surmise that his own story is bolstered by ignoring Pike — the accommodating hunter — who was such a contrast to his own antagonistic ways. The 1830s explorer Back is safe for Jones to mention because his was no threat to the Jones hunting story. Then again, perhaps Jones had never heard of Pike.

11. Easton and Brown, *Lord of Beasts*, 93.

12. *Ibid.*, 103, and Jones with Inman, *Forty Years*, 371. It appears to be a surprise to Jones that muskox circle up and stand their ground to threats from predators.

13. Jones with Inman, *Forty Years*, 398. Editors' Note: We asked Roger Catling, a wolf hunter at Reliance for over thirty years, to comment on the Jones/Rea wolf attack story. He commented: "Now that's a tall tale if I ever heard one! But like all tall tales there is a bit of truth to it. Very occasionally a pack of wolves will circle a camp a few times. Shooting one of them will cause the rest to flee in a hurry and they would never stop to eat the downed one. They may come back and eat the dead one a few days after the camp is gone."

14. Jones with Inman, *Forty Years*, 384. I must add that Jones had wanted to return south with calves not yearlings, but his arrangement to have a milk supply arrive north failed when a travel partner abandoned them for the Alaska gold rush.

15. *Ibid.*, 392.

16. *Ibid.*, 395. But one must pause to wonder how they could know these distances in a yet unmapped land and amid much wandering and snow blizzard travel.

17. Mary Evans, *A Short History of Society: The Making of the Modern World* (Maidenhead, UK: Open University Press, 2008), 44.

18. Rudy Wiebe, *A River of Stone: Fictions and Memories* (Toronto: Random House, 2001), 2.

19. Theodore Roszak, *Person/Plant: The Creative Disintegration of Industrial Society* (New York: Doubleday & Co., 1979), 49.

20. George Grinnell, *A Death in the Barrens* (Toronto: Northern Books, 1996), 99.

21. Steve Paulson, God enough: *www.salon.com/env/atoms_eden/2008/11/19/stuart_kauffman/print.html*, accessed on May 27, 2009.

Chapter 8: J.W. Tyrrell: The Man Who Named Pike's Portage

1. J.W. Tyrrell, Department of the Interior. *Report on an Exploratory Survey between Great Slave Lake and Hudson Bay, Districts of Mackenzie and Keewatin.* Ottawa, ON: Department of the Interior, Government Print Bureau, 1901, 2.

2. *Ibid.*, 16. See David Hanbury, *Sport and Travel in the Northland of Canada* (London: Edward Arnold, 1904).

3. *Ibid.*, 12.

4. *Ibid.*

5. *Ibid.*

6. *Ibid.*, 14.

7. *Ibid.*

8. *Ibid.*, 16–18.

9. *Ibid.*, 24.

10. *Ibid.*, 28.

11. *Ibid.*, 31.

12. *Ibid.*, 32.

13. *Ibid.*

14. *Ibid.*

15. *Ibid.*, 32–33.
16. *Ibid.*, 34.
17. *Ibid.*
18. *Ibid.*, 34–35.
19. *Ibid.*, 35.
20. *Ibid.*, 37.

Part III: On the Trail in the Early 1900s

1. John Sandlos, *Hunters at the Margin* (Vancouver, BC: University of British Columbia Press, 2007), 141.

Chapter 9: The Beaulieu Clan: "Unlettered People"

1. Émile Petitot, *Travels Around Great Slave and Great Bear Lakes, 1862–1882* (Toronto: The Champlain Society, 2005), 52.
2. The Tatsanottine are often referred to in the historic literature as Yellowknife, Redknife, or Copper Indians, a group related to, but distinct from, the Chipewyan. Those descendents of the Tatsanottine, who call themselves Rocher River people, are not part of the present-day Yellowknives Dene. The Tłįcho, until recently, were known as the Dogrib Dene. Danny Beaulieu is a renewable resource officer with the government of the Northwest Territories. He is based in Yellowknife.
3. Chris Hanks, *François Beaulieu II: Son of the Last coureurs de bois in the Far Northwest*, Historic Sites and Monuments Board of Canada, Agenda Paper. n.d.
4. Hanks, *Beaulieu*, 5.
5. Warburton Pike, *The Barren Ground of Northern Canada* (London: Macmillan and Co., 1892), 21.
6. *Ibid.*, 18.
7. Editors' Note: See chapter 6 in this book for further treatment on another sporting gentleman, E.T. Seton.
8. Pike, *Northern Canada*, 21.
9. Guy Blanchet, "Thelewey-aza-yeth," in *The Beaver*, Vol. 28, No.

2 (September 1949), 8–11. Also see David Pelly, *Thelon: A River Sanctuary* (Hyde Park, ON: The Canadian Recreational Canoeing Association, 1996) and David Pelly, *Old Ways North* (St. Paul: Minnesota Historical Society Press, 2008) for insight into the Chipewyan trading routes out of Fort Churchill.

10. Émile Petitot, *Traditions indiennes du Canada nord-ouest* (Paris: Maisonneuve Frères, 1886), 430.

11. Hanks, *Beaulieu*, 10. The Castle, sometimes called Bear Lake Castle, was at or very near the current location for Déline (Fort Franklin). In fact, Franklin's men, when building Fort Franklin, used building materials from the old North West Company post.

12. Kerry Abel, *Drum Songs: Glimpses of Dene History* (Montreal and Kingston: McGill-Queen's University Press, 1993), 86.

13. Hanks, *Beaulieu*, 20.

14. Akaitcho assisted the Franklin expedition of 1819–21. He later supported George Back's 1833–35 expedition down the Great Fish River (Back River) by supplying meat during wintering-over at Fort Reliance.

15. Émile Petitot, *En route pour la mer glaciale* (Paris: Letouzey et ane, 1887), 313.

16. Sheryl Grieve, *North Slave Métis Alliance Scope of Concerns for the Environmental Assessment of the Giant Mine Remediation Project.* (Presented July 23, 2008).

17. Editors' Note: The exact location of the Beaulieu's East Arm trading post named Fond du Lac is difficult to ascertain. As editors, we have searched high and low in the literature, on archival maps, and spoken to local people, as well, in our attempt to pinpoint it. There seems to be consensus that this Fond du Lac was somewhere near Taltheilei Narrows and perhaps where Plummer's Great Slave Lodge sits today. Months ago, Randy Freeman asked Danny Beaulieu where Fond du Lac was; Danny indicated that it was a different location at different times. What is clear is that Fond du Lac was a Beaulieu camp.

18. Hanks, *Beaulieu*, 30.

19. *www.pc.gc.ca/apps/lhn-nhs/det_E.asp?oqSID=1920&oqeName=Beaulieu+II%2C+Fran%E7ois&oqfName=Beaulieu+II%2C+Fran%E7ois* (Parks Canada, accessed May 21, 2009).

20. Petitot, *Travels Around*, 52.

Chapter 10: Guy Blanchet: A Northern Surveyor on Pike's Portage

1. British Columbia Archives (BCA) hereinafter BCA, MS-0498, Box 9, 10.
2. BCA, MS-0498, Box 12, Folder 27.
3. Warburton Pike, *The Barren Ground of Northern Canada* (New York: Dutton, 1917), 23–24.
4. Seton, Ernest Thompson, *Arctic Prairies* (New York: Harper Colophon, 1981), 189.
5. BCA, MS-0498, Box 9, 10.
6. Blanchet, "Exploring with Sousi and Black Basile," in *The Beaver* (Summer, 1960), 34–41.
7. National Archives of Canada, MG 30, Vol. 2, File 11.
8. Blanchet, "Exploring with Sousi and Black Basile."
9. Editors' note: This picture of Guy Blanchet was taken at the headwaters of the Coppermine River in 1924. On his return trip to Great Slave Lake, Guy met John Hornby at Reliance as he was preparing to make his way over the portage with Critchell-Bullock. Gwyneth Hoyle tells the story of their meeting in *Northern Horizons of Guy Blanchet*, 80–81: "Despite his often unkempt appearance, Hornby had some vanity. When they met, Guy was sporting two months growth of whiskers, having just come off a long trip on the Barrens. Hornby, seeing the effect of a beard on his friend's appearance, immediately dashed off to his shack and shaved."
10. Editors' note: For more about the life of Guy Blanchet, see Gwyneth Hoyle, *The Northern Horizons of Guy Blanchet* (Toronto: Natural Heritage Books-Dundurn Press, 2007).

Chapter 11: John Hornby: An Uncommon Man

1. Pierre Berton, *Prisoners of the North* (New York: Carrol and Graff, 2004), 219.
2. Edgar Christian, *Unflinching: A Diary of Tragic Adventure* (London: John Murray, 1937).

3. George Whalley, *The Legend of John Hornby* (Toronto: Macmillan, 1962).

4. Melvill is spelled two different ways in the Hornby literature. It is spelled both as Melvill and Melville.

5. The Melvill party included James Mackinlay, a Hudson's Bay man who had accompanied Warburton Pike in 1889–90.

6. Whalley, *Hornby*, 52.

7. In the fall of 1914, Le Roux and Rouvière were murdered by two Inuit men on a return trip along the Coppermine River to Dease Lake. Hornby had warned Le Roux and Rouvière of the hostilities that were building with the Inuit but was ignored. For more on this story, see McKay Jenkins, *Bloody Falls of the Coppermine: Madness and Murder in the Arctic Barren Lands.* (New York: Random House, 2006).

8. Fort Franklin is located on the southwest shore of Great Bear Lake near the mouth of the Great Bear River. Fort Franklin was built by George Back in the fall of 1825 and Franklin's crew of his Second Land Expedition spent the winters of 1825–26 and 1826–27 at Fort Franklin. Fort Franklin is known today as Déline.

9. Whalley, *Hornby*, 111.

10. *Ibid.*, 113.

11. *Ibid.*, 131.

12. *Ibid.*, 133.

13. Fort Reliance was home to others after George Back built it in 1833 and lived there during the winters of 1833–34 and 1834–35. These others include Anderson and Stewart (1855), Buffalo Jones (1897), J.W. Tyrrell (1900), and E.T. Seton (1907).

14. Whalley, *Hornby*, 154.

15. *Ibid.*, 148.

16. "Make preparations" was a phrase Hornby had used many times in his life of privation in the North, which meant "doing the last things before death." Whalley, *Hornby*, 309.

17. Roger Catling claims that Hornby set up his tent and later built his second cabin on the site that is now Roger's home. Roger Catling, personal communication, April 16, 2009.

18. Malcolm Waldron, *Snow Man: John Hornby in the Barren Lands* (Montreal: McGill-Queens University Press, 1997), 3.

19. Whalley, *Hornby*, 243.
20. Waldron, *Snow Man*, 31.
21. *Ibid.*, 32.
22. *Ibid.*, 226.
23. The story of Hornby and Bullock's winter in the cave is told in *Snow Man* by Malcolm Waldron. See "The Letter," chapter 12 in this book, for Guy Blanchet's humorous story involving a letter from the Hornby/Bullock expedition.
24. Berton, *Prisoners of the North*, 216.
25. Whalley, *Hornby*, 251.
26. *Ibid.*, 28.
27. Robert Common describes finding this cache in Robert Common, "Soviet Satellite Debris Hits Historic Area and Recalls Tragic Hornby Drama of 1927," in *Canadian Geographic*, Vol. 97, No. 1 (August/September, 1978), 8–17. Robert and five other men spent the winter of 1977–78 at Warden's Grove on the Thelon to honour Hornby on the fiftieth anniversary of his death. Among the many stories detailed in this article is the story of the Russian Nuclear-powered Satellite Cosmos 954 that came crashing into their winter of isolation. For more on Robert Common and his winter at Warden's Grove, see Christopher Norment, *In the North of Our Lives*. Camden, ME: Down East Books, 1989.
28. Whalley, *Hornby*, 289.
29. Christian, *Unflinching*, 60.
30. *Ibid.*, 129.
31. Whalley, *Hornby*, 310. Some sources say Christian wrote on a note that was left on the stove, some say a note was hanging on the stove pipe, while others still say he wrote in charcoal on the stove door.
32. Kenneth Dewer was a member of prospecting party that travelled the Thelon River in the summer of 1928. His party had been alerted by the RCMP in Fort Smith about the Hornby party's disappearance and asked to keep a lookout for them. Dewer describes his party finding the cabin and discovering the remains of the bodies. It is a fascinating story. The Dewer party reported their gruesome find to the RCMP at Chesterfield Inlet, and in the summer of 1929 the RCMP sent a party to investigate the site and bury the bodies. It was the RCMP that found Edgar Christian's diary. See Kenneth M. Dewer, "I Found the Bodies of the Hornby

Party," in *Canadian Geographic* (August/September, 1978), 18–23.

33. Christina Sawchuk, "The Myth of John Hornby." Unpublished Honours Thesis, University of Alberta, 2005.

34. Waldron, *Snow Man*.

35. Whalley, *Hornby*.

36. Alex Hall, *Discovering Eden: A Lifetime of Paddling Arctic Rivers* (Toronto: Key Porter, 2003), 144.

37. C.H.D. Clarke, "The Thelon Game Sanctuary." Paper presented at the Arctic Explorers Symposium, Toronto, 1978.

38. Roger Catling, personal communication, August 6, 2006.

39. Waldron, *Snow Man*, x.

40. Whalley, *Hornby*, 264.

41. John Hornby, "Report of the Explorations in the District Between Artillery Lake and Chesterfield Inlet." National Archives of Canada, RG 85, Vol. 740, File 20 — Hornby.

42. David Pelly, *Thelon: A River Sanctuary* (Hyde Park, ON: Canadian Recreational Canoeing Association, 1996), 60.

Chapter 12: The Letter

1. The Letter (Guy Blanchet, "The Letter," *The Beaver* (Spring 1963), 41–44) is reprinted with permission of Canada's National History Society.

2. From the introduction to "The Letter" in the original publication.

   In addition to his work as a surveyor, Guy Blanchet was also an author and contributed ten articles to *The Beaver* between 1936 and 1963. He also authored the book *Search in the North* (Toronto: Macmillan, 1960). Interestingly, when Blanchet first submitted "The Letter" to *The Beaver* magazine, it was rejected. However, after the release of Whalley's book, *The Legend of John Hornby* (Toronto: Macmillan, 1962) "The Letter" was accepted and published in 1963. We chose to include "The Letter" in our collection of stories because we love the story and think it provides light-hearted insight into the bizarre winter that Hornby and Critchell-Bullock spent together in the esker cave as well as the odd relationship they developed during that time. Furthermore, Blanchet tells the story so well that to retell it seemed unimaginable.

Chapter 13: Helge Ingstad: Inspiration for a Life of Adventure in the Land of Feast and Famine

1. Nils Lund, dir. *Helge Ingstad. The Man That Proved the Vikings Were First*. 1999. Videotape.

2. Basic biographical information about Helge Ingstad has been gleaned from the following sources: Susan Barr, "Ingstad, Helge," *Encyclopedia of the Arctic*, Vol. 2, ed. Mark Nuttall (New York & London: Routledge, 2005), 974–75; Birte Svatun, *Anne Stine og Helge Ingstad: Historien om et nysgjerrig par* (Oslo: N.W. Damm & Søn, 2004);Arne Emil Christensen, "Helge Ingstad 1899–2001," *Norsk Geografisk Tidsskrift*, in *Norwegian Journal of Geography*, Vol. 56 (March 2002), 47–48; Douglas Martin, "Helge Ingstad, Discoverer of Viking Site, Dies at 101," *New York Times*, March 30, 2001; Finn Robert Jensen, "Pelsjegeren som endret historien," *Aftenposten*, March 30, 2001, 16.

3. Ragnhild Plesner, "Eventyrerens siste reise," *Aftenposten*, April 6, 2001. Jens Stoltenberg was not the only person to express this sentiment. The title of a full-page article by Finn Robert Jensen that appeared in the major Norwegian newspaper *Aftenposten* the day after Ingstad's death was "Pelsgjegeren som endret historien" ("The Trapper that Changed History"). See page 16 of the March 30, 2001, edition of *Aftenposten*.

4. Ingstad used the term *Caribou Eaters* to describe the group of Dene with whom he lived. This is now an outdated term.

5. Helge Ingstad, Trans. Eugene Gay-Tifft, *The Land of Feast and Famine* (Montreal and Kingston: McGill-Queen's University Press, 1992), xii. This book was originally published as *Pelsjegerliv Blandt Nord-Kanadas Indianere* (Oslo: Gyldendal, 1931). It was first published in English in 1933 by Alfred A. Knopf. The quotations in this chapter are taken from the 1992 McGill-Queen's edition, as are the stories related.

6. See previous note for complete bibliographic information. The literal translation of the original title is "The Life of a Trapper among North-Canadian Indians."

7. Books by Ingstad that are available in English include: *The Apache Indians: In Search of the Missing Tribe* (Lincoln: University of Nebraska

Press, 2004); *The Viking Discovery of America: The Excavation of a Norse Settlement in L'Anse Aux Meadows, Newfoundland* (New York: Checkmark Books, 2001). Anne Stine Ingstad is the co-author; *Land Under the Pole Star: A Voyage to the Medieval Norse Settlements of Greenland and the Saga of a People that Vanished* (London: Cape, 1966); *Nunamiut: Among Alaska's Inland Eskimos* (New York: W.W. Norton, 1954).

8. Fridtjof Nansen (1861–1930) and Roald Amundsen (1872–1928) are perhaps the two most famous Polar explorers that Norway has produced. Nansen was the first person to cross Greenland on skis, and he gained an international reputation for his voyage toward the North Pole in the polar ship *Fram* from 1893–96. He also received the Nobel Peace Prize in 1922 for his humanitarian work. Amundsen was the first person to reach the South Pole, arriving there with his team in 1911, one month before Scott. Amundsen was also the first person to successfully transverse the Northwest Passage (1903–06). Both Nansen and Amundsen published bestselling books based on their groundbreaking feats. (Editors' note: The Norwegian ski-touring company ASNES used the faces of Nansen, Amundsen, and Ingstad as the surface art on a number of their 2009 model skis.)

9. Christensen, *Helge Ingstad 1899–2001*, 47–48.

10. Svatun, *Anne Stine og Helge Ingstad*, 7–9.

11. The literal translation of the Norwegian word *friluftsliv* is "open air living." It describes the Scandinavian approach to relating to nature and outdoor life. For further reading, see Bob Henderson and Nils Vikander, eds. *Nature First: Outdoor Life the Friluftsliv Way* (Toronto: Natural Heritage Books-Dundurn Press, 2007).

12. Christensen, *Helge Ingstad 1899–2001*, 47.

13. Svatun, *Anne Stine og Helge Ingstad*, 10–12.

14. Lund, *Vikings Were First*.

15. *I Helge Ingstads Fotspor*. Dir. Nils Lund and Stein P. Aasheim. Plenum Film, 1998.

16. Ingstad, *The Land of Feast and Famine*, 44.

17. *Ibid.*, 44.

18. Moose Lake is identified on most topographical maps today southwest of Reliance.

19. Lund, *Vikings Were First* (see note 13) is in English and covers a number of Ingstad's accomplishments and adventures. It is more comprehensive than *I Helge Ingstads Fotspor* (see note 14) which is in Norwegian and focuses on Ingstad's years in the eastern Great Slave Lake region. These two projects were filmed in conjunction with each other near the end of Ingstad's life. Helge Ingstad is interviewed in both, and his grandson, Eirik Ingstad Sandberg, is a central figure in both productions.

20. Ingstad, *The Land of Feast and Famine*, 145.

21. *Ibid.*, 287.

22. Lund, *Vikings Were First*.

23. Klondike Bill (Woodney) was a colourful prospector, hunter, and trapper who spent time in the Northwest Territories, Yukon, and Alaska in the early twentieth century. His life served as the inspiration for Ingstad's *Klondyke Bill*, originally published by Ingstad's Norwegian publisher Gyldendal in 1941. The book was translated into English by F.H. Lyon under the same title and published in 1955 by W. Kimber of London.

24. Ingstad, *The Land of Feast and Famine*, 238.

25. *Ibid.*, 236.

26. *Ibid.*, 283–84.

27. *Ibid.*, 318.

28. Lund, *Vikings Were First*.

29. Ingstad, *The Land of Feast and Famine*, 328–29.

30. Lars Monsen, *Nådeløs Villmark: Canada på tvers* (Oslo: Lars Monsen Outdoors, 2002), 150.

31. *Ibid.*, 15.

32. Fridtjof Kjæreng. dir. *Canada på tvers*. NRK, 2004. [Film]. Monsen, *Nådeløs Villmark*, 163.

33. Monsen, *Nådeløs Villmark*, 163. Ingstad died on March 29, 2001.

34. *Ibid.*, 172–73.

35. *Ibid.*, 173.

36. Helge Ingstad, *Sporisneen, Etterlatte dikt* (Oslo: Gyldendal, 2002), 28–32.

37. Lund, *Vikings Were First*.

38. Ingstad, *The Land of Feast and Famine*, 332.

Part IV: On the Trail to the Present

1. Pierre Berton, *The Mysterious North* (New York: Alfred A. Knopf, 1956), 324.

Chapter 14: Gus D'Aoust: Living a Dream on the Barrens

1. Alix Harpelle, *Those Were the Days That I Lived and Loved: A Biography of Gus D'Aoust, A Professional Barrenland Trapper* (Steinbach, MB: Martens Printing, 1984), 48.
2. *Ibid.*, 32.
3. *Ibid.*, 146.
4. Some of the dates and locations may be incorrect. Gus was an aging man when he told these stories to Alix Harpelle, who wrote the book *Those Were the Days That I Lived and Loved: A Biography of Gus D'Aoust, A Professional Barrenland Trapper*. I once asked Roger Catling of Reliance, who had been mentored as a trapper by Gus, if he felt that this book was a true reflection of Gus and his life. Roger thought it was, but indicated that some of the details, such and dates and locations, were incorrect simply because Gus could no longer remember them.
5. Harpelle, *Those Were the Days That I Lived and Loved*, 20.
6. *Ibid.*, 23.
7. For a complete story of the creation of Wood Buffalo Park and its impact on hunting and trapping, as well as other issues of hunting and trapping in the Northwest Territories, see John Sandlos, *Hunters at the Margin: Native People and Wildlife Conservation in the Northwest Territories* (Vancouver: UBC Press, 2007).
8. Harpelle, *Those Were the Days That I Lived and Loved*, 42.
9. *Ibid.*, 71.
10. Pierre Berton, *The Mysterious North* (New York: Alfred. A. Knopf, 1956), 336.
11. Harpelle, *Those Were the Days That I Lived and Loved*, 91.
12. *Ibid.*, 92.
13. *Ibid.*, 96.

14. George Magrum and his two sons also spent many years trapping in that region.

15. A toggle is a stick about five feet long, which the trap was attached to. Its purpose was to keep the trap secure.

16. Harpelle, *Those Were the Days That I Lived and Loved*, 82.

17. *Ibid.*, 60.

18. *Ibid.*, 64.

19. David Pelly, *Thelon: A River Sanctuary* (Hyde Park, ON: Canadian Recreational Canoeing Association, 1996), 33–34.

20. Berton, *The Mysterious North*, 338.

21. Harpelle, *Those Were the Days That I Lived and Loved*, 203.

22. See chapter 15 in this volume, Roger Catling: The Last Wolf Hunter in Reliance.

23. Roger Catling, personal communication, August 9, 2006.

24. *Ibid.*

25. *Ibid.*

26. *Ibid.*

27. Harpelle, *Those Were the Days That I Lived and Loved*, 194.

28. *Ibid.*, 48.

29. Helge Ingstad, *The Land of Feast and Famine* (Montreal: McGill/Queen's Press, 1931/1992), 4.

30. Harpelle, *Those Were the Days That I Lived and Loved*, viii.

31. *Ibid.*, 207.

Chapter 15: Roger Catling: The Last Wolf Hunter in Reliance

1. Kristen Olesen and her husband Dave have lived at the mouth of the Hoarfrost River on the north shore of McLeod Bay for over twenty years. They have two daughters and many sled dogs. For their story, see chapter 16.

2. Old Fort Reliance was built in the fall of 1833 by A.R. McLeod of the Hudson's Bay Company. He accompanied George Back on the 1833–35 expedition in search of Sir John Ross down the Great Fish River (now Back River). As Back went up the Hoarfrost River in August

1833, in search of the headwaters of the Back River, he sent McLeod to build winter quarters at the head of the lake. Back and his crew wintered at Old Fort Reliance for two years, 1833–34 and 1834–35. The Fort was later used by Anderson and Stewart (1855), Buffalo Jones (1897), J.W. Tyrrell (1900), and E.T. Seton (1907). Great Slave Lake's McLeod Bay is named after A.R. McLeod. For more on the George Back story, see chapter 4.

3. Gus D'Aoust was a hunter and trapper who trapped in the region beginning in the 1930s. He left in the 1970s with failing eyesight and deteriorating knees. He was Roger Catling's mentor. For details of D'Aoust's life, see chapter 14.

4. All quotes from Roger are from a personal interview by Morten Asfeldt and Bob Henderson, conducted on August 9, 2006, in Reliance, Northwest Territories, unless otherwise noted.

5. For the complete story, see Christopher Norment, *In the North of Our Lives: A Year in the Wilderness of Northern Canada.* (Camden, ME: Down East Books, 1989).

6. Noel Drybones lived, hunted, and trapped in this region throughout his lifetime. Remains of his cabins, camps, and boats are easily found along Pike's Portage and the shores of Artillery Lake. Many of his family continue to live in Lutsel K'e. For stories of his life, see chapter 2.

7. The route up Pike's Portage to Acres Lake and east to Barrenlands Lake (a local name) has long been a common winter route to the Thelon River. This route is much shorter than the summer route through Artillery Lake to Ptarmingan Lake and down the Hanbury River. This route is possible in winter because the lakes are frozen, making portages irrelevant.

8. Roger Catling, personal communication, December 17, 2008.

9. Thank you to my colleague Varghese Manaloor, associate professor of economics, Augustana Campus, University of Alberta, for this conversion.

10. Roger Catling, personal communication, December 17, 2008.

11. Mark Downey, Fur Harvesters Auction CEO, personal communication, November 17, 2008.

12. Dean Cluff, regional biologist, Government of the Northwest Territories, personal communication, November 27, 2008.

13. Rebecca Grambo, *Wolf: Legend, Enemy, Icon* (Richmond Hill, ON: Firefly Books, 2005).
14. Roger Catling, personal communication, October 25, 2008.

Chapter 16: North of Reliance

1. Editors' note: This chapter is composed of a number of passages from Dave Olesen's book *North of Reliance* (Minocoqua, WI: Northword Press, 1994). The quoted material is used with permission of the author. The last section of the chapter was written by Dave specifically for this book in the spring of 2009.
2. Annie Dillard, *The Writing Life* (New York: HarperPerennial, 1990), 32.
3. John Haines, *The Stars, the Snow, the Fire: Twenty-five Years in the Northern Wilderness: A Memoir* (Saint Paul, MN: Greywolf Press, 2000).
4. See Dave Olesen, ed. *A Wonderful Country: The Quetico-Superior Stories of Bill Magie* (Ely, MN: Raven Productions, 2005).

PART V Epilogue

1. Yi-Fu Tuan, *Space and Place: The Perspective of Experience* (Minneapolis: University of Minnesota Press, 1977), 6.

Chapter 17: Thaidene Nene: The Land of the Ancestors

1. Peter Lee, *Boreal Canada: State of the Ecosystem*. Report for the National Round Table on the Environment and Economy. (Edmonton: Global Forest Watch, 2004); Dirk Bryant, Daniel Nielsen, Laura Tangley, *The Last Frontier Forests: Ecosystems and Economies on the Edge* (Washington, DC: World Resources Institute, 1997).
2. Michael Soule, John Terborgh, Wildlands Project, *Continental Conservation*. (Washington, DC: Island Press, 1999).
3. Javier Beltrán, Adrian Phillips, *Indigenous and Traditional Peoples*

and *Protected Areas: Principles, Guidelines and Case Studies* (Cardiff, UK: IUCN World Commission on Protected Areas, 2000).

4. Dene Nation, *Dene History* (*www.denenation.com/denehistory.html*, accessed May 11, 2009).

5. John Sandlos, *Hunters at the Margin: Native People and Wildlife Conservation in the Northwest Territories*. (Vancouver: University of British Columbia Press, 2007), 75.

6. *News of the North*, July 31, 1969.

7. Thomas Berger was the commissioner of the Mackenzie Valley Pipeline Inquiry, which was initiated by the Government of Canada on March 21, 1974, to investigate the social, environmental, and economic impact of a proposed gas pipeline that would run through the Yukon and the Mackenzie River Valley of the Northwest Territories. Ultimately, Justice Berger recommended against the building of the pipeline, calling for a ten-year moratorium on the project in order to deal with local land claims and environmental issues and concerns. Thomas R. Berger, *Northern Frontier, Northern Homeland: The Report of the Mackenzie Valley Pipeline Inquiry*. Vol. 1 (Ottawa: Supply and Services Canada, 1977).

8. *Lutsel K'e Dene First Nation, Community-Based Monitoring: Final Report*. (NWT: West Kitikmeot Slave Study Society, 2002).

9. A National Park Reserve has the same designate as a National Park pending the completion of any outstanding Aboriginal land claims.

10. Mackenzie Valley Environmental Impact Review Board, *Report of Assessment and Reasons for Decision on UR Energy Inc. Screech Lake Uranium Exploration Project EA 0607-003* (Yellowknife: MVEIRB, May 7, 2007).

11. *Ibid.*

12. David Pelly, letter to MVEIRB re: Ur-Energy, May 30, 2005. The Murray McLauchlan song is called "Out Past the Timberline" and the chorus is "No Canada ain't some cabinet man; In the Rideau club at election time; Oh Canada is somewhere out there; Out Past the timberline." (Timberline Gullwing Music, True North Records, CAPAR, 1983).

Selected Bibliography

Abel, Kerry. *Drum Songs: Glimpses of Dene History.* Montreal and Kingston: McGill-Queen's University Press, 1993.

Anderson, H. Allen. *The Chief: Ernest Thompson Seton and the Changing West.* College Station: Texas A&M University Press, 1986.

Back, George. *Narrative of the Arctic Land Expedition to the Mouth of the Great Fish River and Along the Shores of the Arctic Ocean in the Years 1833, 1834, and 1835.* Boston: Adamant Media Corporation, 2005. Originally published in 1836.

Berton, Pierre. *The Mysterious North.* New York: Alfred. A. Knopf, 1956.

———. *Prisoners of the North.* New York: Carroll & Graf, 2004.

Brody, Hugh. *The People's Land: Eskimos and Whites in the Eastern Arctic.* Markham, ON: Penguin Books, 1975.

Christian, Edgar. *Unflinching: A Diary of Tragic Adventure*. London, UK: John Murray, 1937.

Douglas, George. *Lands Forlorn*. New York: Putnam and Sons, 1914.

Easton, Robert and MacKenzie Brown. *Lord of Beasts: The Saga of Buffalo Jones*. Tucson, AZ: University of Arizona Press, 1961.

Gordon, Bryan. *People of Sunlight, People of Starlight: Barrenland Archaeology in the Northwest Territories of Canada*. Hull, QC: Canadian Museum of Civilization, 1996.

Grambo, Rebecca. *Wolf: Legend, Enemy, Icon*. Richmond Hills, ON: Firefly Books, 2005.

Grinnell, George. *A Death in the Barrens*. Toronto: Northern Books, 1996.

Haines, John. *The Stars, the Snow, the Fire: Twenty-five Years in the Northern Wilderness, A Memoir*. St. Paul, MN: Greywolf Press, 2000.

Hall, Alex. *Discovering Eden: A Lifetime of Paddling Arctic Rivers*. Toronto: Key Porter, 2003.

Harpelle, Alix. *Those Were the Days That I Lived and Loved: A Biography of Gus D'Aoust, A Professional Barrenland Trapper*. Steinbach, MB: Martens Printing, 1984.

Hayball, Gwen. *Warburton Pike: An Unassuming Gentleman*. Poole, Dorset: Gwen Hayball, 1994.

Hearne, Samuel. *A Journey to the Northern Ocean: The Adventures of Samuel Hearne*. Surrey, BC: TouchWood Eds., 2007.

Henderson, Bob and Nils Vikander, eds. *Nature First: Outdoor Life the Friluftsliv Way*. Toronto: Natural Heritage Books-Dundurn Press, 2007.

Hodgkins, Bruce and Margaret Hobbs, ed. *Nastawgan: The Canadian North by Canoe and Snowshoe.* Toronto: Betelgeuse Books, 1987.

Hodgkins, Bruce W. and Gwyneth Hoyle, *Canoeing North into the Unknown: A Record of River Travel: 1874–1974.* Toronto: Natural Heritage Books, 1994.

Houston, C. Stuart. ed. *To the Arctic by Canoe 1819–1821: The Journal and Paintings of Robert Hood, Midshipman with Franklin.* Montreal and London: McGill-Queen's Press, 1974.

–––. ed. *Arctic Ordeal: The Journal of John Richardson Surgeon-Naturalist with Franklin, 1820–1822.* Kingston, ON: McGill-Queen's Press, 1984.

Hoyle, Gwyneth. *The Northern Horizons of Guy Blanchet: Intrepid Surveyor, 1884–1966.* Toronto: Natural Heritage Books-Dundurn Press, 2007.

Ingstad, Helge. *Nunamiut: Among Alaska's Inland Eskimos.* New York: W.W. Norton, 1954.

–––. trans. F.H. Lyon. *Klondyke Bill.* London: W. Kimber, 1955.

–––. *Land under the Pole Star: A Voyage to the Medieval Norse Settlements of Greenland and the Saga of a People that Vanished.* London, UK: Cape, 1966.

–––. trans. Eugene Gay-Tifft, *The Land of Feast and Famine.* Montreal & Kingston: McGill-Queen's University Press, 1992.

–––. and Anne Stine Ingstad. *The Viking Discovery of America: The Excavation of a Norse Settlement in L'Anse Aux Meadows, Newfoundland.* New York: Checkmark Books, 2001.

–––. *The Apache Indians: In Search of the Missing Tribe.* Lincoln, NB: University of Nebraska Press, 2004.

Jenkins, McKay. *Bloody Falls of the Coppermine: Madness and Murder in the Arctic Barren Lands.* New York: Random House, 2006.

Jones, Charles Jesse, *Buffalo Jones' Forty Years of Adventure.* London, UK: Sampson Low, Marston and Company, 1899.

Keller, Betty. *Black Wolf: The Life of Ernest Thompson Seton.* Vancouver: Douglas and McIntyre, 1984.

McDonald, T.H., ed. *Exploring the Northwest Territory: Sir Alexander Mackenzie's Journal of a Voyage by Bark Canoe from Lake Athabasca to the Pacific Ocean in the Summer of 1789.* Norman: University of Oklahoma Press, 1966.

Monsen, Lars. *Nådeløs Villmark: Canada på tvers.* Oslo: Lars Monsen Outdoors, 2002.

Morris, Brian. *Ernest Thompson Seton, Founder of the Woodcraft Movement, 1860–1946: Apostle of Indian Wisdom and Pioneer Ecologist.* Lewiston: The Edwin Mellen Press, 2007.

Mowat, Farley. *People of the Deer.* Toronto: McClelland & Stewart-Bantam, 1980.

Munn, Henry Toke. *Prairie Trails and Arctic Byways.* London, UK: Hunt and Blackett, 1932.

Norment, Christopher. *In the North of Our Lives.* Camden, ME: Down East Books, 1989.

Olesen, Dave. *Cold Nights, Fast Trails.* Minocoqua, WI: Northword Press, 1989.

———. *North of Reliance: A Personal Story of Living Beyond the Wilderness.* Minocqua, WI: Northward Press, 1994.

———. ed. *A Wonderful Country: The Quetico-Superior Stories of Bill Magie*. Ely, MN: Raven Productions, 2005.

Pelly, David. *Thelon: A River Sanctuary*. Hyde Park, ON: The Canadian Recreational Canoeing Association, 1996.

———. *Old Ways North*. St. Paul: Minnesota Historical Society Press, 2008.

Petitot, Émile. *Travels Around Great Slave and Great Bear Lakes, 1862–1882*. Toronto: The Champlain Society, 2005.

Pike, Warburton. *The Barren Ground of Northern Canada*. London: MacMillan and Co., 1892.

———. *Through the Subarctic Forest*. New York: Arno Press, 1967. Originally published in 1896.

Powell-Williams, Clive. *Cold Burial*. New York: St. Martins, 2002.

Redekop, Magdalene. *Ernest Thompson Seton*. Don Mills: Fitzhenry and Whiteside, 1979.

Sandlos, John. *Hunters at the Margin: Native People and Wildlife Conservation in the Northwest Territories*. Vancouver: University of British Columbia Press, 2007.

Seton, Ernest Thompson. *Life Histories of Northern Animals*. 2 Vols. New York: Charles Scribner's Sons, 1909.

———. *The Arctic Prairies*. New York: Harper Colophon Books, 1981. Originally published in 1911.

———. *The Book of Woodcraft and Indian Lore*. New York: Doubleday, 1912.

———. *Trail of an Artist-Naturalist: The Autobiography of Ernest Thompson Seton*. New York: Charles Scribner's Sons, 1940.

———. *Lives of Game Animals* 4 Vols. Boston: Charles T. Banford Co., 1953.

Steele, Peter. *The Man Who Mapped the Arctic: The Intrepid Life of George Back, Franklin's Lieutenant.* Vancouver: Raincoast Books, 2004.

Struzik, Ed. *Ten Rivers: Adventure Stories from the Arctic.* Toronto: CanWest Books, 2005.

Svatun, Birte. *Anne Stine og Helge Ingstad: Historien om et nysgjerrig par* (Oslo: N.W. Damm & Søn, 2004).

Wadland, John. *Ernest Thompson Seton: Man in Nature and the Progressive Era, 1880–1915.* New York: Arno, 1978.

Waldron, Malcolm. *Snow Man: John Hornby in the Barren Lands.* Montreal: McGill-Queens University Press, 1997.

Whalley, George. *The Legend of John Hornby.* Toronto: Macmillan, 1962.

———. ed. *Death in the Barren Ground.* Ottawa, ON: Oberon Press, 1980.

Whitney, Casper. *On Snow-Shoes to the Barren Grounds.* New York: Harper and Brothers, 1896.

Wiebe, Rudy. *A River of Stone: Fictions and Memories.* Toronto: Random House, 2001.

Index

About the Contributors

Guy Blanchet was born in Ottawa in 1884 and became a distinguished Canadian surveyor who spent a great deal of his working life in the North surveying Great Slave Lake and the Barrens as well as laying the path for the CANOL pipeline in the 1940s. Blanchet wrote many articles that were published in *The Beaver* and also published a book called *Search in the North* (Toronto: Macmillan, 1960). Gwyneth Hoyle, author of chapter 10 in this book, has written *The Northern Horizons of Guy Blanchet: Intrepid Surveyor, 1884–1966* (Toronto: Natural Heritage Books-Dundurn Press, 2007), which is an outstanding unveiling of his life.

Peter Carruthers has a professional background in anthropology, archaeology, geography, and land-use planning. Currently in private practice, he continues a career in cultural and natural heritage conservation and planning — locally, nationally, and internationally. He is the past chair of the board of Heritage Toronto, has recently served two terms on the board of the Canadian Association of Heritage Professionals (CAHP), and is active in other heritage conservation organizations. Since 2001, Mr. Carruthers has been the principal of

Linsmore Associates, a small firm that works collaboratively to carry out projects in support of heritage conservation for the private and public sector, and he is also a senior associate with Archaeological Services Inc. He lives in Toronto, Ontario.

Randy Freeman is a Yellowknife-based heritage consultant, writer, and broadcaster. In 1985, after completing his master's degree in historical geography, he was enticed north by the Government of the Northwest Territories to establish and manage their Toponymy Program. It was through that work that he discovered the often exciting, unusual, and unbelievable history of the North. Over the past thirteen years he has researched and written more than five hundred northern history scripts and columns for both CBC North Radio and *UpHere* magazine. Whether it's digging deep into archival records or reading newspapers a hundred years out of date, Randy has a nose for long-forgotten northern history.

René Fumoleau was born in France in 1926 and came to the Canadian North as an Oblate priest in 1953. Long a legend in northern circles, he has chronicled Dene life in his poems, stories, films, and photographs. *As Long As This Land Shall Last* (Calgary: University of Calgary Press, 2004), his critically acclaimed study of Native treaties in Canada, brought Fumoleau to national attention in 1975. The work was reissued in a new edition in 2004. Fumoleau is also the author of *The Secret* (Ottawa: Novalis, 1997) and *Here I Sit* (Ottawa: Novalis, 2004). He lives in Yellowknife, Northwest Territories.

Gwyneth Hoyle began researching canoe routes into the North well before the publication of *Canoeing North into the Unknown* (Toronto: Natural Heritage Press, 1994) with her co-author, Bruce Hodgins. Northern travellers continued to be her great interest, resulting in two other books, *Flowers in the Snow* (Lincoln, University of Nebraska Press, 2001), the life of a remarkable Scottish woman, and *The Northern Horizons of Guy Blanchet* (Toronto: Natural Heritage Books-Dundurn Press, 2007). Gwyneth is a research associate of the Frost Centre at Trent University in Peterborough, Ontario.

Larry Innes is the executive director of the Canadian Boreal Initiative (CBI), a national conservation organization based in Ottawa, Ontario. He is also a lawyer practising environmental and Aboriginal law for First Nations across Canada. Larry has worked extensively on protected-area establishment in Canada's North, from the Yukon to Labrador. As an advocate for effective ecological and cultural representation in new park designations, he is proud to support the efforts of the Lutsel K'e Dene First Nation to bring forward their vision for protecting Thaidene Nene. Larry lives in Goose Bay, Labrador.

John McInnes has enjoyed twenty-six canoe trips in the Northwest Territories — primarily on its "small rivers" north of Great Slave Lake — over the past thirty years. Included among his travels are a total of six routes leading to the East Arm of Great Slave Lake — one of which followed Pike's Portage. John lives in Edmonton, Alberta.

Dave Olesen was born and raised in northern Illinois. He graduated *summa cum laude* from Northland College in 1979 with a BA in humanities and northern studies. He first travelled to the Northwest Territories in 1980, on a six-week dog-team expedition with his friend Will Steger from Ely, Minnesota. In 1987, he immigrated to Canada and settled at the mouth of the Hoarfrost River on Great Slave Lake, Northwest Territories. With his wife, Kristen Gilbertson, he has lived there year-round ever since. They have two daughters. Together the family runs a small outfitting business for winter dog-team adventures, and a charter-air service with two bush planes. Meanwhile, they try to keep up with the demands of an eighty-five-year-old Danish sailboat, thirty-nine hungry Alaskan huskies, and one very lucky black cat.

Brenda Parlee is assistant professor and Canada Research chair at the University of Alberta in Edmonton, Alberta. She lived and worked for the community of Lutsel K'e from 1996 to 2001, during which time she was involved in a diversity of land-based research projects in and around Desnethché (Reliance and Pike's Portage). Her experiences in Lutsel K'e were fundamental to her understanding of the North and prompted a number of interdisciplinary and collaborative research projects on the effects of mining on community well-being, changing barren ground caribou populations, and the social-economy of the North. Recognizing that the proposed national park will bring many travellers to the area, her chapter in this book is a personal reflection on the way that we (as scholars) come to know "place." It is hoped that it will challenge others to consider their own relationship to the community, history, and significance of the area to the Denesoline as they journey through Thaidene Nene. Brenda currently lives in Edmonton, Alberta, with her husband, Scott, and their two boys, Eric and Alex.

David Pelly is the author of *Thelon: A River Sanctuary* (Hyde Park: Canadian Recreational Canoeing Association, 1996), the complete account of the region's storied history. He has also written many other books and articles on Canada's North, the land, its people, and its history. His most recent book is *The Old Way North* (St. Paul, MN: Minnesota Historical Society Press, 2008), about a different but equally significant and even longer-standing access route into the Barrenlands. David has paddled various parts of the Thelon watershed on several occasions over the past thirty years, has walked in James W. Tyrrell's footsteps beside the Mary Frances River, and has long been an admirer of Tyrrell's remarkable fortitude in the Barrenlands. David lives in Ottawa, Ontario.

Ingrid Urberg is associate professor of Scandinavian studies at the University of Alberta-Augustana Campus in Camrose, Alberta. In addition to teaching Norwegian language and Scandinavian literature and culture, Ingrid co-teaches an interdisciplinary course called "Explorations of the Canadian North," which involves a winter homestead stay on the East Arm of Great Slave Lake. Her research focuses on personal narratives and polar literature, and has taken her to northern Norway, Greenland, and Svalbard. She was awarded the Augustana Distinguished Teaching Award in 2002. Ingrid lives in Camrose, Alberta.

John Wadland is professor emeritus in the Department of Canadian Studies at Trent University. His Ph.D. dissertation, *Ernest Thompson Seton: Man in Nature and the Progressive Era, 1880–1915* (New York: Arno Press, 1978), dealt only marginally with Seton's travels in the eastern Great Slave Lake region. Renewed national and international scholarly interest in Seton has prompted Professor Wadland to revisit and rethink his earlier study. He has chosen *The Arctic Prairies* (New York: International University Press, 1943) as a launching pad for this project. It is his hope that this brief paper will be a useful, if modest, support for the Lutsel K'e Dene First Nation's proposal for a national park to protect Thaidene Nene. John lives in Peterborough, Ontario.

About the Editors

Morten Asfeldt spent his childhood years in northern Newfoundland and the Yukon. Roaming wild places and reading stories of those who had gone before him began at a young age and have remained a constant throughout his life. Morten has travelled extensively in the Yukon, Northwest Territories, and Nunavut on personal canoe, hiking and dogsled adventures, as a commercial canoe and raft guide, and with students as part of his teaching at the University of Alberta's Augustana Campus in Camrose, Alberta. Morten has published in academic journals and magazines, and has contributed a chapter to *Nature First* (Toronto: Natural Heritage Books-Dundurn Press, 2007). In addition, Morten's photographs from the North appear in a number of books, magazines, brochures, and websites. Morten lives in Camrose, Alberta, with his wife, Krystal, and their two children, Jasper and Kaisa.

Bob Henderson began his passion for outdoor life as a camper and later as a member of the staff at Camp Ahmek in Algonquin Park, Ontario. Later, as a canoe tripping and winter travel guide with family

Bob Henderson and Morten Asfeldt in the evening light on Charlton Bay.

and friends and with students at McMaster University, Bob began exploring Canadian trails coast to coast. He has taught outdoor education at McMaster for twenty-eight years, often sharing stories on the trail involving characters and events related in this book.

Bob is the author of *Every Trail has a Story: Heritage Travel in Canada* (Toronto: Natural Heritage Books-Dundurn Press, 2005) and co-editor with Nils Vikander of *Nature First: Outdoor Life the Friluftsliv Way* (Toronto: Natural Heritage Books-Dundurn Press, 2007). Bob lives in Uxbridge, Ontario.

By the Same Author

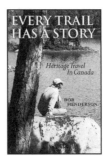

**NATURE FIRST: OUTDOOR LIFE
THE FRILUFTSLIV WAY**
Edited by Bob Henderson
and Nils Vikander
978-1-89704-521-3 $29.99

**EVERY TRAIL HAS A STORY:
HERITAGE TRAVEL IN CANADA**
Bob Henderson
978-1-89621-997-4 $26.95

Nature First combines the Scandinavian approach to creating a relationship with nature (known as *friluftsliv*) with efforts by Canadian and international educators to adapt this wisdom and apply it to everyday life experiences in the open air. This is a book for parents, travel guides, educators and anyone who participates in outdoor pursuits, and provides a compellingly fresh approach to life in the "out-of-doors."

Canada is packed with intriguing places for travel, where heritage and landscape interact to create stories that fire our imagination. Scattered across the land are incredible tales of human life over the centuries. Here Bob Henderson, the traveller, captures our living history in its relationship to the land.

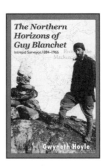

Of Related Interest:

**NORTHERN HORIZONS: THE
INTREPID SURVEYOR, 1884–1966**
Gwyneth Hoyle
978-1-55002-759-4

Tell us your story! What did you think of this book? Join the conversation at www.definingcanada.ca/tell-your-story by telling us what you think.

The working life of the distinguished surveyor Guy Blanchet reflects the story of northern Canada in the first half of the twentieth century. His life was rich in contacts with First Nations people, and his friendships included most of the well-known northern travellers of the time. While Blanchet published a number of articles about his experiences, this is the first time his fascinating life story has been told in book form.

Available at your favourite bookseller

DUNDURN PRESS
www.dundurn.com